THE CURIOUS
BOOK OF
MIND-BOGGLING
TEASERS, TRICKS,
PUZZLES & GAMES

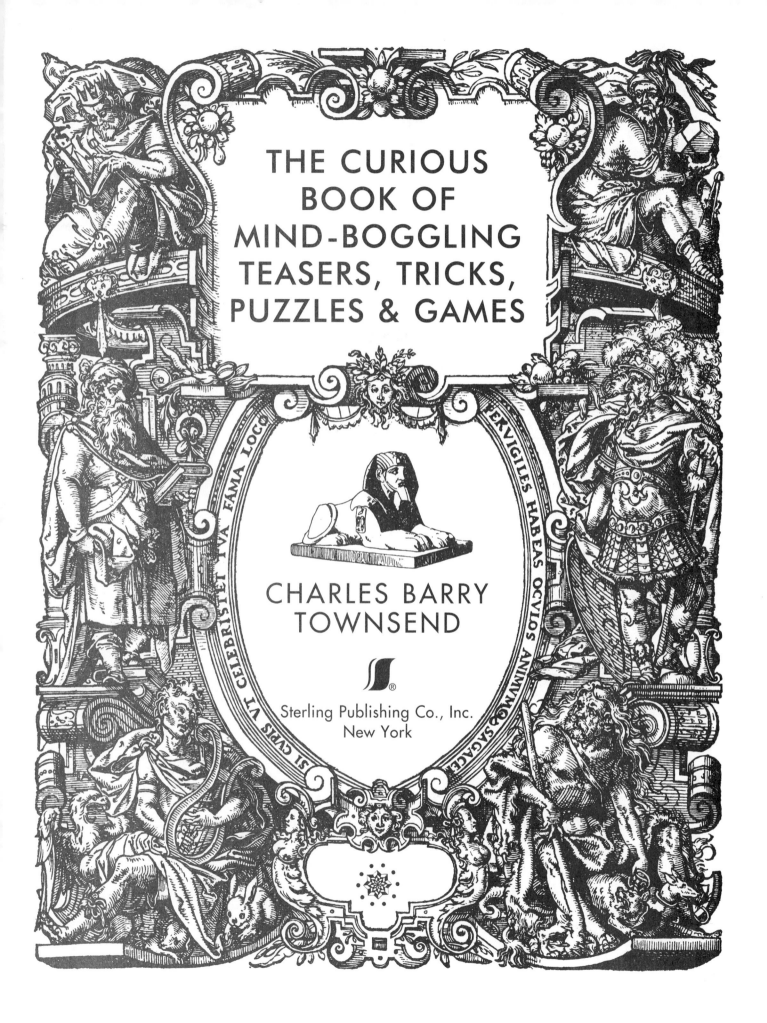

THE CURIOUS BOOK OF MIND-BOGGLING TEASERS, TRICKS, PUZZLES & GAMES

CHARLES BARRY TOWNSEND

Sterling Publishing Co., Inc.
New York

to
**Maryann
Markham
Christian**

Published in 2003 by
Sterling Publishing Co., Inc.
387 Park Avenue South, New York, NY 10016
Copyright © 2000 by Charles Barry Townsend
Originally published under the title *Merlin's Big Book Of Puzzles, Games & Magic*,
a compilation of the previously published *Merlin's Puzzler, Merlin's Puzzler 2*,
and *Merlin's Puzzler 3*.
Distributed in Canada by Sterling Publishing
c/o Canadian Manda Group, One Atlantic Avenue, Suite 105
Toronto, Ontario, Canada M6K 3E7
Distributed in Great Britain by Chrysalis Books
64 Brewery Road, London N7 9NT England
Distributed in Australia by Capricorn Link (Australia) Pty. Ltd.
P.o. Box 704, Windsor, NSW 2756 Australia

Sterling ISBN 1-4027-0214-0

CONTENTS

FOREWORD

"Land Ho," cries out the helmsman. We'll soon be typing up at the docks on Merlin's Isle, so stow your gear and be ready to go ashore. For those of you who have never been to Merlin's Isle, I welcome you all and promise you an exciting few days of mind-challenging experiences. This is our fourth trip to this fascinating enigma. We first visited this fabulous island in 1976. Our last visit was in 1981 when Merlin commissioned us to compile a magic book for him. Merlin's Isle is a place of the mind, suspended in time and space. Here, Merlin can summon up people and places from the past to perplex and entertain us with a myriad of puzzles, games, and magical entertainments. Merlin's goal has always been to compile in one set of writings a veritable encyclopedia of the best of these mental amusements. In the present volume he has come very close to realizing this task.

Within the pages of this book you will find over 575 items of interest presented with hundreds of fanciful illustrations. This book is Merlin's way of celebrating the start of the new millennium.

During our stay on the island we will once again be challenged by that master of Victorian puzzlers, the one-and-only Professor Hoffmann. We will also drop in to the famous turn-of-the-century theater, Maskelyne's Egyptian Hall in Piccadilly, for an evening's entertainment of magic and mystery. You'll learn to perform many feats of legerdemain and even the secret of how to construct mathematical magic squares in your head.

Our old friends Mr. Sherlock Holmes and Dr. Watson will be on hand with problems of deductive reasoning. The "Word Professor," Willard Wordsworth, will test our word powers, and Mr. Will Goldston will teach us how to juggle with plates and coins.

All things considered, I think that we are in for a great visit. We're tying up to the dock now, so line up along the rail and prepare to disembark. All right, you first, step lively down the gangplank and into one of the carriages that Merlin has sent to take us to the palace . . .

Your editor,

Charles Barry Townsend

(Pictured below is your editor flanked by his two junior assistants, Mark and Chris, circa 1980.)

ACKNOWLEDGMENTS

I wish to thank the New-York Historical Society for permission to use the illustration on page 5. This illustration previously appeared in *This Fabulous Century — 1900-1910*, © 1969 by TIME-LIFE Books.

Grateful acknowledgment is made to Dover Publications, Inc. for permission to use illustrations from the following works:

Alphabets and Ornaments, Ernst Lehner. Copyright 1952 by Ernst Lehner. New York: Dover Publications, Inc.

Amusements in Mathematics, Henry E. Dudeny. New York: Dover Publications, Inc., 1917.

Baroque Cartouches for Designers and Artists, Johann Ulrich Krauss. New York: Dover Publications, Inc., 1969.

Cartouches and Decorative Small Frames, edited by Edmund V. Gillon, Jr. New York: Dover Publications, Inc., 1975.

Decorative Alphabets and Initials, edited by Alexander Nesbitt. Copyright 1959 by Dover Publications, Inc.

G & D Cook & Co's Illustrated Catalogue of Carriages and Special Business Advertiser. New York: Dover Publications, 1970.

Handbook of Ornament, Franz Sales Meyer. New York: Dover Publications, Inc., 1957.

Panorama of Magic, Melbourne Christopher. New York: Dover Publications, Inc., 1962. By permission of author.

Symbols, Signs & Signets, Ernst Lehner. Copyright 1950 by Ernst Lehner. New York: Dover Publications, Inc.

The Complete Woodcuts of Albrecht Dürer, edited by Dr. Willi Kurth. New York: Dover Publications, 1963.

The Crystal Palace Exhibition Illustrated Catalogue London 1851. New York: Dover Publications, Inc., 1970.

Other books from which material was drawn include:

Puzzles Old and New, Professor Hoffmann. London & New York: Frederick Warne and Co., 1900.

The Universal Self-Instructor and Manual of General Reference, edited by Albert Eller Berg. New York: Winter House Ltd., facsimile of the 1883 edition, 1970.

Will Goldston's Who's Who in Magic, Will Goldston. London: Aladdin House, 1920.

rthur's Castle, The Knights of The Round Table, Camelot, Merlin, Lancelot, Guinevere. These places and people conjure up in our minds visions of great events, daring deeds and subtle intrigue. A whole, rich world alive and vibrant which seems as real to us today as it was 1,400 years ago. Or was it real? Did it all really happen? It is said that when the end came to Camelot and Arthur's dream was shattered, his adviser Merlin, saddened by the knowledge that even his vast powers were unable to help Arthur in his hour of greatest need, retreated to a place called the "Isle of Merlin." Today the Isle of Merlin, like the Scottish village of Brigadoon, exists only in time and space. The Isle of Merlin is inhabited by people and animals. It has both farms and cities, rivers and mountains. It is great and it is small and completely without precedent. Merlin and his Isle are able to travel through time visiting both the past and the future. It was while visiting the present and seeing the current interest in the Arthurian legend that Merlin decided to make available for publication his notes concerning some of the great interests of his life, namely puzzles, games and magic. This first volume, along with the volumes to follow, will constitute an encyclopedic collection of the best puzzles, games and magic that have amused and entertained the world since the dawn of recorded history.

Quantity is not the emphasis here, but rather quality. We want to preserve in one set of writings the very best example of these arts. Merlin also feels that these secrets are deserving of better illustrations than have formerly been accorded to books of this nature. To this end your editor has drawn heavily on the works of the master engravers of the past to help in the graphic presentation of Merlin's problems.

That completes my introduction to this first volume of Merlin's puzzles. I have had a grand time putting it all together and I am confident that you will enjoy the challenges propounded by Merlin. Happy puzzling to you!

Your Editor,

Charles Barry Townsend

Mr. Sherlock Holmes

"I say, Holmes," rumbled Watson as their train sped towards London, "now that this beastly business of the Oxston Creeper has been taken care of perhaps you would be good enough to answer something that has been puzzling me for the last week."

"Of course, Watson, old chap," replied Holmes. "What would you like to know about the Creeper?"

"It's not the Creeper that has my mind all muddled, it's your brother, Mycroft. The last time he came around to Baker Street he propounded that confounded puzzle with the water pitcher and crystal goblets. I can't make head or tail of it."

"But it's elementary, my dear Watson, elementary. The problem is simple. You have a water pitcher which is filled with exactly two gallons of water. The larger goblet holds eight and a half ounces of liquid. The smaller one just four ounces of liquid. You are to fill both goblets to the brim with water from the pitcher and yet still have two gallons of water left in the pitcher."

"Really, Watson," said Holmes while lighting his pipe, "at times your powers of deduction greatly disappoint me." (See page 1 for puzzle setup). "Now just a minute, Mr. Holmes," interjected Inspector Lestrade from his seat in the corner. "You're being a bit 'ard on Dr. Watson. I've solved many a case for Scotland Yard in my time, but that problem makes no sense at all to me. Now, if it's answers to puzzles you're after, then I'd suggest that you start with the one Professor Moriarty sent to you in the mail concerning his next crime."

"Quite right, Inspector," said Holmes. "The Problem of the Ten Tigers, I believe Watson calls it. The puzzle states that the London Zoo, after having been given ten tigers, had them placed all together in a circular cage (Fig. 1). Next they wished to erect three circular fences within this cage in such a way that each tiger would be isolated from every other tiger. The fences could cross each other at any point. I'll give you both until we arrive at Paddington Station to solve these puzzles. If you're still in the dark by then, I suggest that you go and see my landlady, Mrs. Hudson. She solved both of these in ten minutes."

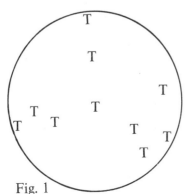

Fig. 1

Professor Moriarty

SANTA'S DILEMMA

The
Tucker ▶
House

The Vaka House ◀

anta is about to leave the North Pole on his yearly journey around the world. He has paused to study his flight plan for the town of Pleasant Dale. There are 64 homes in Pleasant Dale, all neatly laid out in the pattern depicted above. Every house in town is on his list. Santa wishes to start with the Tucker house and end with the Vaka house. In between, his route should always be in a straight line, moving horizontally or vertically from house to house, never backtracking or crossing any previous line of flight.

Can you help Santa draw up a flight plan so he can get under way? Who knows, he might even be bringing me a new set of golf clubs.

MERRY

CHRISTMAS !!!

THE FESTIVAL OF PUZZLES

It's festival time once again on the Isle of Merlin. The puzzle experts from all parts of the island are converging on the capital. In the press release picture on the next page we see Merlin arriving aboard his flagship, *Merlin 1*. The city is decked out with puzzles on the buildings, bridges and airships. Let's move in for a closer look at some of the more outstanding problems.

High atop one of the twin towers in front of Merlin's ship they have erected a new television antenna (1). The instructions in the festival's convention catalogue read as follows: "The design of this antenna can be drawn using one continuous line and without any line crossing any other line." That should keep the contestants busy for a while.

The office personnel on the other twin tower came up with an equally interesting problem (2). They have hung the numerals 1, 6 and 3 on the outside of their building. "You are to arrange these numbers into one number that can be evenly divided by seven." Merlin particularly likes the ingenious solution to this puzzle.

Hanging on the Park Plaza office building is the face of a gigantic six-sided clock (3). "The puzzler may run out of time attempting to solve this puzzle. The challenge is simple. Merely rearrange the numbers on the clock so that the sum of each of the six sides totals 17."

Moving down the picture we find that the bridge workers have put up a giant Tinker Toy-like structure on top of one end of the King Arthur Bridge (4). Our guidebook reads, "This toy-like structure is composed of 9 equal-size triangles. By removing 5 of the girders reduce the number to 5 equal-size triangles."

To the left of the bridge, painted on the top side of the giant passenger dirigible (5), is an Indian puzzle. "Take the four Indian arrowheads and arrange them in such a way as to have five arrowheads."

Finally, Merlin noted from his airship that nine of his escort balloons were flying in such a formation that there were 3 rows with 4 balloons in each row. Some of the balloons, of course, were in more than one row. "I'll have to add this puzzle to the convention's itinerary" thought Merlin.

Well, readers, there are some of the festival problems for this year. Come along now and join the fun. The shuttle dirigible for the Park Plaza is leaving in five minutes.

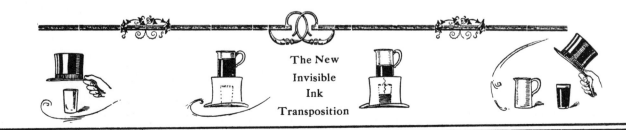

The New
Invisible
Ink
Transposition

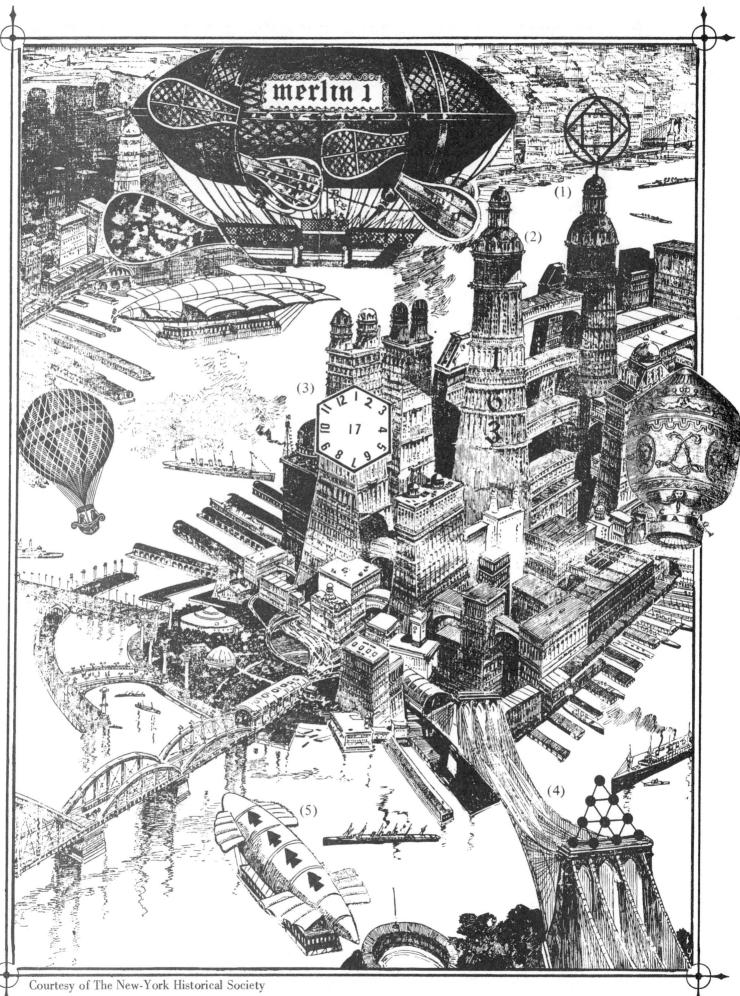

merlin 1

(1)

(2)

(3)

11 12 1 2 3
10 4
17
9 5
8 7 6

6
3

(4)

(5)

5

acing us on the next page is a section of the temple wall among the ruins of Absurdium on the Isle of Merlin. Upon examining the site, our scholars found that the artifacts illustrated five of the puzzles that the novice was required to solve during his early training.

The first puzzle we will try to solve is found in the center of the drawing and was known as the Problem of the Wandering Planets. Resting on seven crystal bases, we have: to the left, three black spheres (Mercury, Venus, Earth); the center unoccupied; to the right, three white spheres (Mars, Jupiter and Saturn). The problem is to transpose the black and white spheres so that the three black ones will be on the right and the three white ones will be on the left. Using dimes and pennies and the layout at the top of the page, test your skill. The rules of movement are:

(1) Each sphere can only be moved one space at a time.
(2) Spheres must be moved in a forward direction only; i.e., black, left to right, white, right to left.
(3) If a counter is divided from a vacant space by a single counter only, it may jump over the counter to occupy this space.

Above and to the left of the Wandering Planets we find nine arrowheads pointing downwards. Here you must draw four straight lines that will pass through all the arrowheads without lifting your pencil from the paper.

To the right of the arrowheads we find a nest of triangles. A powerful sign to the ancient puzzlers, it has to be drawn without lifting your pencil from the paper or having any of the lines cross one another.

On the wall below the problem of the Wandering Planets is a square divided into nine smaller squares. You are charged with the task of creating a magic square using the numbers one through nine. Each line, whether horizontal, vertical or diagonal, must add up to 15.

The last problem has to do with the two urns to the right of the magic square. The first urn holds five gallons of wine while the second holds five gallons of water. We measure out a gallon of wine, pour it into the water and mix thoroughly. Then we measure out a gallon of the mixture from the second urn and pour it into the first urn. Question: is there more or less water in the first urn than there is wine in the second urn?

castle of cards can become a very puzzling structure when built with a deck of playing cards from the Isle of Merlin. Each card depicts a puzzle. Solve all three and win the game.

At the top of the castle is the Ace-of-Puzzlers. The three squares in the diagram are built using 12 matches. Problem: by moving only three matches, form five squares.

In the middle we have the King-of-Puzzlers. The problem here is to arrange the figures so that they form a perfect triangle.

On the bottom we find the Jack-of-Puzzlers. Pictured on the card is a hexagon. Can you turn it into a cube?

On the next page is a Japanese feudal baron contemplating the family crests of his enemies. Together, their strength is great enough to crush him; divided, each can be easily defeated. With three straight cuts of his sword the baron can divide the page into seven pieces, each one containing a whole crest. If only his enemies could be divided so easily. Where would he make the cuts to divide the crests?

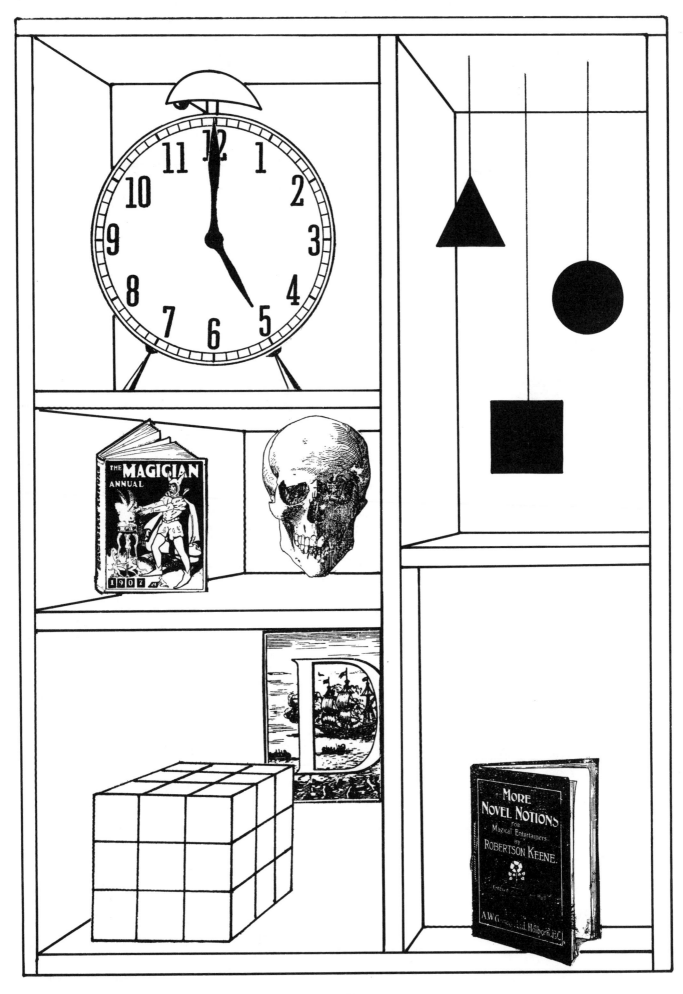

Merlin's Notes

The clock on the left shows five o'clock. At what time during the next hour will:

(A) both hands coincide?

(B) both hands first stand at right angles to one another?

The other day I found a piece of wood that had been carved into a strange shape. When placed at various angles before a light source it would cast a shadow in the shape of a circle, a square or a triangle. What was the shape of this piece of wood?

Place the books together on the bottom shelf. Put them in the following order. To the left, *The Magician's Annual.* To the right, *More Novel Notions.* A bookworm starts eating at page 1 of *The Magician's Annual* and chews his way in a straight line to the last page of *More Novel Notions.* If each cover is 1/8 inch thick and the inside of each book is 1 inch thick, how far will the bookworm travel?

A six-inch wooden cube can be divided into 27 two-inch cubes using six saw cuts along the lines shown in the drawing. By overlapping some of the pieces after each cut, is it possible to come up with 27 cubes in less than six saw cuts? If not, explain why.

THE PALACE OF PUZZLES

Below is a puzzle-niche in the reception hall of Merlin's Palace of Puzzles. The Greek-cross design in the tapestry hanging above the chariot scene illustrates a very old problem. The puzzle is to cut the cross into four pieces using two straight cuts and then reassemble these pieces to form a perfect square. On the table in the foreground stands a marble sculpture representing a panel of wood containing three square holes. The problem is to saw the panel into two pieces of equal size and shape which when placed together will form a perfect square with no holes in it.

The target shows the numbers: 16, 17, 23, 24, 39, 40

ere we find Friar Tuck, that roguish monk of Robin Hood's band of outlaws, slumbering through the afternoon when he is supposed to be keeping an eye on the castle of the Sheriff of Nottingham. Earlier in the day he had been trying, with his bow and arrows, to win a bet he has made with Robin. The problem is to shoot a number of arrows into the target so that the score will total exactly 100. Judging by the smile on his face, I'd guess that Friar Tuck thinks he knows the answer and can already taste the prize. Do you know how many arrows it would take to score 100?

Mr. Sherlock Holmes

ow, Watson, pay careful attention to what I say. Across the street there are five houses, each of a different color and inhabited by men of different nationalities with different pets, drinks and cigarettes. Two of these men are wanted in connection with the Bayswater Bank embezzlement. Here are the clues.

1. The Englishman lives in the red house.
2. The Spaniard owns the dog.
3. Coffee is drunk in the green house.
4. The Ukrainian drinks tea.
5. The green house is immediately to the right (your right) of the ivory house.
6. The Old Gold smoker owns snails.
7. Players are smoked in the yellow house.
8. Milk is drunk in the middle house.
9. The Norwegian lives in the first house on the left.
10. The man who smokes Chesterfields lives in the house next to the man with the fox.
11. Players are smoked in the house next to the house where the horse is kept.
12. The Lucky Strike smoker drinks orange juice.
13. The Japanese smokes Parliaments.
14. The Norwegian lives next to the blue house.

Now, Watson, who drinks water and who owns the zebra? These are the men we are after.

rom the archives of the National Puzzle Museum on the Isle of Merlin come the following problems:

(1) You are required to rearrange the five triangular pieces of cardboard (Fig. 1) into a perfect square. One of the pieces may be cut in two.

Fig. 1

(2) In Figure 2 we find 3 cups and 6 lumps of sugar. Our problem is a simple one. We are required to place the 6 lumps into the cups in such a way that each cup will contain an uneven number of lumps. All six lumps must be used. The lumps cannot be broken up.

Fig. 2

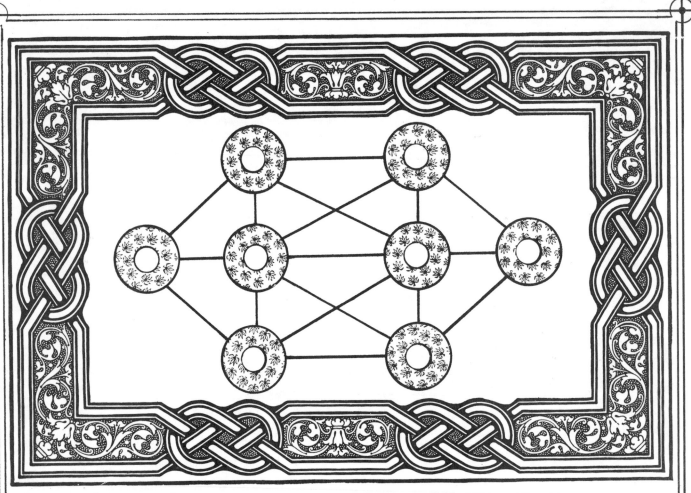

From our neighbor, Bill Iorio, a scion of the famous Iorio glass founding family of Flemington, New Jersey, comes an interesting problem. In the illustration above I have laid out eight glass plates. There are several connecting lines between them. Your puzzle is to arrange the numbers 1 through 8 on the plates in such a manner that no two consecutive numbers will be joined by any one of the lines. If your thinking cap is on straight you should solve this one in five minutes.

The Rhino's Riddle

Since all the animals on the Isle of Merlin can speak, it is not unusual to be quizzed by a passing specimen. Rupert the Rhino has been perplexing travelers for years by challenging them to arrange eight 8's so that when they are added up they total 1,000.

Rupert will bet you a bale of hay that you can't do it.

 hile browsing in a used book store I came upon an interesting old copy of a Funk and Wagnalls Dictionary from 1915. Below is a list of 18 words from it. Can you match 12 of them to the pictures I've used to make up a sample page from this old tome?

(A) Stereoscope

(B) Parbuckle

(C) Catalo

(D) Xat

(E) Fiacre

(F) Adjutant

(G) Char-a-banc

(H) Ballista

(I) Bark

(J) Cutter

(K) Juggernaut

(L) Peccary

(M) Bittern

(N) Uhlan

(O) Coot

(P) Sphygmograph

(Q) Cowl

(R) Roentgen Rays

everal years ago the leading archaeologists of the Isle of Merlin discovered the ruins of an ancient civilization off the coast of their island. One hundred feet beneath the sea divers came upon many relics scattered about the ocean floor. After studying the many stone plaques that were brought up during the expedition, it was found that the city had once been a part of the fabled land of Atlantis and that the people had been great puzzle enthusiasts. In the drawing on the next page we see that some of the ruins consisted of ornate pillars topped with puzzle designs that had once stood in the streets and gardens of Atlantis. Test your skill by trying to solve the following four Atlantian puzzles:

(1) Our first problem is a difficult one. Draw the figure below (a circle with a dot in the center) with one continuous line — that is without lifting your pencil from the paper.

(2) Lying on the sand at the bottom of the next page are six Atlantian coins. Arrange them in the form of a cross with four coins in each row.

(3) Once again, as in problem one, you must use a continuous line to solve this puzzle. Draw a line that will cross every line once, and only once, in the figure below. You can start anywhere.

(4) I've saved the best for last. Can you place eight dots on the target below in such a way as to have two dots on every circle and two dots on each straight line?

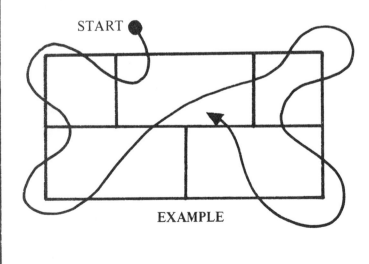

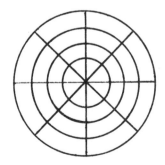

The Haunted House

he old MacAllister mansion outside of Lloydville has stood empty and forlorn now for many years owing to its ghostly inhabitants. To shed some light on the subject a committee of experts from P.O.P. (Pals of Poltergeists) spent a night there this summer. They met five ghosts who locked them in the main hall and would not set them free until they had correctly answered a problem put to them by each of the apparitions. Let's see how long you would have been held a prisoner in the MacAllister house. (See page 21 for picture of main hall.)

(1) The first ghost pointed to the plaque on the wall above the fireplace and said "On that plaque is the MacAllister family motto. Ten of the letters have fallen off. Tell me what the original motto said."

```
S_R K_  W_I E  _H_
   I_O S  H_T
```

(2) The second ghost pointed a finger at a spider's web high above our heads and asked, "If the arc of that web describes a quarter of a circle and is 20 inches long, what is the area covered by the web in square inches?"

AREA ←
ARC ←

(3) The third specter pointed to the sections of chain which lay upon the floor and said, "Last night I found these nine sections of chain down in the dungeon. The original chain was composed of fifty links. If it costs 25¢ to open a link and 50¢ to close and weld it, what is the least amount of money it will cost me to have it put back together again?"

(4) The fourth shade placed a small checkerboard on the table and positioned nine checkers on the numbered squares. "You must remove eight of the checkers from the board leaving the ninth one in the center square. You remove a checker by jumping another one over it to the vacant square beyond. You can jump in any direction using any checker. Any number of jumps in succession with the same checker will count as one move. Your problem is to do it in the least number of moves."

(5) With an eerie laugh, the last ghost pointed around the room at the three clocks and whispered "Yesterday, June 15, 1974, at 12:00 noon these three clocks were set going at precisely the same time. Twenty-four hours later the first clock was found to be one minute slow, the second clock one minute fast, and the third exactly on time. If the clocks are allowed to keep running on, losing or gaining a minute each day, on what date and what time of day will all three clocks show twelve o'clock again at the same instant?"

SRK WIE H
IOSHT

21

A Detective Quiz

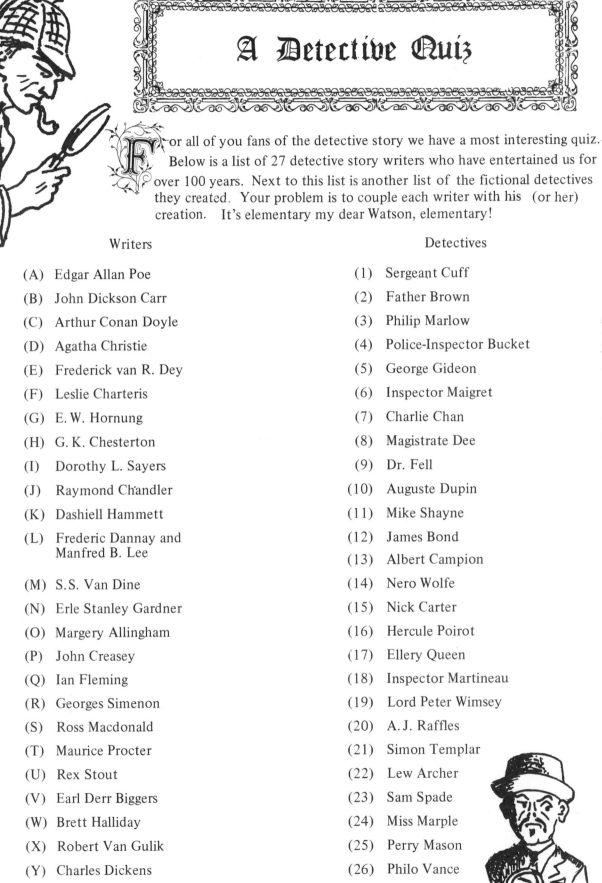

For all of you fans of the detective story we have a most interesting quiz. Below is a list of 27 detective story writers who have entertained us for over 100 years. Next to this list is another list of the fictional detectives they created. Your problem is to couple each writer with his (or her) creation. It's elementary my dear Watson, elementary!

Writers	Detectives
(A) Edgar Allan Poe	(1) Sergeant Cuff
(B) John Dickson Carr	(2) Father Brown
(C) Arthur Conan Doyle	(3) Philip Marlow
(D) Agatha Christie	(4) Police-Inspector Bucket
(E) Frederick van R. Dey	(5) George Gideon
(F) Leslie Charteris	(6) Inspector Maigret
(G) E. W. Hornung	(7) Charlie Chan
(H) G. K. Chesterton	(8) Magistrate Dee
(I) Dorothy L. Sayers	(9) Dr. Fell
(J) Raymond Chandler	(10) Auguste Dupin
(K) Dashiell Hammett	(11) Mike Shayne
(L) Frederic Dannay and Manfred B. Lee	(12) James Bond
	(13) Albert Campion
(M) S.S. Van Dine	(14) Nero Wolfe
(N) Erle Stanley Gardner	(15) Nick Carter
(O) Margery Allingham	(16) Hercule Poirot
(P) John Creasey	(17) Ellery Queen
(Q) Ian Fleming	(18) Inspector Martineau
(R) Georges Simenon	(19) Lord Peter Wimsey
(S) Ross Macdonald	(20) A. J. Raffles
(T) Maurice Procter	(21) Simon Templar
(U) Rex Stout	(22) Lew Archer
(V) Earl Derr Biggers	(23) Sam Spade
(W) Brett Halliday	(24) Miss Marple
(X) Robert Van Gulik	(25) Perry Mason
(Y) Charles Dickens	(26) Philo Vance
(Z) Wilkie Collins	(27) Sherlock Holmes

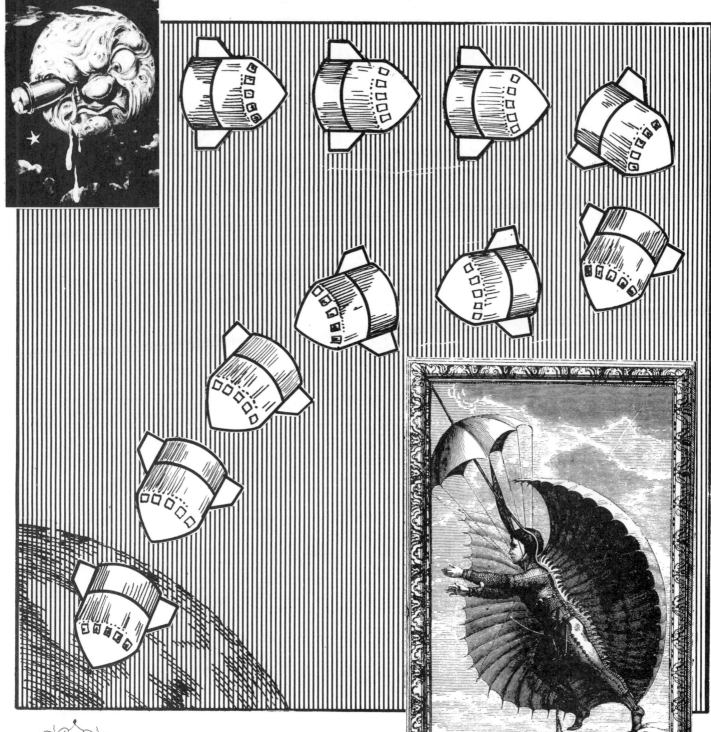

surprising fact was brought to my attention the other day. It seems that outside of the Isle of Merlin no one else on Earth seems to be aware that in the not too distant past this planet was attacked by warships piloted by the dreaded Birdmen of Venus. Thanks to our puzzle experts we were able to predict what type of formation their ships would be flying in when they attacked Earth. Knowing this, our forces easily defeated them. The one thing we knew about the Birdmen was that they always placed 10 ships in each attacking group in such a way that they formed five rows with four ships in each row. There are two ways to do this. Can you come up with the same solutions that enabled us to stop the Birdmen?

The Pharaoh's Curse

When the tomb of the Egyptian Pharaoh Riddles the IV was opened it was found to be guarded by the triple curse of Thoth. Whoever gazes upon the resting place of the pharaoh (and that now includes you since by this time you have looked at the drawing on the next page) must correctly answer the following three questions. If you fail to answer all of them you may be in for a visit from Anubis, guardian of the netherworld.

Question 1 – The problem is to place eleven coins on the black dots which encircle the shield of Hammurabi. Starting at any dot, count six sixth dot. Continue this on different dots. a coin on it is dot and counted dots and place a coin on the until all coins have been placed When counting, a dot with treated like an empty along with the rest.

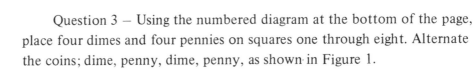

Question 2 – This question is very easy. How many triangles are there in the figure below?

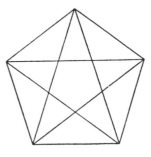

Question 3 – Using the numbered diagram at the bottom of the page, place four dimes and four pennies on squares one through eight. Alternate the coins; dime, penny, dime, penny, as shown in Figure 1.

Fig. 1 ⭕⚫⭕⚫⭕⚫⭕⚫☐☐

When the coins have been set up, move them, two at a time, so that after four moves they are positioned as shown in Figure 2.

Fig. 2 ☐☐⚫⚫⚫⚫⭕⭕⭕⭕

1	2	3	4	5	6	7	8	9	10

SEND
+MORE
———
MONEY

A
B C D
E F G
H

Merlin's Notes

On the opposite page we have four puzzles from Merlin's personal notebook. They are all challenging, but I think he enjoys the third puzzle most of all.

The first problem deals with a fantastically accurate German cuckoo clock. If the clock takes six seconds to strike six, how many seconds will it take to strike nine? You have sixty seconds to solve the puzzle.

The far-out picture in frame two is a complicated box designed to hold the new, top secret Mark XII Pizza making machine. The box has 14 corners and 21 edges. How many faces does the box have?

Send More Money — the cry of the impoverished college student. A cry that this time will be answered if only his father can decipher the message. Each letter of the message represents a digit (zero through nine). How much, in dollars and cents, does his son need?

The fourth puzzle has nothing to do with Roman helmets. I just had four of them left, so I threw them in for decoration. Here the puzzle is to rearrange the letters A through H in the squares so that no two consecutive letters are adjacent to one another (not even diagonally).

hile touring the back country of his domain that Prince of Puzzlers, Merlin, chanced upon the ruins of a forgotten inn. Because of the great age of the buildings, Merlin eagerly set about exploring them for any ancient puzzles that may have been forgotten down through the centuries. The first puzzle he came to was cast in bronze and mounted on the stone wall by the entrance door.

"Eight farmers," read the instructions, "were given a parcel of land to farm. They were to divide it up into eight plots, all of the same shape and size. Before dividing up the land each farmer built his home. In the drawing the farmers' homes are represented by chess pawns and the land by half a chessboard. Show how the farmers divided up the land so that each plot was of the same size and shape and contained one house."

fter carefully recording the above puzzle in his notebook, Merlin was about to enter through the door in the wall when he noticed that the face on the clock above the door was broken into four pieces and that the Roman numerals on each piece added up to twenty. "This will make a fine puzzle to put before the Royal Court," thought Merlin. See if you can figure out how the clockface was broken.

aving passed through the gate into the courtyard, Merlin paused and studied the banner which hung above the entrance to the inn. "Everywhere I go I find puzzles," he mused. "Even the banner of the family which ran this inn was designed after one of the famous old continuous line puzzles."

Your problem is to duplicate the design of the banner by drawing one continuous line without lifting your pencil from the paper and without crossing one line over another. Folding the paper is not allowed.

ounting the steps to the inn door, Merlin halted and looked at the graffiti on the wall above the door. "This too, is an old puzzle," he thought to himself. "Let me see now, how did it go? Ah yes, the puzzle is to write the number 55 using five fours." Smiling over the answer, Merlin entered the inn. You too will be able to smile if you can solve this one.

Professor Hoffmann wrote many books dealing with magic, puzzles and home entertainment in the latter part of the 19th and early 20th centuries. His outstanding work was *Modern Magic*. There is great charm and ease of manner in his style of writing which creates a lasting friendship between reader and author. My favorite selection is *Puzzles Old and New*, which runs to 394 pages of the most varied and excellent of material. I have selected my favorite puzzles from this great book, along with many of the fine illustrations to be found therein. On the next 16 pages you will have the treat of matching wits with the good professor.

Good luck my friends, the professor is a hard man to beat.

THE "ENGLISH SIXTEEN" PUZZLE

A clever puzzle, under the above title, is issued by Messrs. Heywood, of Manchester.

A board, as illustrated on the next page, is used, with eight white and eight red counters. These are arranged on the black squares, the red to the right, the white to the left, the central square, No. 9 in the drawing, being left vacant. The problem is to transpose the red and white counters, the men to be moved according to "draughts" rules — i.e., forward only; the whites towards the spaces occupied by the reds, and the reds towards the spaces occupied by the whites. The men move only on the black squares, and therefore diagonally. A white man can pass over a red man, or a red man over a white man, provided that the space next beyond is vacant.

A SINGULAR SUBTRACTION

Required, to subtract 45 from 45 in such manner that there shall be 45 left.

A MYSTERIOUS MULTIPLICAND

Required, to find a number which, multiplied by 3, 6, 9, 12, 15, 18, 21, 24, or 27, shall in each case give as the product the same digit, three times repeated.

AN UNMANAGEABLE LEGACY

An old farmer left a will whereby he bequeathed his horses to his three sons, John, James and William, in the following proportions: John, the eldest, was to have one-half, James to have one-third, and William one-ninth. When he died, however, it was found that the number of horses in his stable was seventeen, a number which is divisible neither by two, by three, or nine. In their perplexity the three brothers consulted a clever lawyer, who hit on a scheme whereby the intentions of the testator were carried out to the satisfaction of all parties.

How was it managed?

A NOVEL CENTURY

Required, by multiplication and addition of the numbers 1 to 9 inclusive, to make 100, each number being used once, and once only.

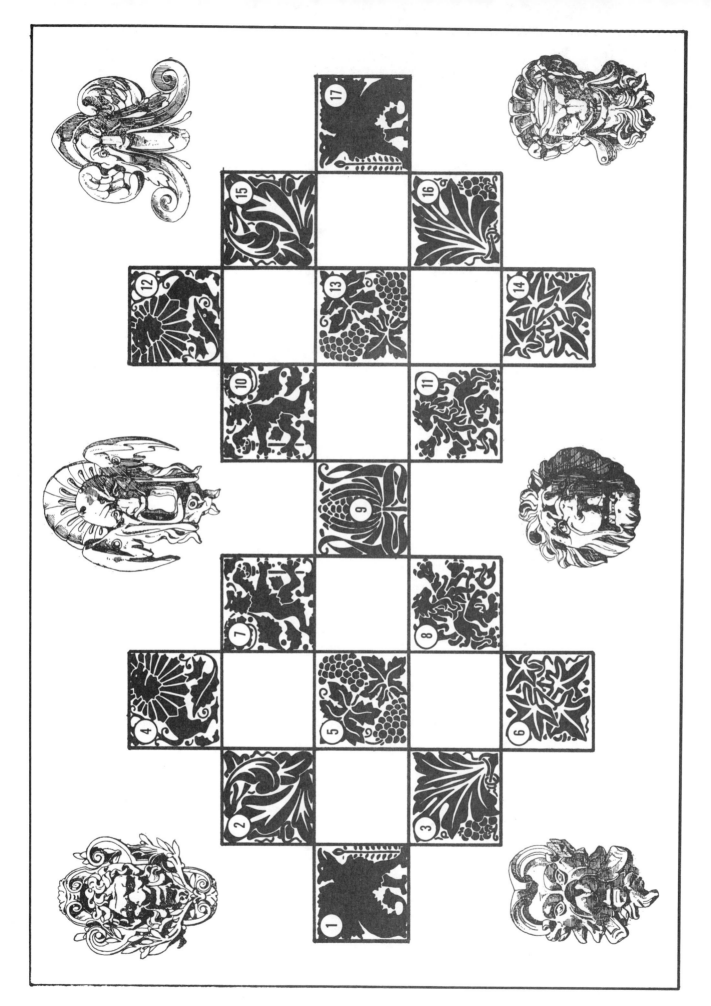

he following is from *Who's Who In Magic* by Will Goldston. "Professor Hoffmann, one of the greatest and grandest figures in modern magic, was by profession a barrister. His real name was Angelo Lewis. In addition to his living at Bar, Hoffmann was a free-lance journalist, and a reader for Messrs. Routledge, the London publishers. He wrote books on games under his real name and that of Hoffmann. From these, his interest turned to magic, and although well into adult years, magic became an obsession with him. He read such magical books as were in existence at his time, and thought them very poor. He examined the state of the professional stage, and was staggered at the number of imitators that were then bringing magic into disrepute. He personally appealed to these performers, urging them to change the stereotype nature of their programmes, but was met with abuse and ridicule at every hand. As a last resort, he threatened to expose their magical secrets: and this threat he eventually put into effect, with the assistance of Professor Bland, a magical dealer, who owned a store in Oxford Street, London. Hoffmann's articles in the London *Boy's Own Paper* created a sensation, and in spite of many threats, he continued with them. Eventually, they had the desired effect of creating variety in the performances of professional magicians. These articles were embodied, with additional exposes, in Hoffmann's first great magical work, entitled *Modern Magic*. It was, and still is, a standard work on magical principles, and through it many of the world's greatest performers have been attracted to magic. Curiously, Hoffmann as a performer was never impressive. His repertoire was small, and his execution rather clumsy. Nevertheless, his theoretical knowledge was immense. He followed *Modern Magic* with such important works as *More Magic, Later Magic,* and *Puzzles Old and New*. His *Latest Magic,* which Houdini persuaded him to publish, was his one mistake. It was badly written and conveyed very little valuable information; as a result Hoffmann lost something of his reputation as an author. About 1903, Hoffmann moved from London to Hastings, there to live in semi-retirement. He died in 1917.

THE EIGHT-POINTED STAR PROBLEM

Given, an eight-pointed star, as shown on page 33, and seven counters. You are required to place the counters on seven of the points of the star, in so doing strictly following the rule following – viz., Each counter is to be drawn from a vacant point along the corresponding line to another vacant point, and there left. You then start from another vacant point, and proceed in like manner till the seven points are covered.

CAN YOU NAME IT?

Required, to find a number which is just so much short of 50 as its quadruple is above 50.

ANOTHER CENTURY

Required, by addition only of the numbers 1 to 9 inclusive to make 100, each number being used once, and once only.

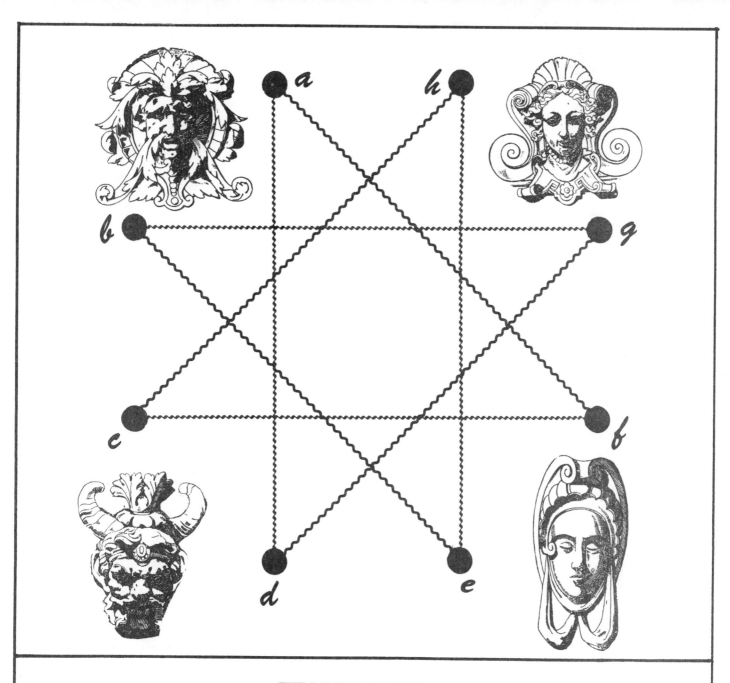

THE LUCKY NUMBER

Many persons have what they consider a "lucky" number. Show such a person the row of figures subjoined – 1, 2, 3, 4, 5, 6, 7, 9, (consisting of the numerals from 1 to 9 inclusive, with the 8 only omitted), and inquire what is his lucky or favourite number. He names any number he pleases from 1 to 9, say 7. You reply that, as he is fond of sevens, he shall have plenty of them, and accordingly proceed to multiply the series above given by such a number that the resulting product consists of sevens only.

Required, to find (for each number that may be selected) the multiplier which will produce the above result.

THE HUNDRED BOTTLES OF WINE

An innkeeper sold in eight days 100 bottles of wine, each day overpassing by three bottles the quantity sold on the previous day.

How many did he sell on the first, and on each of the succeeding days?

he puzzles on this page are from the book *Puzzles Old and New.*

JUST ONE OVER

A man, being asked how many sovereigns (coins) he had in his pocket, replied, "If I divide them by 2, by 3, by 4, by 5, or by 6, I shall always have one over."

What number had he?

A WEIGHTY MATTER

With how many weights, and of what denominations respectively, can you weigh any number of pounds from 1 to 127 inclusive?

THE EXPUNGED NUMERALS

Given, the sum following:

```
  111
  333
  555
  777
  999
```

Required, to strike out nine of the above figures, so that the total of the remaining figures shall be 1111.

BEHEADED WORDS

1. Behead a tree, and leave the roof of a vault.
2. Behead "on high," and leave the topmost story.
3. Behead "thrown violently," and leave an organ of the body.
4. Behead a preposition, and leave a contest.
5. Behead your own property, and leave ours.
6. Behead "to delete," and leave "to destroy."
7. Behead a reproach, and leave a relative.
8. Behead "to annoy," and leave comfort.
9. Behead an occurrence, and leave an airhole.

The deleted initials, taken in the above order will give the name of an American general after whom a well-known street in Paris is named. (To behead a word you drop the first letter of the word).

NINE COUNTERS

Required, to arrange nine counters (coins) in such a manner that they shall form ten rows, with three counters in each row.

THE MENAGERIE

The proprietor of a menagerie was asked how many birds and how many beasts it included. He replied, "Well, the lot have 36 heads and 100 feet."

How many of each were there?

THE TWO NUMBERS

There are two numbers, such that twice the first plus the second equals 17, and twice the second plus the first equals 19. Find the numbers.

Photograph of Professor Hoffmann

The Chess Master

Chess problems, in the ordinary sense, are interesting only to chess-players. But there is one particular chess puzzle, the so-called Knight's Tour, which requires no knowledge of chess, and may be attempted with success even by a person quite unacquainted with the game.

We may take it for granted that every reader knows that the chessboard consists of 64 squares (eight rows of eight squares each, black and white alternately). Some readers may, however, not be aware of the nature of the knight's move. The knight at chess moves in a rather peculiar way — viz., two squares straight (either forward, backward, or sideways), and one square to the right or left from the square thus reached, forming a sort of zigzag. Thus, assuming the knight to be placed on the square marked K in Fig. 1, he might be moved to any of those indicated by an asterisk.

The problem known by the name of The Knight's Tour is to move the knight from square to square of the board in such manner that he shall, in the course of 64 moves, have rested (once and once only) on every square.

The experimenter is to start with square number one, top left-hand corner. It is sometimes also made a condition that he should finish within a single move of the square from which he started. We will use this condition in our puzzle. Before attempting to solve the puzzle, the reader is recommended, if using the actual chessboard, to provide himself with a supply of small counters, and to place one by way of "mark" on each square to which he moves the knight, so that there may be no doubt as to which squares have or have not been visited.

Fig. 1

he following puzzles may be as hard to solve as getting loose from a Chinese Magic handcuff.

THE "TWENTY-SIX" PUZZLE

This is a magic square with a difference, the four corner places being omitted. The problem is to arrange the numbers 1 to 12 inclusive in the form of a cross, as shown in Fig. 1, so as to make 26 in seven different ways — viz., the two horizontal and the two vertical rows, the group of squares marked aaaa, the group marked bbbb, and group marked cccc, each making the above-mentioned total.

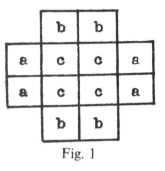

Fig. 1

MANY FIGURES, BUT A SMALL RESULT

Required, of the numbers 1, 2, 3, 4, 5, 6, 7, 8, 9, 0, to compose two fractions, whose sum shall be equal to 1. Each number to be used once, and once only.

THE CAPTIVES IN THE TOWER

An elderly queen, her daughter, and little son, weighing 195 pounds, 105 pounds, and 90 pounds respectively, were kept prisoners at the top of a high tower. The only communication with the ground below was a cord passing over a pulley, with a basket at each end, and so arranged that when one basket rested on the ground the other was opposite the window. Naturally, if the one were more heavily loaded than the other, the heavier would descend; but if the excess on either side was more than 15 pounds, the descent became so rapid as to be dangerous, and from the position of the rope the captives could not check it with their hands. The only thing available to help them in the tower was a cannonball, weighing 75 pounds. They, notwithstanding, contrived to escape.

How did they manage it?

A DIFFICULT DIVISION

A wine merchant has in his celler 21 casks. Seven are full of wine; seven half-full, and seven empty.

How can he divide them (without transferring any portion of the liquid from cask to cask) among his three sons — Dick, Tom, and Harry — so that each shall have not only an equal quantity of wine, but an equal number of casks?

NOTHING LEFT

There is a certain number from which, if you subtract ten, multiply the remainder by three, find the square root of the product, and from such square root subtract eighteen, nothing is left. What is the number?

THE THREE TRAVELLERS

Three travellers, accompanied by their servants, arrive at the bank of a river and desire to cross. The only means of transit is a boat which carries two persons. The travellers have reason to believe that the servants have entered into a conspiracy to rob and murder them, should they be able to get the upper hand. It is therefore essential that a single master should not be left alone with two of the servants, or two masters with all three of the servants.

How can the transit be arranged so as to avoid either of the above conditions?

DROPPED-LETTER PROVERBS

Supply the missing letters, and each of the series following will be found to represent a popular proverb. Each dash represents either a dropped letter or the space between two words. In some of the examples one dash stands for two dropped letters.

1 — A-t-t-h-n-t-m-s-v-s-n-n-.
2 — H-l-g-s-b-s-w-o-a-g-s-l-t.
3 — C-l-r-n-d-f-o-s-p-k-h-t-t-h.
4 — W-e-t-e-w-n-s-n-h-w-t-s-t.
5 — H-n-s-y-s-t-b-s-p-l-c-.

A PUZZLE WITH COUNTERS

Required, to arrange eleven counters in such a manner that they shall form twelve rows, with three counters in each row.

NO TWO IN A ROW

With an ordinary checkerboard, and eight checkers.

Required, so to dispose the eight checkers upon various squares of the board that no two shall be in the same line, either vertically, horizontally, or diagonally.

A CARD PUZZLE

Taking the four "fives" from a pack of cards, you are required to arrange them, face upwards, in such manner that only four pips of each shall be visible.

THE FOUR WINEGLASSES

Given, four wineglasses, of the same shape and size.

Required, so to arrange them that the centre of the foot of any one of them shall be equidistant from all the rest.

The "Forty-Five" Puzzle

The number 45 has some curious properties. Among others, it may be divided into four parts, in such manner that if you add two to the first, subtract two from the second, multiply the third by two, and divide the fourth by two, the result will in each case be equal. What are they?

Squares, Product, and Difference

Required, to find two numbers the sum of whose squares is greater by 181 than their product, and whose product is greater by 161 than their difference.

The Two Ages

Father and son are aged 71 and 34 respectively. At what age was the father three times the age of his son; and at what age will the latter have reached half his father's age?

The Shepherd and His Sheep

A shepherd was asked how many sheep he had in his flock. He replied that he could not say, but he knew if he counted them by twos, by threes, by fours, by fives, or by sixes, there was always one over; but if he counted them by sevens, there was none over. What is the smallest number which will answer the above conditions?

When Will They Get It?

Seven guests at a restaurant came, the first every day, the second every other day, the third every third day, and so on to the seventh, who came once a week only. The host, in a liberal mood, declared that on the first day all came together he would treat them to a dinner gratis. How soon, according to the above order of rotation, would they be in position to claim his promise?

The Two Sons

An elderly mathematician was asked what were the ages of his two sons. He replied, "The one is five and a quarter years older than the other, and six times the age of the elder, added to five times the age of the younger, would be 301."

What was the age of each?

Crossette

Arrange in the form of a circle ten smaller circles (see Fig. 1).

Starting from any circle you please, and calling such circle 1, the next 2, and so on, place a coin on the fourth. Then start again from any uncovered circle you please, count 1, 2, 3, 4, and place a coin on the fourth. Proceed as above until all but one has a coin on it. You may count either backwards or forwards. Circles with coins on them are to be reckoned in the counting, but the count of "four" must in each case fall upon a circle which does not have a coin upon it.

Fig. 1

The Orchard Puzzle

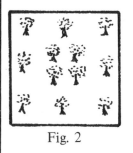

Fig. 2

A farmer had an orchard, wherein were twelve fruit trees in the positions shown in Fig. 2. He directed that on his decease the orchard should be equally divided between his four sons, with the proviso that the portion taken by each was to be of the same size and shape, and to contain three of the twelve fruit trees. How was it done?

Single-Stroke Figures

A good deal of ingenuity may be exercised in the attempt to describe geometrical figures without taking the pencil from the paper, or passing over any line for the second time. (see Fig. 3). The double crescent (Fig. 4), or so-called Seal of Mahomet, is another pretty example, the legend being that the prophet was accustomed to describe it with one stroke of his scimitar, by no means a difficult feat, notwithstanding its apparent complexity.

Fig. 3

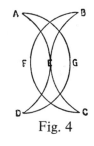

Fig. 4

The Two Travellers

Traveller A

A and B are travelling the same road, A going four miles an hour, B five miles an hour. But A has two and a half hours' start. In what length of time will B overtake A, and how far from the starting point?

Traveller B

The "Right and Left" Puzzle

This is a very excellent puzzle and has the special recommendation of being very little known. Using the board provided on the next page, place 17 white counters on the left side of the board and 17 black counters on the right side of the board. The puzzle is to transpose the black and white counters, so that the 17 white shall be in the right hand, and the 17 black in the left hand spaces. This is to be done in accordance with the following conditions – viz.:

1. Each counter can only be moved 1 space at a time.
2. If a counter is divided from a vacant space by a single counter, it may pass over it into the vacant space.
3. Counters may only be moved in a forward or up and down direction (black to the left, white to the right). A move once made cannot be retracted.

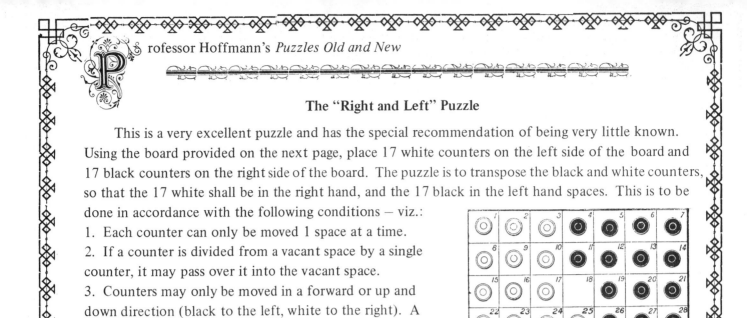

Skihi

This also is sold as a game, but comes more properly within the category of puzzles. It is a patent, and the property of the Skihi Novelty Company, London, W.C. The set consists of 48 square cards, 2 inches each way, and of various colors. Each card has four slots cut in it, as shown in Fig. 1. There are also 10 circular cards, each with three slots, as shown in Fig. 2. These cards may be utilized to form an almost unlimited number of fanciful designs. We subjoin a few examples (see Figs. 3-6), which will give some idea of the very wide capabilities of this clever toy. All of these may be constructed with a single set. By using three or four sets in conjunction, very much more ambitious designs may be executed.

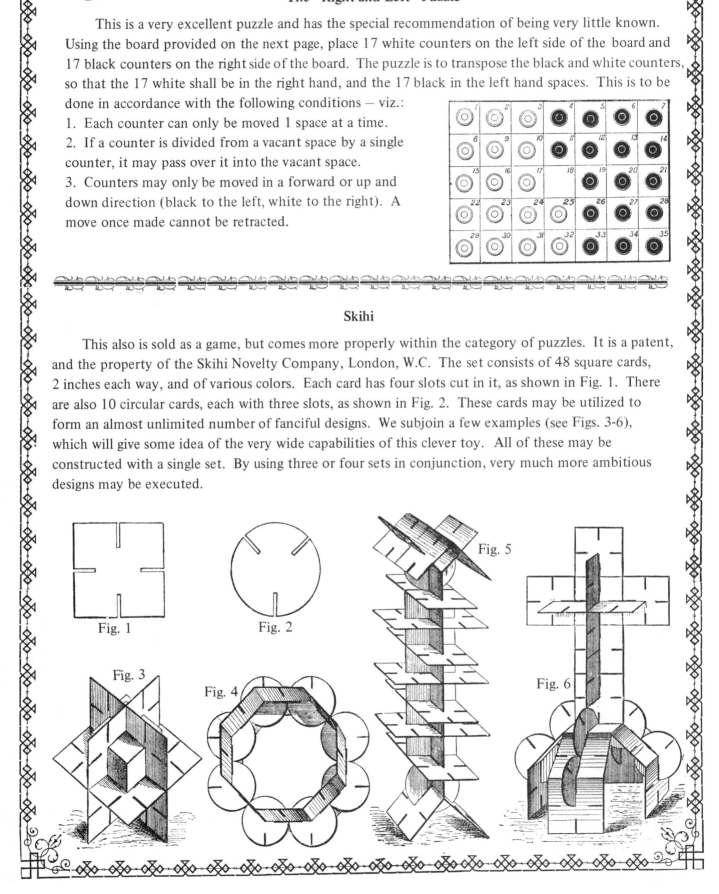

Fig. 1

Fig. 2

Fig. 5

Fig. 3

Fig. 4

Fig. 6

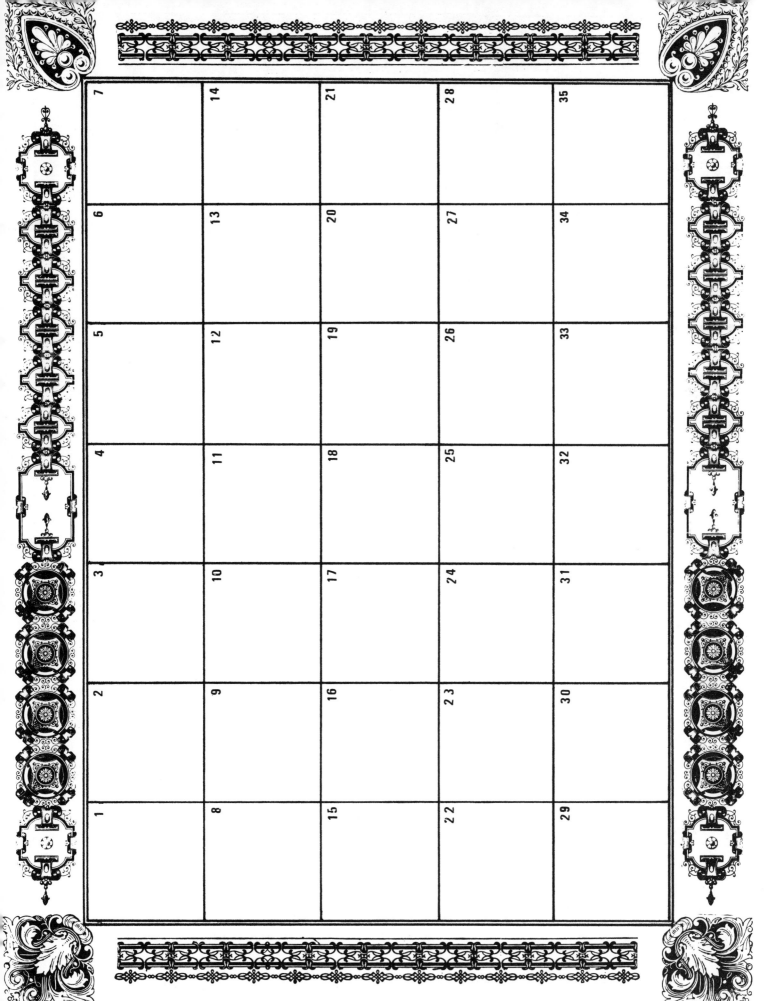

he Treasure at Medinet

This puzzle comes from Germany, but is said to be of Oriental origin.

The legend accompanying it is to the effect that an Eastern prince, Haroun al Elim, in far back times ruled over a range of country with eight sugar-loaf hills, on each of which was erected a fortress. Each fortress, with the surrounding district, was under the command of a governor, but the jealousies of the eight governors and their respective underlings led to affrays and bloodshed whenever they chanced to meet. To lessen the chance of such meetings, Haroun made a number of roads, eight crossing his kingdom in one direction, eight more at right angles to them, and others crossing diagonally.

These were so arranged with reference to the castles that the occupants of each castle had a clear road in each direction through and out of the prince's territory without passing any other castle.

The castles, says the legend, are now in ruins and the roads no longer traceable; but a plan of them is still preserved among the archives of the Mosque Al Redin, at Medinet on the coast of the Red Sea. Unfortunately, the plan, which was folded in four, has been worn by age into four separate fragments, and the utmost skill of the Cadi of the mosque has failed to discover their proper relative positions. He has therefore offered a reward – The Great Sword of Basra, reputed to have once belonged to the mighty Saladin, now preserved at Medinet – to anyone who may succeed in placing the four fragments in their original positions – viz., with no two castles on either road, either horizontal, vertical, or diagonal.

For the use of the Infidel, the severed map has been reproduced on four separate cards, A, B, C, and D. See page 274 for a duplication master.

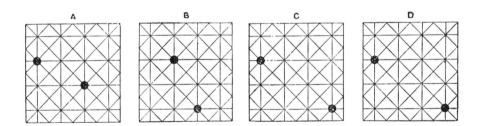

The Market Woman and her Stock

A woman selling apples met three boys. The first bought half her stock, and gave her back 10; the second bought a third of what she had then remaining, and gave her back 2; and the third bought half of her then remaining store, and gave her back 1; after which she found that she had 12 apples left.

How many had she at first?

The Three Arabs

Two Bedouin Arabs halted in the desert to eat their midday meal. Their store consisted of eight small loaves, of which five belonged to the first and three to the second. Just as they sat down, a third Arab overtook them and asked to be permitted to share their meal, to which they agreed. Each ate an equal portion of the eight loaves, and the third Arab, at the close of the meal, handed the others eight pieces of money in payment. A dispute arose as to the division of the money, the first Arab maintaining that as he had had five loaves and the other three only, the money should be divided in the same proportion. The other maintained that as all had eaten equally, each should take half the money between them. Finally, they agreed to refer the matter to the third Arab, who declared that both were in the wrong, and pointed out the proper division.

What was it?

The Three Market Women

Three peasant women went to market to sell apples. The first had 33, the second 29, and the third 27 only. Each of them gave the same number of apples for a penny, and yet, when they got home, they found that each had received an equal amount of money.

How could such a result come to pass?

An Aggravating Uncle

An uncle with a turn for figures presented his youthful nephew with a box of soldiers, but made it a condition that he should not play with them till he could discover, on arithmetical principles, how many the box contained. He was told that if he placed them three in a row, there would be one over; if he placed them four in a row, there would be two over; if five in a row, three over; if six in a row, he would have four over. The total number was under 100.

How many soldiers did the box contain?

The False Scales

A cheese put into one of the scales of a false balance was found to weigh 16 lbs. When placed in the opposite scale it weighed 9 lbs. only. What was its actual weight?

The Divided Square

Given, a square of cardboard of, say, two inches each way. Required, to divide it into five equal squares.

43

A Box of Puzzles

ome eighty years ago Mr. J. Bland, of New Oxford Street, sold a most wonderful assortment of puzzles. The good Professor has assembled a few of the more readily constructed mechanical puzzles for you to build. Coat hanger wire should suffice for the construction of the wire puzzles, while cardboard, plywood and lattice strips will do for the other items.

The Triangle

The wire is here bent into a triangle, or rather succession of triangles, the one within the other, and terminates on the outside in a ring passing round the next adjacent portion of the wire (see Fig. 1). From the triangle hangs a long wire loop, like a lady's hairpin, save that it is secured by a sort of crossbar at the opposite end.

The puzzle is to detach the loop from the triangle.

The Interlaced Triangles

The wire is in this case so manipulated as to form five triangles, four of them in pairs, lying one above the other; the fifth of smaller size, connected with the larger triangles by a tiny ring, and forming a "stop" to a larger ring, which it is the "crux" of the puzzle to disengage (see Fig. 2).

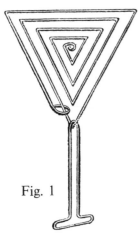

Fig. 1

Fig. 2

The United Hearts

We have here (see Fig. 3) the representation, in copper wire, of a couple of hearts, the one interlaced within the other. The problem is to separate them.

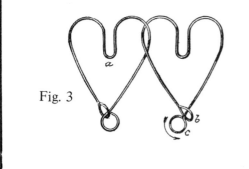

Fig. 3

The Heart Puzzle

This is a very easy puzzle. It consists of a heart-shaped piece of boxwood, through which is threaded a silken cord terminating in a glass ball, as shown in Fig. 4. The problem to be solved is the detaching of the cord and ball from the heart.

The Chinese Ladder

This is a puzzle of a different kind, the "loop" element being in this case wanting. It is said to be a genuine importation from China. It consists of a small wooden ladder of four steps (see Fig. 5). Each step has two holes in it. A silken cord a yard in length, secured at top with a knot and glass bead, is threaded through each hole in succession (down one side and up the other). Between each pair of holes it is also threaded through a hole in a bone counter, so that there are two counters in each compartment. To the free end of the cord is attached a stout needle.

The puzzle is to bring the whole of the counters *together* on the cord.

Fig. 4

The Imperial Scale

This is a puzzle of a more difficult character, though, like many others, easy enough when you know it. It consists (see Fig. 6) of a flat piece of boxwood, three inches square, with eight holes in it, four in the centre and one at each corner. Through each of the corner holes passes a silken cord about four inches in length, secured by a glass bead on the under side and united with the rest in a knot at top. A fifth cord, of rather more than double length is passed downwards through two of the centre holes, then up again through the other two and through the loop formed by the passage of the cord through the first pair of holes, the two ends then being made to form part of the general knot at top. Between the loop and the standing part of the central cord is secured a ring, of bone or metal.

Fig. 5

The problem is, without untying either of the knots, to detach the ring from the cord, and again to restore it to its position.

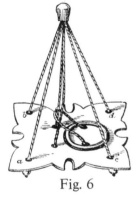

Fig. 6

The Cross-Keys or Three-piece Puzzle

This (Fig. 7) is a very ingenious puzzle of its kind. It is one of the simplest, in one sense, being composed of only three pieces of wood, but they are interlocked with extreme ingenuity, and the endeavour to separate them will give a good deal of trouble. Indeed, one's first impression on a casual inspection is that the whole must have been carved out of a single piece.

Contrary to the usual rule, the reconstruction of the puzzle will here be found easier than its separation.

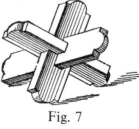

Fig. 7

(1)
OANNES

(2)
NIMROD

(3)
NISROCH

long the banks of the Tigris and Euphrates rivers some 4,000 years ago, the people of Babylon played a game called Mazda. The greatest player of all time was the great law giver, King Hammurabi. He left a record of his playing system engraved upon the back of the diorite monument which recorded his famous set of laws.

On the next page is a copy of the moves and countermoves he used. Using this table we can match wits, at this late date, with the Grand Master of Mazda. The rules of play are simple. Set up the playing board by placing 3 shekels (coins) on Oannes (1), 4 shekels on Nimrod (2) and 5 shekels on Nisroch (3). Play alternates between two players. During a player's turn he *must* remove at least one coin from one of the three piles. He can remove the whole pile or any part of the pile. The player can remove coins from only one pile at a time. The loser is the one who is *forced* to remove the last coin from the board. Now that you know the rules try a game with Hammurabi. At the top of each column of moves on the next page is the key "1 2 3 P T." The "1 2 3" stands for each one of the piles of coins. The "P" stands for the word PILE and the "T" stands for the word TAKE. Here's how we use this key: If you start the game by removing 2 coins from pile 3, the board setup would be 3 coins in pile 1, 4 coins in pile 2 and 3 coins in pile 3 (3-4-3). To find Hammurabi's countermove look down the columns under 1 2 3 until you find (3-4-3). Then look to the right (under P T) and you will find 2-4. This is the countermove and means "From PILE 2 TAKE 4 coins". Remove 4 coins from pile 2 and it's your turn again. If you wish Hammurabi to go first remove 2 coins from pile 1. This was always his opening move.

1 2 3	P T	1 2 3	P T	1 2 3	P T	1 2 3	P T	1 2 3	P T
3-4-5	1-2	3-0-5	3-2	2-1-5	3-2	1-2-5	3-2	0-3-5	3-2
3-4-4	1-3	3-0-4	3-1	2-1-4	3-1	1-2-4	3-1	0-3-4	3-1
3-4-3	2-4	3-0-3	3-1	2-1-3	1-1	1-2-3	2-1	0-3-3	3-1
3-4-2	2-3	3-0-2	1-1	2-1-2	2-1	1-2-2	1-1	0-3-2	2-1
3-4-1	2-2	3-0-1	1-3	2-1-1	1-1	1-2-1	2-1	0-3-1	2-3
3-4-0	2-1	3-0-0	1-2	2-1-0	1-2	1-2-0	2-2	0-3-0	2-2
3-3-5	3-5	2-4-5	1-1	2-0-5	3-3	1-1-5	3-4	0-2-5	3-3
3-3-4	3-4	2-4-4	1-2	2-0-4	3-2	1-1-4	3-3	0-2-4	3-2
3-3-3	3-3	2-4-3	2-3	2-0-3	3-1	1-1-3	3-2	0-2-3	3-1
3-3-2	3-2	2-4-2	2-4	2-0-2	3-1	1-1-2	3-1	0-2-2	3-1
3-3-1	3-1	2-4-1	2-1	2-0-1	1-2	1-1-1	3-1	0-2-1	2-2
3-3-0	2-1	2-4-0	2-2	2-0-0	1-1	1-1-0	2-1	0-2-0	2-1
3-2-5	3-4	2-3-5	3-4	1-4-5	2-1	1-0-5	3-5	0-1-5	3-5
3-2-4	3-3	2-3-4	3-3	1-4-4	1-1	1-0-4	3-4	0-1-4	3-4
3-2-3	2-2	2-3-3	3-2	1-4-3	2-2	1-0-3	3-3	0-1-3	3-3
3-2-2	1-3	2-3-2	3-1	1-4-2	2-1	1-0-2	3-2	0-1-2	3-2
3-2-1	2-1	2-3-1	1-1	1-4-1	2-3	1-0-1	3-1	0-1-1	3-1
3-2-0	1-1	2-3-0	2-1	1-4-0	2-4	1-0-0	lost	0-1-0	lost
3-1-5	3-3	2-2-5	3-5	1-3-5	3-3	0-4-5	3-1	0-0-5	3-4
3-1-4	3-2	2-2-4	3-4	1-3-4	3-2	0-4-4	3-1	0-0-4	3-3
3-1-3	3-1	2-2-3	3-2	1-3-3	1-1	0-4-3	2-1	0-0-3	3-2
3-1-2	3-1	2-2-2	3-2	1-3-2	3-1	0-4-2	2-2	0-0-2	3-1
3-1-1	1-2	2-2-1	3-1	1-3-1	2-2	0-4-1	2-4	0-0-1	lost
3-1-0	1-3	2-2-0	2-1	1-3-0	2-3	0-4-0	2-3		

The Wizard

rom The Wizard comes this puzzle to mystify your friends. After getting two people to step forward from your audience, announce that you are going to conduct a paper-cutting race. Pick up a three-foot loop of paper from the table (Loop A) and pierce the center with the point of a pair of scissors. Cut along the center line of the loop until you reach the starting point. You will now have two *separate* loops. Tell the contestants that they must do the same with their loops and that the first one to finish will receive $5.00. Give them each a pair of scissors and a loop of paper 15 feet long and start the race. Sad to say, neither party will win. Your paper loop had no twist in it when it was made, so when it was cut it became two separate loops. Loop "B" was made with one twist in it and when cut around the middle will become a single loop twice as long as it was before being cut. Loop "C" was made with two twists in it, and when it is cut around the middle it will become two *interlocking* loops, not separate as specified. Make the loops out of newspaper or adding machine tape 3 or 4 inches wide. With loops 15 feet long the twists in the paper will not be noticeable.

Loop A   Loop B   Loop C

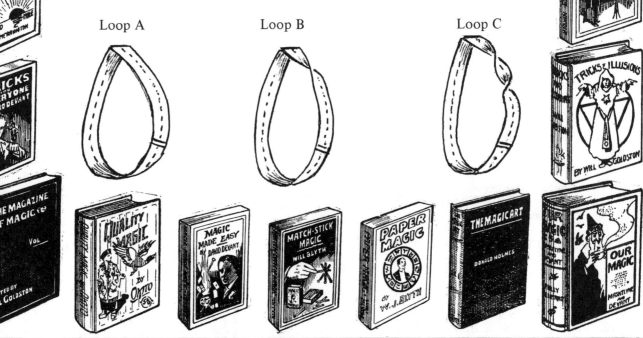

irates' Gold" is a game of rummy played in days gone by. It is said that many a king and buccaneer lost his fortune pursuing this game. The fascination for it is easily understood, for once you have played it you will see that here is a game that is far superior to many other forms of rummy. It can be played by two players or as many as eight or more. When a great number of people play you can use two decks.

The rules of play are as follows:

1. The complete game consists of 13 hands of rummy.

2. In the first hand aces are wild. In the second, twos are wild, and so on up through the thirteenth hand when kings are wild.

3. When you lay down a meld, it can be 3 or 4 of a kind but no more than 4. A straight must be 3 or more cards of the same suit. You can use your wild cards when melding.

4. You cannot play cards off on another person's meld, or exchange a card for a wild card, unless you already have a meld of your own down.

5. If during your turn twos are wild, and someone has a meld down with two tens and a two and you have a ten in your hand, you can substitute your ten for his two and then use this wild card in your hand to make up a new meld.

6. Each player gets 7 cards to start. The dealer gets 8 and discards one face-up to begin the play.

7. The hand ends when someone has melded all of his cards.

8. After a hand ends, all of the other players add up the points in their respective hands. Ace is one point, all face cards count 10 points and each wild card counts 25. The player who went out gets zero points. The points for each player are entered on a score sheet.

9. After 13 hands have been played the player with the lowest score wins.

ver a thousand years ago a giant wave raced across the Pacific and crashed upon the shores of the Japanese island of Miyako Shima.

When the islanders, who had taken refuge in the hills beyond the coast, returned to their village they were astonished to see that their homes still stood and that their fishing boats lay at anchor, undamaged. A miracle had saved them. A mysterious miracle. For down on the beach they found 10 shields bearing the crests of the leading samurais of Japan. They had been en route from Formosa to Kyushu when the wave had smashed their sailboat and all on board had been lost to the sea. The shields lay in the sand exactly as pictured on page 51. A monk by the name of Eisai, after seeing the crests, said that they were a sign showing that the peaceful villagers were favored by the gods above the warlike samurai. To commemorate their deliverance the monk created a puzzle that all the people of Miyako Shima must solve every year on the anniversary of The Great Wave. If you care to test your skill against the residents of Miyako Shima the rules are simple. Place 2 white counters on shields 1 and 2, and 2 red counters on shields 9 and 10. The puzzle is to make the red and white counters change places. You can slide the counters along a straight line one at a time in any order you like. No jumping allowed. The only thing you are not allowed to do is to have a red and white counter standing on the same line at the same time. To illustrate this point, your first move can only be from 1 or 2 to 3, or from 9 or 10 to 7.

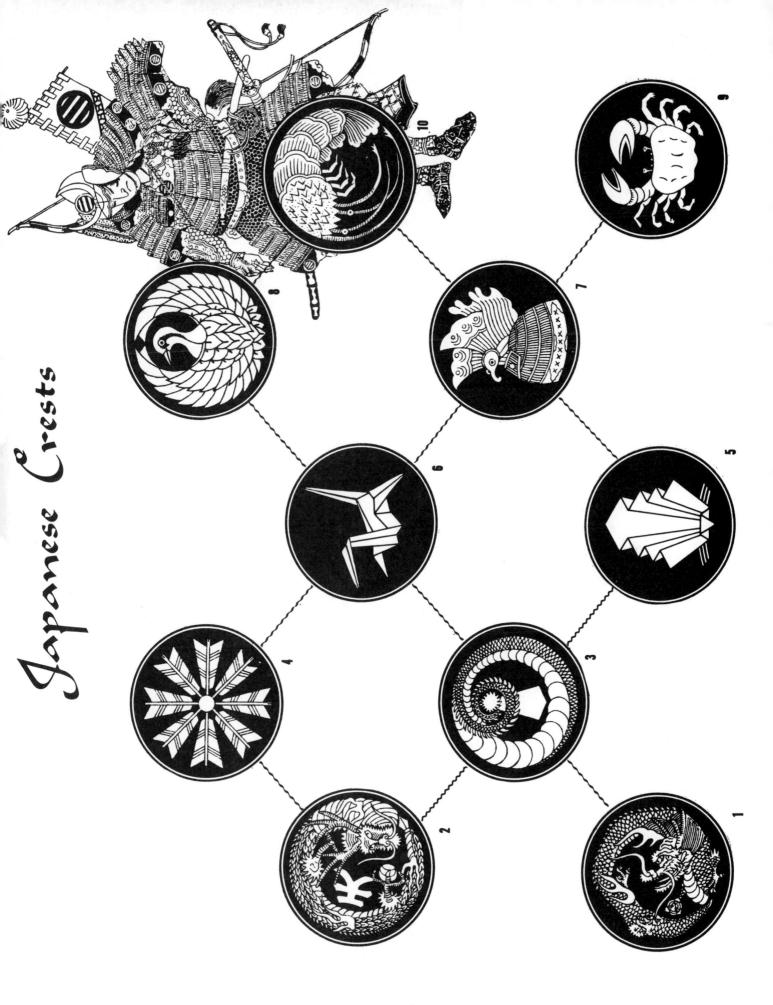

Japanese Crests

O n page 53 of this book you will find the layout for a solitaire game I call The Lion. It is a very ancient puzzle sometimes known as Central Solitaire. I call it The Lion because it is certainly one of the most enduring of puzzles, appearing again and again in the literature of puzzledom. Very often the problem is made up in the form of a circular wooden board with holes drilled in the top to hold marbles which serve as counters.

To play this game you will need 32 counters (small poker chips, or pennies will do). Place a counter on every numbered space except the center one, No. 17. The problem is to remove 31 of the counters from the board, leaving the last one in the center space. Just as in the game of checkers, you are allowed to jump one counter over the next one to a vacant space beyond. The counter that was jumped over is then removed from the board. Every move must be a jump. Thirty-one moves would clear all but the last counter from the board. Just as in checkers you can jump more than one counter during any given move, making it possible to solve this problem in a good deal less than 31 moves. Our solution uses 19. No diagonal jumps are allowed; you can only jump in the direction of the lines. Good luck.

VOLTAIRE'S RIDDLE. What is the longest and yet the shortest thing in the world; the swiftest and the slowest; the most divisible and the most extended; the least valued and the most regretted; without which nothing can be done; which devours everything, however small, and yet gives life and spirit to all things, however great?

THE FOX AND RABBITS

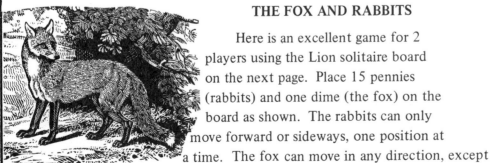

Here is an excellent game for 2 players using the Lion solitaire board on the next page. Place 15 pennies (rabbits) and one dime (the fox) on the board as shown. The rabbits can only move forward or sideways, one position at a time. The fox can move in any direction, except diagonally, one position at a time. Just as in checkers, the fox can take a rabbit by jumping over him into a vacant position beyond. The object of the game is to bottle-up the fox so that he cannot make a move in any direction.

THE  LION

A KEGLERS DELIGHT

One game that has steadily gained in popularity down through the years is bowling. Now happily, we can all play this game at home. All you need are five pairs of dice and an empty can with one end cut off to use as a dice cup. The play is very simple. When it is your turn to bowl place the ten dice in the cup. Shake the dice and spill them onto the table. If none of the 10 dice has a six up, then you have thrown a strike. If three of the dice have a six up, then this indicates that three pins have been left standing and that you have to bowl again and try for a spare. You would then take the three dice with the sixes up and place them in the cup. Shake these dice and spill them onto the table.

BOWLING.

STRIKE

If none of the three dice have a six up then you have made your spare. If one of the dice has a six up then your score for the frame comes to nine and you pass the dice to the next player. That's all there is to playing this game. Scoring is the same as in bowling. Have a good time.

A CIRCLE OF COINS

Start with six coins of the same value placed in two rows with all coins touching. The problem is to reform them into a *perfect* circle by moving just one coin at a time. It can be done in only three moves.

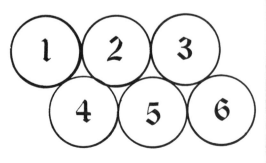

he above drawing is a cartouche by the famed baroque artist, Johann Ulrich Krauss (1655-1719). Framed within this cartouche is a puzzle which was a favorite of King Louis XIV of France. The Sun King had great success in perplexing nearly everyone he challenged with it except his wily superintendent of finance, Nicolas Fouquet. This gentleman dashed off the answer so quickly that the king became suspicious of his honesty and had Colbert, the minister of finance, check his books for any misappropriation of funds. This Colbert did, and history attests to the fact that Fouquet quickly found himself imprisoned. What is this puzzle then that proved to be the petard that Fouquet did hoist himself upon?

Simply take the digits 1 through 11 and place them in the circles so that they add up to the same amount in any direction. That is, the sum of the three circles on any line will always be the same. Simple? Well, don't solve it too quickly or someone's suspicion may fall upon you.

The Hampton Court Maze

Start

abyrinths, or mazes, have been a source of entertainment and confusion ever since Theseus slew the Minotaur on the island of Crete. Architectural and decorative mazes abound in all ages of history. One of the favorite devices of old was the giant garden mazes created by royalty for the amusement of the court. The famous Hampton Court Maze, built by William III, is pictured above. It was made up of paths and thickly trimmed hedges some eight to ten feet high. As a challenge on paper I am sure you will have no difficulty in finding your way to the center and back out again. There is, however, a method which may be employed that will unerringly guide the maze traveler into the center of the garden and back out again. It is this device that I challenge the puzzler to find. The solution is as cunning as the mind of Daedalus, yet as simple as the thread of Ariadne.

Illustration from *Amusements in Mathematics*, by H.E. Dudeny

56

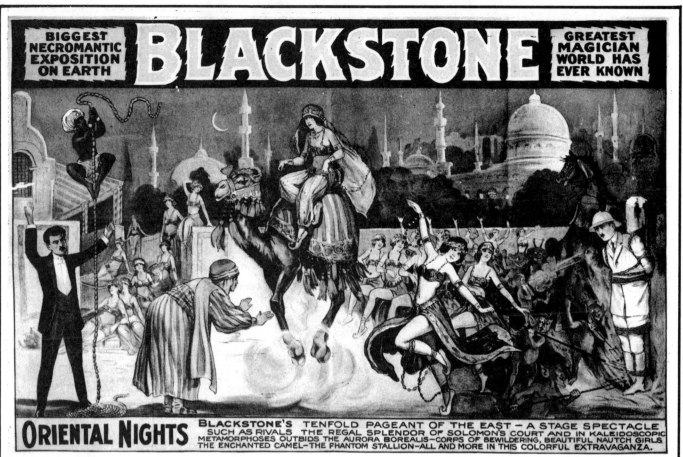

BLACKSTONE

BIGGEST NECROMANTIC EXPOSITION ON EARTH

GREATEST MAGICIAN WORLD HAS EVER KNOWN

ORIENTAL NIGHTS

BLACKSTONE'S TENFOLD PAGEANT OF THE EAST — A STAGE SPECTACLE SUCH AS RIVALS THE REGAL SPLENDOR OF SOLOMON'S COURT AND IN KALEIDOSCOPIC METAMORPHOSES OUTBIDS THE AURORA BOREALIS—CORPS OF BEWILDERING, BEAUTIFUL NAUTCH GIRLS THE ENCHANTED CAMEL—THE PHANTOM STALLION—ALL AND MORE IN THIS COLORFUL EXTRAVAGANZA.

rom the ancient books of magical learning comes this pretty problem in paperclip prestidigitation. The items needed to perform this parlous trick are a bill (the larger the denomination the better) and two paperclips. Fold the bill carefully, as shown in the illustration, and place the two paperclips in position. Remark to your audience that all of the great magicians of the past, Houdini, Thurston, Blackstone, had astonished one and all alike by linking and unlinking solid steel rings. Their secret is now in your possession and you will show them how easy it is for you to do by linking these two paperclips together. Fitting your action to your words, smartly pull the ends of the bill apart. The paperclips will fly into the air and fall to the table joined together. Just follow the illustration and the trick works itself. It is also possible to link three paperclips in this fashion but the method for doing so I leave for you to discern.

ZAP

The Earl's Puzzle

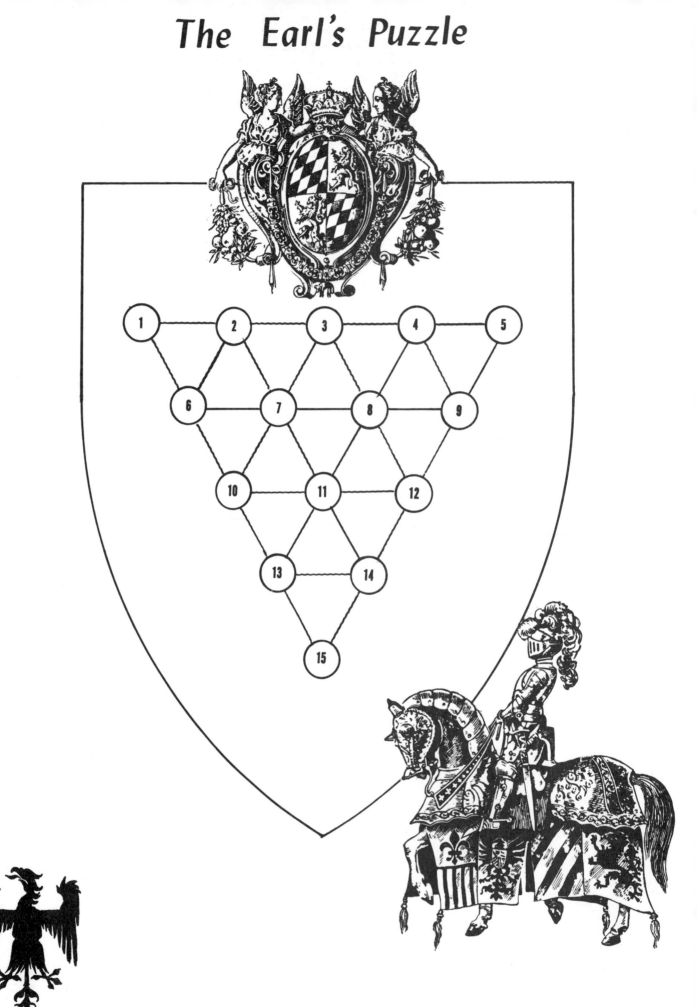

n page 58 you will find a picture of The Earl of Puzzledom and his battle shield, which is decorated with his official family puzzle. This is the equivalent of a coat of arms on the Isle of Merlin. To solve this puzzle you must first place a coin on each of the circles numbered 1 thru 14, leaving 15 empty.

The object is to remove all the coins but one from the board. You play by jumping one coin over another. The space beyond the coin that is jumped must be empty. You then remove the coin that was jumped. You can only jump in a straight line.

Those are the rules, folks. We give you a half an hour to solve it. Good luck.

Alice in Puzzleland

	A		EF	HI	KLMN
BCD		G		J		OP

ell, Alice, my dear," said the Duchess, "put down that croquet mallet and give me your attention. You will need more than five minutes to solve my puzzle. Framed in the picture above, we have a portion of the alphabet. Some of the letters are above the line and some are below the line. You are to write the remaining letters, placing them correctly either above or below the line. I will meet you at the Palace when you have finished.

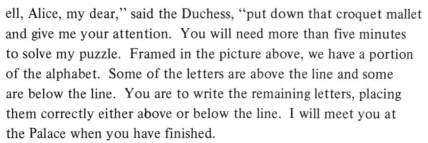

59

INDIA
Squares

Here is an interesting magic square from India. If you add up the 5 numbers in each spoke of the wheel in Fig. 1 you will see that the total in each case is 65. Also, if you add up the 5 numbers in each circle you will find that they, too, will total 65. You can make this magic square up in the form of a mechanical puzzle that will perplex and delight your friends. Cut out 5 circular pieces of cardboard, each smaller than the last, and fasten them together with a small staple through the middle. Print 5 numbers on each disc, just as they appear in Fig. 1. Now move the 5 discs around the staple in different directions, so that the numbers no longer add up to 65 in each spoke. Hand the puzzle to someone and see if he can reposition the discs so that they once more add up to 65 along each spoke. To make it harder do not show him the puzzle setup as you see it in Fig. 1 before he tries to solve it.

See page 273 for a duplication master.

Fig. 1

The emperor Wu Ch'uan-Chih of the Yuan dynasty brings to us this fascinating puzzle using a very old Chinese chessboard. The problem is to place 9 coins upon various squares of the board in such a way that no two shall be in the same line, vertically, horizontally or diagonally. It should be stated that the indentations on either side of the board do not affect the conditions. Thus, two counters placed respectively in the left-hand top and bottom corner squares would be regarded as being in the same line, notwithstanding that there is a break of continuity between them.

A Monstrous Problem

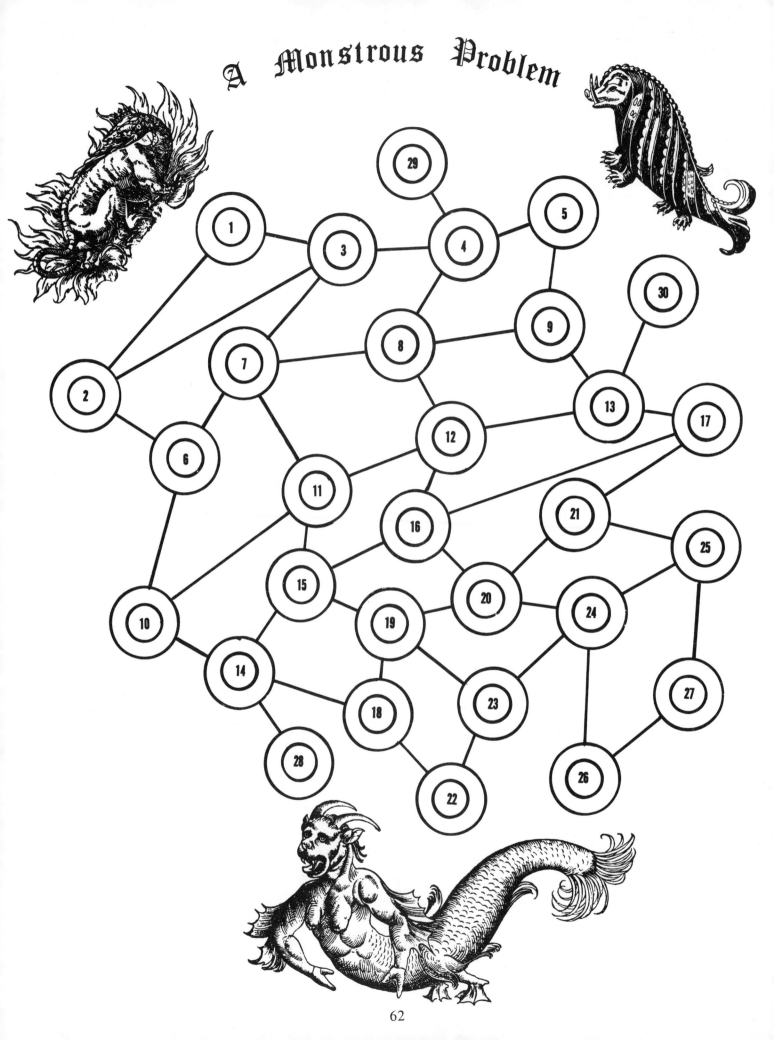

ye, lads, there is a monstrous problem to be solved, for there be a Thing, we know not what, which prowls the Glen at night. Now, the villagers are gathering at the ruins of Carfax Abbey tonight, and from this point they will enter the Glen and seek out this devil. Will they find and capture it? Could you lead them to success where so many have failed in the past? Let us make a game of it and see if you can triumph over the forces of darkness?

Using the game board on page 62, place a black checker on position 12; this will represent the monster. Place a red checker on position 26; this is the starting point for the villagers at Carfax Abbey. The numbered positions on the board are the intersections of the many paths that run through the forest. The game is won when the red checker can be moved to the same position the black checker occupies. The game always begins by moving the red checker first. The play then alternates between the black and the red. Each move consists of moving a checker from one position to an adjacent position along one of the paths that join them together. At first it will appear that if the black side is careful in its choice of moves that it can always stay one position ahead of the pursuing red forces and thus cause a stalemate. Fortunately this need not be the case, for there is a way that the red forces can always be sure of scoring a victory over the black. It is this secret that you must fathom before the Glen can be returned to the peace and tranquility it enjoyed in the past.

THE SPHINX

n June 6th, 1865, Professor Stodare presented before The Prince of Wales a marvelous illusion called The Sphinx, or The Talking Head. The Sphinx, which reposed in a box upon a table in the middle of the stage, answered all questions put to it by the assembled spectators. Then the Sphinx, in its turn, propounded a series of puzzles and riddles for the audience to answer. The following questions are a sampling of these problems.

1. Prove that seven is half of twelve.

2. Place three sixes together so as to make seven.

3. What lives in winter, dies in summer and grows with its roots upwards?

4. Required: to express 100 by repetition of the same figure six times over.

5. What is the surest way of keeping water from entering your house?

6. Five herrings were divided among five persons. Each had a herring and yet one remained in the dish. How was this managed?

7. What gets bigger the more you contract it?

8. Prove that two sixes make eleven.

9. What speaks all languages?

10. You undertake to show another person something which you never saw before, which he never saw before, and which, after you both have seen it, no one else will ever see again. How is it to be done?

11. You undertake to put something into a person's left hand which he cannot possibly take in his right. How is it to be done?

12. Required: to take one from nineteen and leave twenty. How is it to be done?

The Wizard

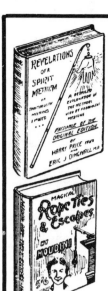

On three sides of this page we find displayed many of Merlin's favorite books on legerdemain, sleight of hand and puzzles. He has graciously consented once again to test our powers of perception with a problem well calculated to perplex the most astute puzzle aficionado. Below we find six glasses, three filled with liquid and three empty. Can you rearrange the order of glasses, by moving or touching only one glass, so that they stand in the following order: (1) filled (2) empty (3) filled (4) empty (5) filled (6) empty. The answer is quite surprising.

Alice in Puzzleland

lice, as usual, was late for her afternoon tea with the Mad Hatter. Also, as usual, she had lost her way. The first person she met was Humpty Dumpty. "Mr. Dumpty, could you please tell me the way to the Mad Hatter's house?" "Only if you can solve this eggtraordinary puzzle. I have five eggs all exactly the same in shape but no two of them is of the same weight. Using only a simple balancing scale, you must arrange them in order of weight from the lightest to the heaviest. This must be done in no more than seven weighings." Alice solved the problem in five minutes and was on her way in the direction given to her by Humpty Dumpty. In less than five minutes she was lost again. Presently she came across the Walrus and the Carpenter arguing on the beach. "I say it can't be done," said the Walrus. "And I say it can if I could only remember how," rejoined the Carpenter. "What are you talking about?" asked Alice. "He says that he can take a board one foot wide by five feet long and cut it into five pieces that can then be rearranged into a perfect square. I don't believe it." "That's simple," said Alice, "and I'll tell you the answer if you direct me to the Mad Hatter's house." "I don't know where he lives," replied the Walrus, "but Tweedledum and Tweedledee can tell you and I can tell you how to find them." "Very well," said Alice and showed him how to cut the board.

A few minutes later Alice found the brothers in the woods standing by a fork in the path. "The Walrus told me that one branch of this path would lead me to the Mad Hatter's house and that the other would take me to the den of the Jabberwock, a place I certainly don't want to go. He said that you boys know the right path to take. He also warned me that one of you always tells the truth. and that the other one always tells lies. He also says that I can only ask one of you one question." Alice then phrased her question in such a way that she was sure to get a correct answer regardless of which brother she asked.

Continuing on her way Alice soon found herself, not at the tea party, but in the Queen's garden. "Please Mr. Five, can you tell me how to get to the Mad Hatter's house? I'm ever so late for the party." "Don't tell her, Five," said the Seven, "unless she tells us how to make a card square." (See Fig. 1, page 68) "That's right Alice, you solved everybody else's problem, now you must solve ours." "All right, but please hurry," cried Alice. "You must take ten cards, ace through ten, counting the ace as one, and arrange them in a square in such a way that the points along each side of the square will add up to 18. Each corner card will be counted in two rows." "That's easy," said Alice, quickly arranging the cards. "Now which way do I go?"

Two minutes later Alice arrived at the party and took her seat. "You're late, you're late," cried the Mad Hatter, "and for that you must solve the puzzle just propounded to us by the Dormouse or else you will get no tea." (Continued on page 68)

A TRICKY TRANSPOSITION

Philatelically speaking, our problem has absolutely nothing to do with postage stamps. However, as your editor had accumulated some interesting examples of stamps, I felt they would give added decoration to the game board used in this puzzle. Enough said. Getting on with the problem at hand, we are once again faced with a transposition puzzle. Place three red counters on stamps 1, 2 and 3, and three black counters on stamps 10, 11 and 12. In just 22 moves you should be able to cause them to change places. The rules of play are as follows:

Alternately move one counter at a time along the lines from one stamp to another.

At no time can a counter of one color be on a stamp that a counter of the opposite color could move to on the next move. This prevents you from moving either the counter on 11 or the counter on 2 when making the first move of the game. It also prevents you from moving 10 to 9, 12 to 7, 1 to 6 or 3 to 4 on the first move.

Only one counter can be on a stamp at any one time.

You should have fun with this problem as it is a fine old puzzle.

Alice in Puzzleland continued:

"Oh, no," sighed Alice. "I'm so tired of doing these silly puzzles. But, I'm also very thirsty, so get on with it." "Now listen closely," said the Mad Hatter. "The Dormouse has arranged ten cups and saucers on the table so that they are in three rows with four cups and saucers in each row (see Fig. 2). By moving only two cups and saucers, make four rows with four cups and saucers in each row."

Fig. 1

Fig. 2

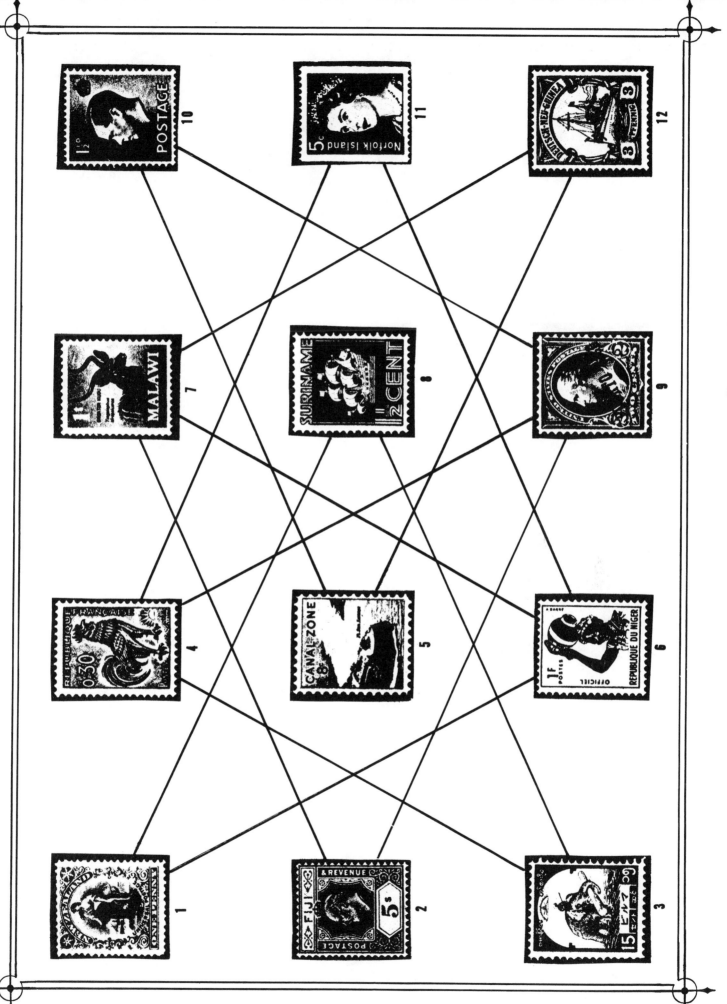

The Rhino's Riddle

 upert the Rhino has just returned from a spelling bee and he is seeing spots before his eyes. Rupert's problem was to use the letters in the spots to make first a one-letter word, then a two-letter word, and so on up to a ten-letter word. Rupert won the contest and so can you!

ell, laddies, I hope that your game is on today for we are going to play the Old Course. Make sure that you have plenty of golf balls because every hole on the front nine has a water hazard. And, to make things worse, some prankster replaced all of the flags on the greens with blank flags. Your problem, starting at the new Pro Shop, is to plot a route around the course that will allow you to end up at the Snack Bar on the island after finishing the ninth hole. One small point to remember is that you cannot pass over any bridge more than once and that you cannot cross over the rivers between holes in any other way than by using the bridges. You are on the tee now. I hope we see you back here before sundown.

 elcome, lads, to the Whaler's Cove. 'Tis a snug harbor to rest in. Now Cookie, here, has a bit of a problem on his hands. He wishes to divide the eight gallons of cider he has in the barrel into two lots of four gallons each. He has two measures; one is for five gallons and the other is for 3 gallons. How can he divide the cider up so that he will end up with four gallons in the five gallon measure and four gallons in the barrel? I saw a man in Borneo do it in seven moves and another in Port Said do it in seven hours. Now, you look like a bright lad to me. I'll wager you a gold sovereign you cannot solve it in seven minutes.

The Old Course

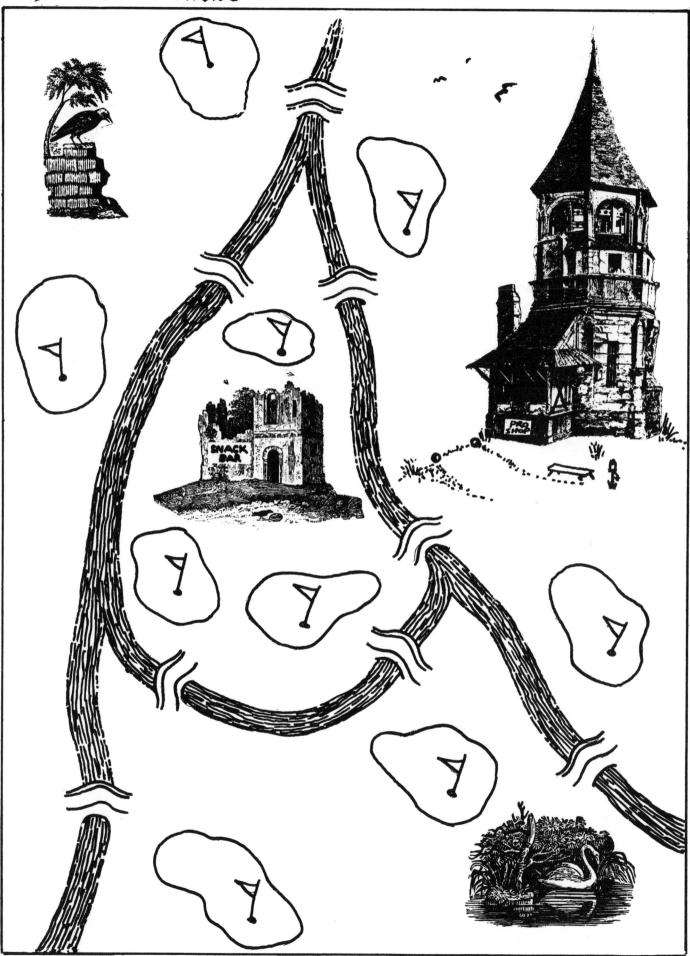

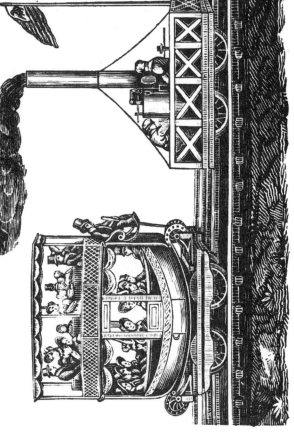

TOM THUMB'S TRAVELS

hen Peter Cooper built his famous locomotive, the Tom Thumb, there were only about 13 miles of railroad track in the United States. Near Baltimore there was a funny little siding that caused all kinds of mixups. In the diagram below, T is the engine and A and B are two cars on the siding. Position C is only long enough to hold one car or the engine. Your first problem is to move car A to B and car B over to A and end up with the engine back where it started from. In the second problem, C is big cars but not for the

enough for two big enough engine.

THE WAYWARD INN

Author unknown

Ten weary footsore travelers
   All in a woeful plight,
Sought shelter in a wayside Inn
   One dark and stormy night.

"Nine beds — no more," the landlord said,
   "Have I to offer you;
To each of eight a single room,
   But the ninth must serve for two."

A din arose. The troubled host
   Could only scratch his head;
For of those tired men no two
   Could occupy one bed.

The puzzled host was soon at ease —
   He was a clever man —
And so to please his guests devised
   This most ingenius plan.

A B C D E F G H I

In room marked A two men were placed;
   The third he lodged in B:
The fourth to C was then assigned —
   The fifth retired to D.

In E the sixth he tucked away
   And in F the seventh man;
The eighth and ninth in G and H
   And then to A he ran.

Wherein the host, as I have said,
   Had laid two travelers by,
Then taking one — the tenth and last —
   He lodged him safe in I.

Nine single rooms — a room for each —
   Were made to serve for ten,
And this it is that puzzles me,
   And many wiser men.

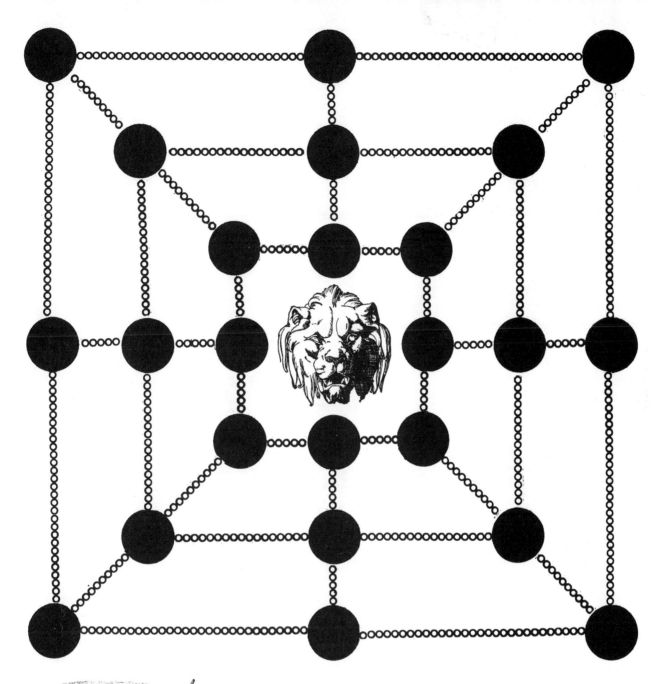

O ne of the most ancient of all games that is still being played today is called Nine Men Mars (also The Mill, Nine-Mens Morris, Meg Merrylegs, etc.). It was played by the early Greeks and Romans. Each player gets nine checkers, one side red, the other side black. Each in turn plays one counter on the black dots on the board. The object is for a player to get three of his checkers in a row. Every time a player succeeds in doing so he may remove one of the other player's checkers from the board. When all the men have been placed on the board, the play continues by moving the checkers along the lines one space at a time. In this way a new line of three can be formed. When one player has lost all of his checkers, the other player is declared the winner.

or many centuries the Vikings sailed across the northern reaches of Europe and America seeking their fortunes in one way or another. To while away the long hours that they spent at sea the Norsemen invented many ingenious puzzles. Let us try a couple.

The Coins of Odin

Place six coins in a row upon the table in the following order: tail, tail, tail, head, head, head. In our problem, when you make a move it must be with two coins at a time. Also, the two coins must be adjoining one another. The puzzle is for us to rearrange the order of the coins so they are now head, tail, head, tail, head, tail. This must be accomplished in just three moves.

The Impossible Coin Puzzle

"Do this puzzle," thundered Odin, "and I will speed you safely home. Fail, and you are doomed to wander forever through the never ending seas of the Land of Always Night." With an alternative like that, the Vikings had to solve this puzzle. What is the problem? Take five coins, all of the same size, and arrange them so that each coin touches every other coin. That's all you have to do. If you try this puzzle I hope you have lots of winter clothing just in case your answer is wrong.

uring the Third Crusade (1189-92), Prince Charles of the Isle of Merlin came to the Holy Land and was captured by the forces of Saladin during the battle for Acre. When he was brought before the mighty lord, Saladin, he was informed that a ransom of 200,000 pieces of gold had been placed upon him and another 50,000 upon his horse.

"Great Saladin," spoke Charles, "I labor here at a great disadvantage. In my own country a prisoner is given a chance to do battle with his wits. Two questions are put to him, and if he can answer them both correctly, he and his horse are set free. If he fails, then the ransom is doubled."

"So be it, then," replied Saladin. "I accept your challenge; now answer these puzzles if you can. On this table we have nine coins. Eight of them are genuine and weigh the same. The ninth coin is counterfeit and is heavier. Find the counterfeit coin, using this simple balance scale, in two weighings."

"Your second test is like the first, but this time we will use 12 coins. One of these coins is also counterfeit, but it is not known whether it is lighter or heavier than the other coins. You must find it, using only three weighings with the scale."

"You have until morning to solve these puzzles" ... so do our readers.

Fig. 1

Fig. 2

Fig. 3

Fig. 4

Merlin's Notes

For our first problem (Fig. 1) on page 76 we have an interesting puzzle using a wooden match, a coin and a very old eggcup. (Instead of an eggcup use any wide-mouth bottle). Break the match in the middle, but do not separate the two halves. Place the match on top of the bottle. Rest the coin on top of the match. The problem is now for you to make the coin drop into the bottle without your touching the match, coin or bottle.

Problem number 2 is a tricky piece of Flatland puzzlement. Without lifting your pencil from the paper, you are to draw six straight lines which will pass through all sixteen dots in the diagram.

You will need twelve checkers, six red and six black, for brain buster number 3. Line them up as shown in Fig. 3. Now, by touching only one checker, make all the vertical rows of checkers either all red or all black instead of the alternate arrangement they are in now.

How much does a brick and a half weigh? In Fig. 4 you will find a drawing of a very heavy brick. Just how heavy is for you to determine. Study the following clue carefully. If a whole brick weighs 9 pounds and half a brick, then what is the weight of a brick and a half?

Merlin's Library

 ow here is an after dinner trick that Merlin loves to show his guests. All you need are two hats (Merlin uses 2 fezzes) and seven walnuts. The hats represent the barns on the estate of the Sheriff of Nottingham. Five of the walnuts are five of his sheep and the other two walnuts are two hungry serfs. One night the serfs became so desperate that they decided to steal the five sheep and kill them in the barns. Practice well the following moves.

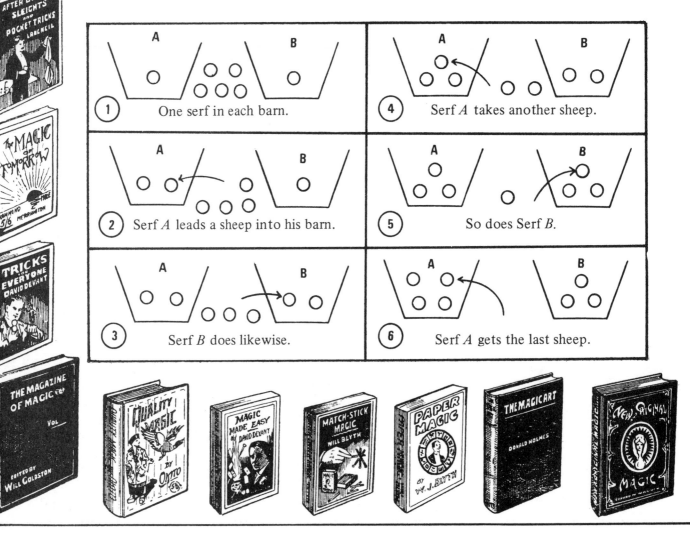

1. One serf in each barn.

2. Serf *A* leads a sheep into his barn.

3. Serf *B* does likewise.

4. Serf *A* takes another sheep.

5. So does Serf *B*.

6. Serf *A* gets the last sheep.

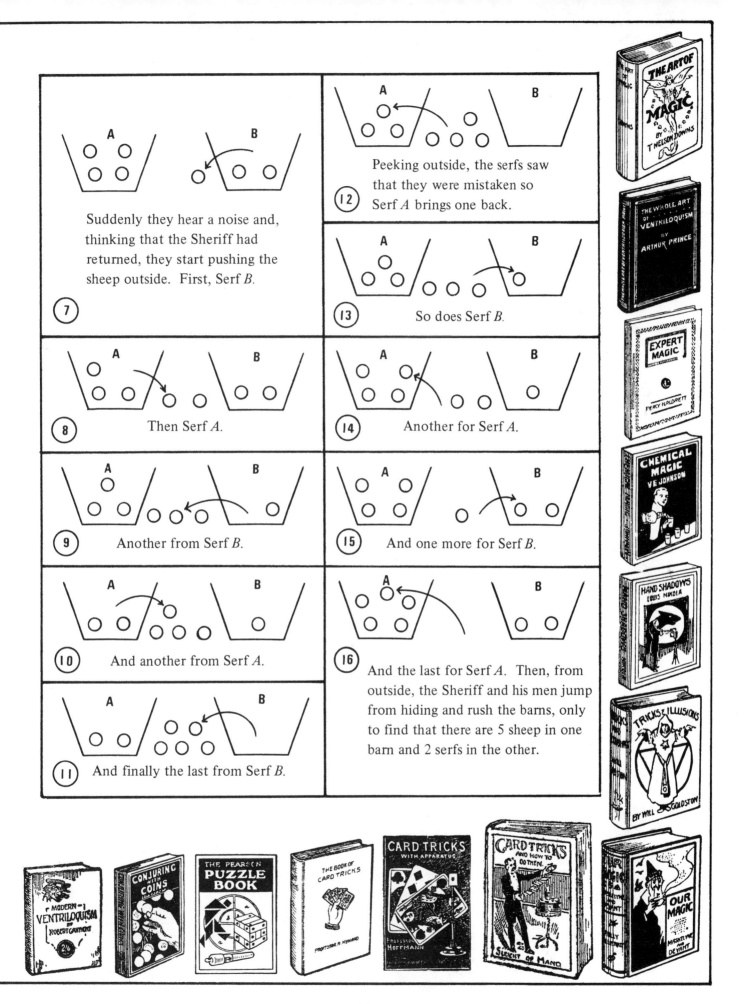

7 Suddenly they hear a noise and, thinking that the Sheriff had returned, they start pushing the sheep outside. First, Serf *B*.

8 Then Serf *A*.

9 Another from Serf *B*.

10 And another from Serf *A*.

11 And finally the last from Serf *B*.

12 Peeking outside, the serfs saw that they were mistaken so Serf *A* brings one back.

13 So does Serf *B*.

14 Another for Serf *A*.

15 And one more for Serf *B*.

16 And the last for Serf *A*. Then, from outside, the Sheriff and his men jump from hiding and rush the barns, only to find that there are 5 sheep in one barn and 2 serfs in the other.

Alice in Puzzleland

he Cheshire cat has perched himself above a puzzle monument on the Isle of Merlin. He is busy explaining to Alice what the problem is (next page). "Many years ago a farmer had a square field. He sold one-quarter of his land (the shaded area) to buy farm equipment. When the farmer grew older, he decided to divide what was left of his farm into four parcels of land, each exactly the same shape and size. How was this accomplished?"

"I'm sure the answer is very simple," said Alice, "but I can't for the life of me see how he did it."

"It can't be done, it can't be done," cried the Mad Hatter.

"Hurry up readers, don't be late. I give you five minutes the answer to relate," challenged the White Rabbit before darting off.

---

 thousand years ago a caravan from far off Samarkand came to Merlin's island with a puzzle to delight Merlin and his court. To solve the puzzle you have to arrange the numbers so that no number appears twice in any row or column. Also, no number can appear twice across the two diagonals. Let us see how good you are at solving the Square of Samarkand.

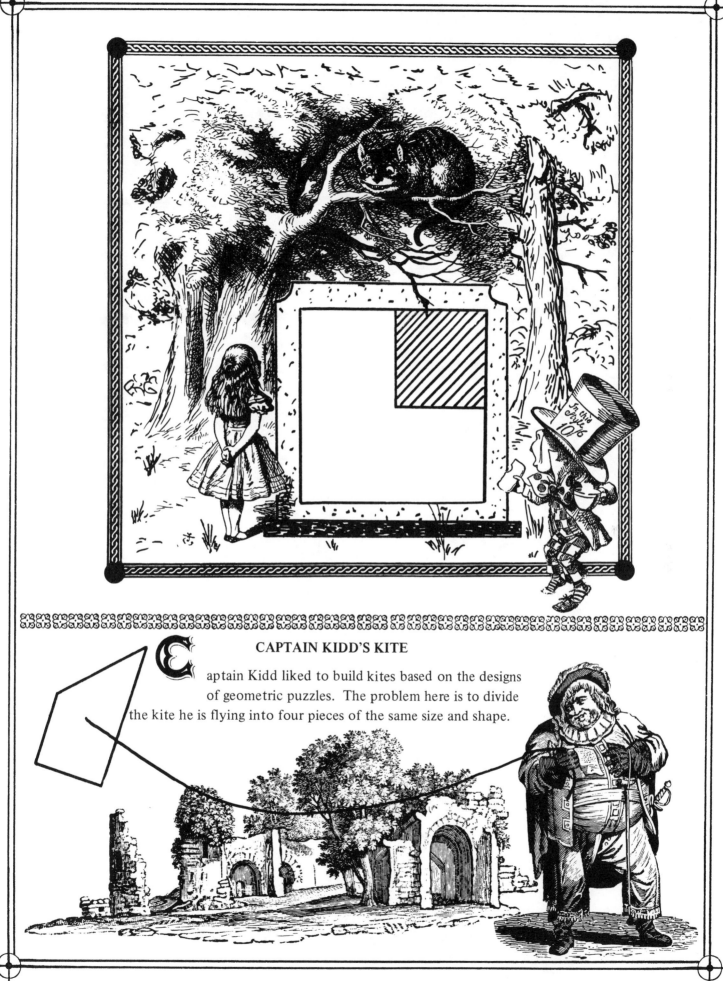

CAPTAIN KIDD'S KITE

Captain Kidd liked to build kites based on the designs of geometric puzzles. The problem here is to divide the kite he is flying into four pieces of the same size and shape.

Fig. 1

Fig. 2

Fig. 3

Fig. 4

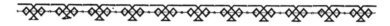

et us start off with one of Merlin's favorite stumpers. In Fig. 1 on page 82 are six ice cream sticks. Try arranging them in such a way that each stick will be touching all of the other sticks.

or centuries the Sphinx (Fig. 2) has looked down upon the many travelers who have come to Egypt to seek wisdom or plunder, adventure or solitude. It is said that at one time the Sphinx had the power of speech and that it would challenge the traveler who passed beneath it to answer a riddle. If he answered it correctly he was allowed to go on in peace. If he failed, well, that's another story.

The riddle most often asked by the Sphinx was as follows; "What walks on four legs in the morning, two legs in the afternoon and three legs in the evening?" I hope you have the answer!

welve Coins in the Fountain." That's what Merlin calls this puzzle (Fig. 3). Could you toss twelve coins into a fountain in such a way that they would form six rows, each row having four coins in it? (Hint: each coin will be in more than one row.)

less me, Holmes," exclaimed Dr. Watson, "It seems all so simple after you have explained it. I didn't have the foggiest as to who or what could have made those confounded tracks in the snow."

Holmes and Dr. Watson were taking a constitutional one evening after dinner when they chanced upon some very strange tracks in the snow. (See Fig. 4). Holmes, of course, had known immediately what had caused the tracks and had challenged Watson to use his powers of deductive reasoning to arrive at a solution. Once again Watson failed. Can you do better?

THE BISHOP'S PUZZLE

own the corridors of time comes Kempelen's Automaton Chess Player to perplex the puzzlers of today. Over a century ago this automaton was exhibited throughout Europe and the United States, where it seldom failed to beat the best chess players of the time. When presented with specially contrived puzzles, the automaton never failed to perceive the answer. Here is the first in a series of problems that were solved by this mechanical marvel. It is entitled "The Bishop's Puzzle."

On the next page is a segment of a chessboard with four black bishops at the top and four white bishops at the bottom. The problem is to make the white bishops change places with the black bishops, using bishop chess moves (they move and capture along diagonals only) and alternating the play, first white then black. No two pieces can occupy the same square at the same time. No bishop may be left in a position where it could be taken by an opposing bishop. See if you can solve this puzzle in no more than 36 moves.

A TIGHT SQUEEZE

ere is a problem that has fooled many students of puzzledom. Needed: a piece of heavy cardboard and a quarter. Cut a hole the size of a dime in the center of the cardboard. The problem you have to solve is how to push the quarter through the hole without tearing or folding the cardboard. It sounds impossible, but I assure you that it can be done.

overs of puzzles old and new will recognize this classic of ancient times. A pyramid of six coins is built upon Circle 1. From the bottom up, the coins used are: (1) silver dollar, (2) half-dollar, (3) quarter, (4) nickel, (5) penny, (6) dime. The object of the puzzle is to move the pyramid from Circle 1 to either Circle 2 or Circle 3. You can move one coin at a time to either an empty circle or to a circle with a coin in it that is larger in diameter than the coin you are moving.

THE BISHOP'S PUZZLE

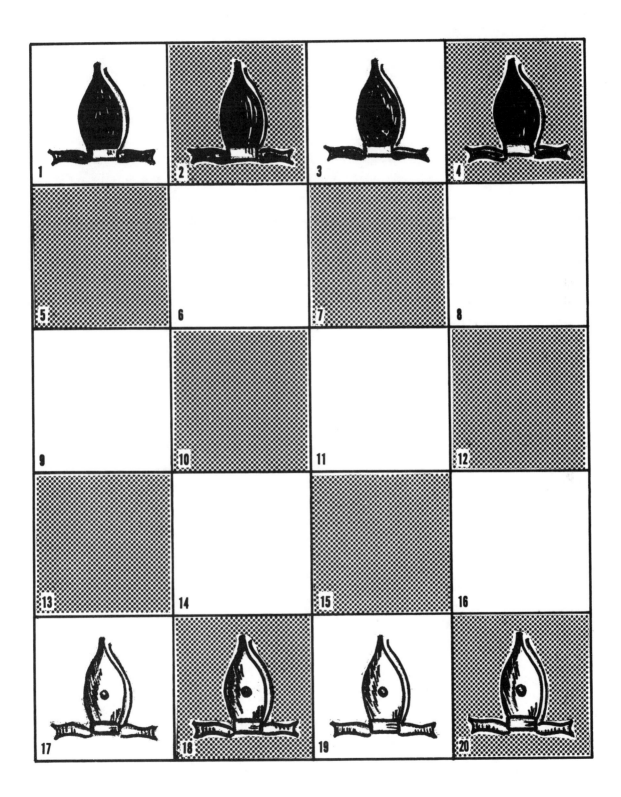

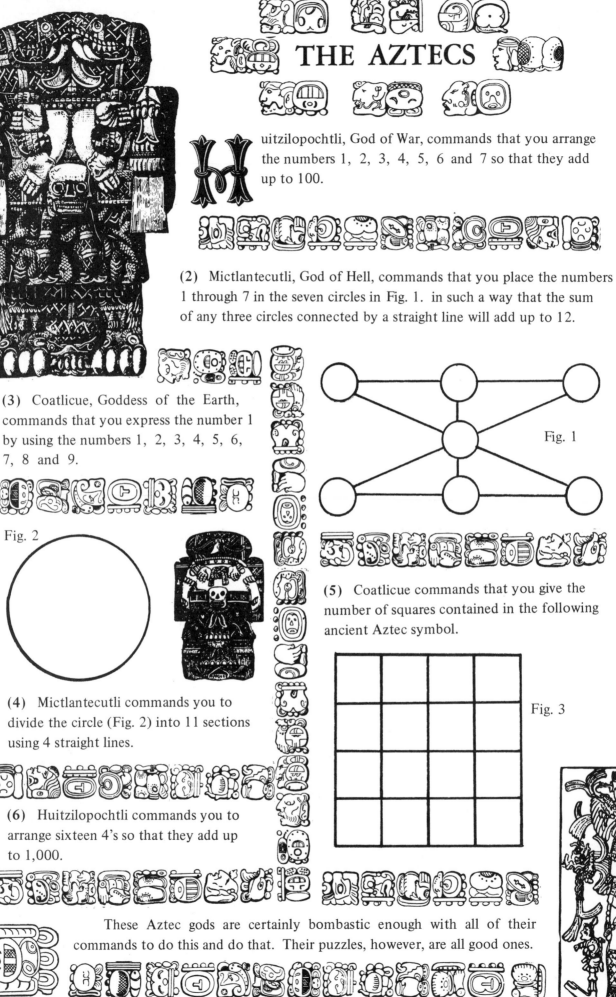

THE AZTECS

Huitzilopochtli, God of War, commands that you arrange the numbers 1, 2, 3, 4, 5, 6 and 7 so that they add up to 100.

(2) Mictlantecutli, God of Hell, commands that you place the numbers 1 through 7 in the seven circles in Fig. 1. in such a way that the sum of any three circles connected by a straight line will add up to 12.

(3) Coatlicue, Goddess of the Earth, commands that you express the number 1 by using the numbers 1, 2, 3, 4, 5, 6, 7, 8 and 9.

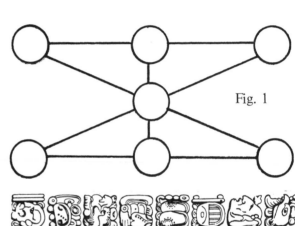

Fig. 1

Fig. 2

(4) Mictlantecutli commands you to divide the circle (Fig. 2) into 11 sections using 4 straight lines.

(5) Coatlicue commands that you give the number of squares contained in the following ancient Aztec symbol.

Fig. 3

(6) Huitzilopochtli commands you to arrange sixteen 4's so that they add up to 1,000.

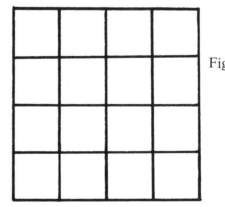

These Aztec gods are certainly bombastic enough with all of their commands to do this and do that. Their puzzles, however, are all good ones.

THE SPHINX

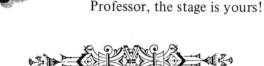

Once again Professor Stodare presents that magnificent enigma, the Talking Sphinx, to challenge your minds with another series of puzzles and riddles.

Professor, the stage is yours!

1. What was it that Adam never had and never saw yet gave to his children?

2. What number gives the same result whether you divide it by 5 or deduct 5 from it?

3. When does a chair hate you?

4. Which candles burn the longer, wax candles or tallow candles?

5. What kind of a clock shows the exact time of day twice a day, but is wrong at all other times?

6. What question can never be answered by "yes"?

7. Four fat women under one small umbrella in a terrible storm. Why didn't they get wet?

8. What is bought by the yard yet is worn by the foot?

9. How far can you go into the woods?

10. If a telephone and a piece of paper had a race, who would win?

11. What will go up a chimney down but will not go down a chimney up?

12. Can you arrange thirteen threes to total 100?

13. Can you change a dollar into 50 coins?

14. Can you walk 50 miles north, 1,000 miles west and 50 miles south and arrive back at your starting point?

15. Why is Ireland the wealthiest country in the world?

16. Why is a man who doesn't go to the races and bet just as bad as one who does?

ere we have a transpositional problem that has been a great favorite of puzzle enthusiasts for many generations. In the drawing above we find a segment from a chessboard with two white knights in squares 1 and 3 and two black knights in squares 7 and 9. The problem, using only knight's moves, (see page 35) is to exchange the positions of the black and white pieces. Can you accomplish this in seven moves?

(1) White to move and win.

(2) White to move and win.

(3) Black to move and win.

(4) Black to move and win.

Kempelen's Automaton Chess Player has a surprise for all of you puzzlers. He is challenging you to solve these four checker problems. If you haven't played checkers since your school days, here is an opportunity for you to sharpen up your game. Look for the double and triple jumps.

Fig. 1

Fig. 2

Fig. 3

Fig. 4

Merlin's Notes

The first problem on the opposite page is one of Merlin's favorite puzzles (Fig. 1). You are to connect the dots with one continuous line until you have formed a cross. When complete there should be 8 dots remaining outside the cross and 5 dots remaining inside. The cross should look like this:

You should find this next test quite easy to solve. Merely take the seven twos you see within the arch in Fig. 2 and arrange them in such a manner that their arithmetical value is equal to two.

So much for the easy puzzles. Now it's time for you to do some work. A chessboard (Fig. 3) is made up of 18 intersecting lines. Can you calculate how many different squares and rectangles are contained within this board? In other words you have to figure out all the different ways it is possible to make a square or a rectangle using the lines as they exist on the board. Try to work out a formula for solving this type of puzzle.

Figure 4 presents the puzzler with a pretty and perplexing problem pertaining to perambulating pieces. Make up a facsimile of the 20-square game board shown in the drawing. Place a chess knight in the upper left-hand square (the one marked S). The object is to move the knight from square S to square F. You can only use knight's moves (see page 35). The knight must land within every square on the board. Each square must be landed on only once. The last move must find the knight sitting in square F.

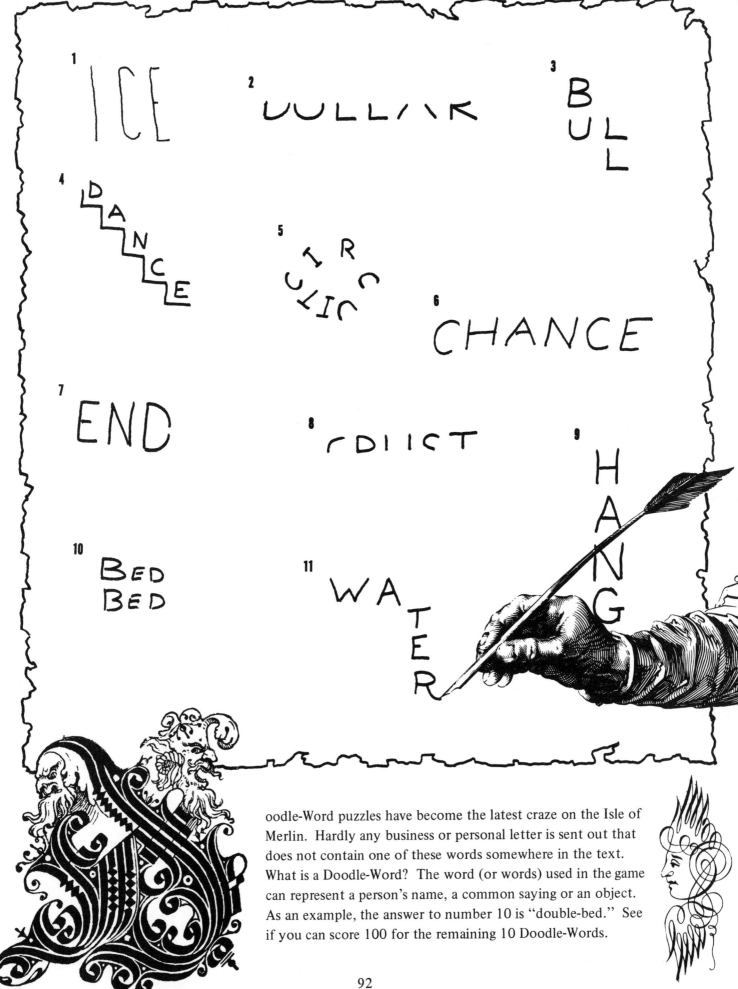

1 ICE

2 DOLLAR

3 B
U
L
L

4 DANCE

5 CIRC
U
L
I
C

6 CHANCE

7 END

8 CRUST

9 H
A
N
G

10 BED
BED

11 WA
T
E
R

oodle-Word puzzles have become the latest craze on the Isle of Merlin. Hardly any business or personal letter is sent out that does not contain one of these words somewhere in the text. What is a Doodle-Word? The word (or words) used in the game can represent a person's name, a common saying or an object. As an example, the answer to number 10 is "double-bed." See if you can score 100 for the remaining 10 Doodle-Words.

92

The Rhino's Riddle

upert came upon a barrel partly filled with water. Without using any kind of measuring stick, Rupert determined whether the barrel was more than half-full, less than half-full or exactly half-full. How did he do it?

ount The Squares

Here's an easy puzzler (?). How many *squares* are there in the drawing to the right? You have a time limit on this one. Two minutes should be all you need to solve it.

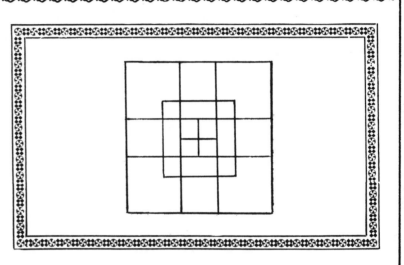

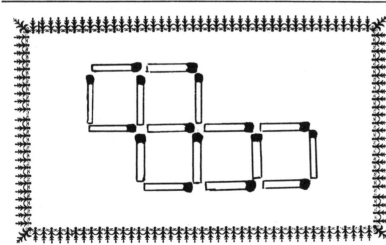

here Did The Square Go?

This is one of the best of the many match-square puzzles. Arrange sixteen matches to form five squares. The problem is to rearrange two of these matches so that instead of having five squares, we now have four squares of similar size.

The Artist's Dilemma

imply put, your task is to draw the figure at the right without crossing a line, without taking your pencil from the paper and without retracing a line.

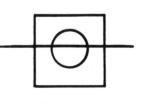

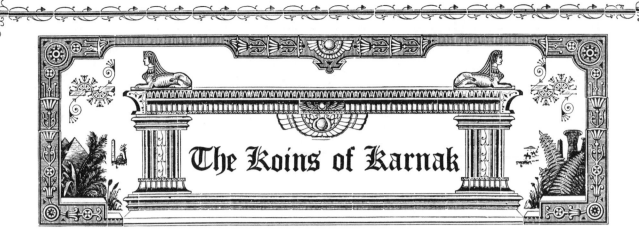

The Koins of Karnak

overs of games step forward and harken to what I have to say. From a far-off land Merlin brings to us an ingenious game he calls "The Koins of Karnak." It is named after the vast temple complex that was at the center of that famous city of ancient Egypt, Thebes. Now Merlin claims that they played this game over 3,000 years ago. Since I wasn't there I'll not dispute his word. To set up the game, lay out twenty-five coins in five rows of five coins each. You can use the game board pictured in the Egyptian stele on page 95. Play alternates between players. In your turn you can remove any number of coins from any row or column. There cannot be, however, a gap between any of the coins removed. For example, if I remove the middle three coins in the top row my opponent cannot remove the two end coins on the left and right. He can, however, remove either one of them. Play continues until all the coins have been

removed. The loser is the player who is forced to remove the last coin. This is a very popular old game and Merlin feels that you should have many enjoyable hours attempting to master it. In my own research into its origins I find that the underlying theory as to skillful play has yet to be worked out by the mathematicians who have interested themselves in it.

One last thought before leaving you. Merlin feels that all of us should be more inventive in our approach to the fascinating diversions that are to be found within this book. When you have become proficient with this game, try it with six coins in six rows or four coins in eight rows. The possibilities are limitless.

Have fun.

DAVENPORT

r. Davenport hired a new window dresser the other day. The first window he arranged (see above) proved to be his last, for Mr. Davenport abhors an unsymmetrical display of any kind. "Imbecile," shouted Mr. Davenport, "the 12 objets d'art should be in the 36 spaces so that there will be just two items in each horizontal row, vertical row and the two corner diagonals." If you can solve Mr. Davenport's puzzle I am sure he will give you the job.

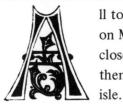

ll too soon, good readers, we have come to the end of our stay on Merlin's island. Merlin has asked the good Professor to close with a couple of puzzles and a feat of conjuring. Goodbye, then, until we meet again on our next journey to this enchanted isle.

Another Single-Stroke Figure

Describe the following geometrical figure (Fig. 1) without taking the pencil off the paper or passing over any line for the second time.

The Entangled Scissors

Pass the loop end of a piece of doubled string through one of the bows of a pair of scissors, then pass the opposite ends through the loop, thence through the second bow, and finally tie them round a walking stick or ruler, as shown in Fig. 2.

The puzzle is to disengage the scissors without untying the cord or slipping the string off the stick.

If preferred, the ends of the cord may be held by a second person, in which case the use of the stick will be unnecessary.

From *Puzzles Old and New*.

Fig. 1

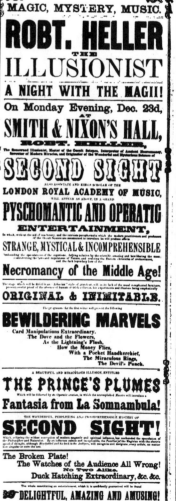

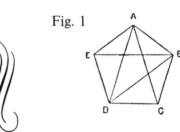

Fig. 2

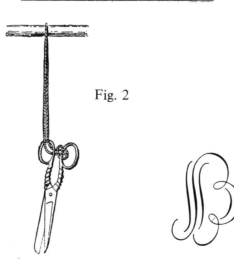

The Magic Cards

hese are usually presented as a conjuring trick, but they also form a very effective puzzle, for it is clear that the secret must lie in the cards themselves, and, given sufficient acuteness, must be discoverable.

Prepare seven cards with numbers on them as follows:

I.	II.	III.	IV.	V.	VI.	VII.
1 33 65 97	2 34 66 98	4 36 68 100	8 40 72 104	16 48 80 112	32 48 96 112	64 80 96 112
3 35 67 99	3 35 67 99	5 37 69 101	9 41 73 105	17 49 81 113	33 49 97 113	65 81 97 113
5 37 69 101	6 38 70 102	6 38 70 102	10 42 74 106	18 50 82 114	34 50 98 114	66 82 98 114
7 39 71 103	7 39 71 103	7 39 71 103	11 43 75 107	19 51 83 115	35 51 99 115	67 83 99 115
9 41 73 105	10 42 74 106	12 44 76 108	12 44 76 108	20 52 84 116	36 52 100 116	68 84 100 116
11 43 75 107	11 43 75 107	13 45 77 109	13 45 77 109	21 53 85 117	37 53 101 117	69 85 101 117
13 45 77 109	14 46 78 110	14 46 78 110	13 46 78 110	22 54 86 118	38 54 102 118	70 86 102 118
15 47 79 111	15 47 79 111	15 47 79 111	15 47 79 111	23 55 87 119	39 55 103 119	71 87 103 119
17 49 81 113	18 50 82 114	20 52 84 116	24 56 88 120	24 56 88 120	40 56 104 120	72 88 104 120
19 51 83 115	19 51 83 115	21 53 85 117	25 57 89 121	25 57 89 121	41 57 105 121	73 89 105 121
21 53 85 117	22 54 86 118	22 54 86 118	26 58 90 122	26 58 90 122	42 58 106 122	74 90 106 122
23 55 87 119	23 55 87 119	23 55 87 119	27 59 91 123	27 59 91 123	43 59 107 123	75 91 107 123
25 57 89 121	26 58 90 122	28 60 92 124	28 60 92 124	28 60 92 124	44 60 108 124	76 92 108 124
27 59 91 123	27 59 91 123	29 61 93 125	29 61 93 125	29 61 93 125	45 61 109 125	77 93 109 125
29 61 93 125	30 62 94 126	30 62 94 126	30 62 94 126	30 62 94 126	46 62 110 126	78 94 110 126
31 63 95 127	31 63 95 127	31 63 95 127	31 63 95 127	31 63 95 127	47 63 111 127	79 95 111 127

A person is requested to think of any number from 1 to 127 inclusive and to state on which one or more of the seven cards it is to be found. Any one knowing the secret can instantly name the chosen number.

How is the number ascertained?

See page 272 for a duplication master.

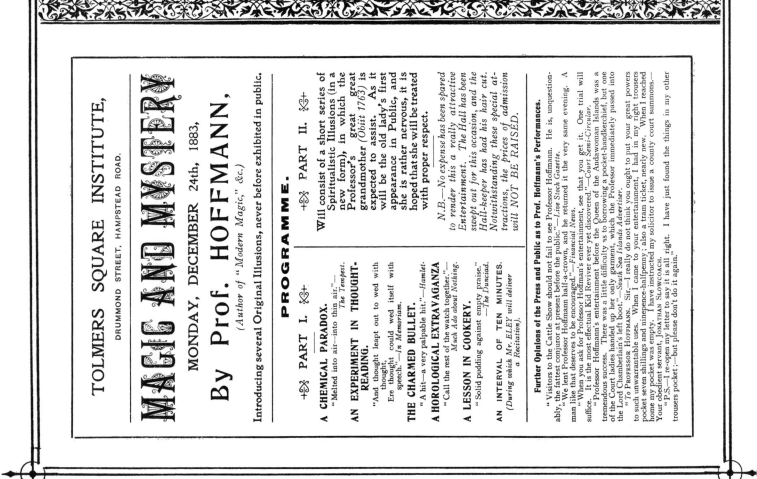

No. 126.   The Latest Egg
Vanish.

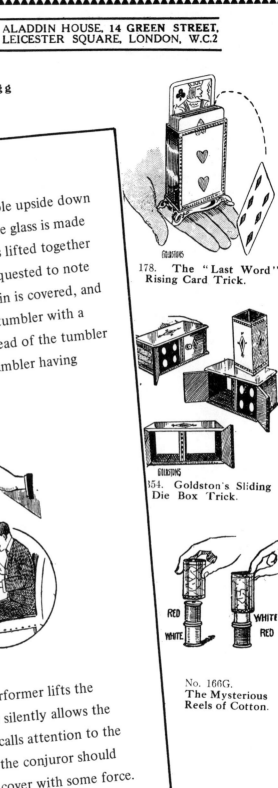

178.   The "Last Word"
Rising Card Trick.

354.   Goldston's Sliding
Die Box Trick.

No. 164. **The Fack
of Oards of En-
ohantment.**

The Famous Linking
Rings.

RED WHITE

WHITE RED

No. 166G.
**The Mysterious
Reels of Cotton.**

WATCH THE COIN.

An ordinary tumbler is placed on the table upside down over a borrowed coin. A cover to fit over the glass is made out of a sheet of newspaper. The tumbler is lifted together with the paper cover — the company are requested to note that the coin is head upward. Again the coin is covered, and the conjuror brings down his hand on the tumbler with a thud; to the surprise of the company, instead of the tumbler being smashed, the paper crumples, the tumbler having vanished.

EXPLANATION: When the performer lifts the tumbler covered with the paper, he silently allows the glass to fall out on to his lap as he calls attention to the coin. To make the trick effective, the conjuror should bring his hand down on the paper cover with some force.

A trick from Will Goldston's old "Catalogue of Magic", circa 1930.

No. 332.   **The Chair or Table
Lifting.**

No. 351.   **The Plush Changing
Bag.**

Merlin's Library

On the first page of this book the Wizard is showing us some of the magical apparatus that is to be found in Merlin's collection. Also outstanding is Merlin's library of magical literature. Let us sample two of the tricks to be found in this treasure trove.

Magicians are forever sawing women in half or cutting ropes into many, many pieces. Merlin has a method for restoring a cut rope that will leave your friends truly baffled. To perform it, you will need an easily made gimmick. (A gimmick is an aid to performing a trick that your audience knows nothing about.) Cut a five-inch piece of rope from a clothesline. Make a loop of this piece and tape the ends together (Fig. 1). Next, attach a piece of elastic cord twelve inches or more in length, depending on how long your arm is, to the taped loop. Insert the loop and elastic into the right sleeve of your suit jacket and lower it down until the end of the loop is about four inches from the end of the sleeve (Fig. 2). Take a safety-pin and attach the end of the elastic to the inside of your coat at the point where it enters the sleeve. Now put your coat on. Reach into the right sleeve with your left-hand and pull the loop down into your right hand (Fig. 3). When performing this trick you must keep the back of your right hand to the audience at all times.

To perform, walk onto the stage with the loop already palmed in your right hand. With your right hand, pick up one end of a five-foot piece of clothesline from the table. With your left hand, pull the rope halfway through your right hand. Open your left hand and let the end of the rope drop. Reach into your right hand and apparently pull the middle of the rope up a couple of inches so that you can cut it into two pieces with a pair of scissors. What you actually do is to pull the concealed loop (the gimmick) up into view (Fig. 4). You now cut this loop with the scissors. Replace the scissors on the table. With the left hand reach down, take the two ends of the rope and place them in the right hand next to the two cut ends of the loop. Now say the appropriate magical incantation and throw the rope towards the ceiling. The moment you open up your hand to release the rope, the cut loop will fly up your sleeve never to be seen again. The movement of your arm and the speed of the elastic will effectively screen the secret of the illusion from the eyes of your audience. Another miracle is performed.

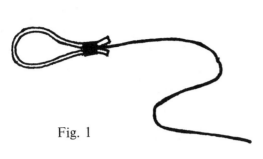

Fig. 1

Fig. 2

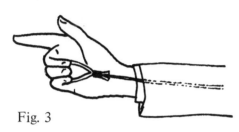

Fig. 3

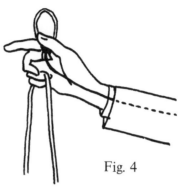

Fig. 4

THE COIN UNDER THE GLASS PUZZLE

Prestidigitators are always fond of doing coin tricks. Here is a trick that Merlin especially likes. I grant you that it is more of a puzzle than a trick, but I think you will enjoy performing it.

Place two quarters on the table far enough apart so that you can balance an inverted glass upon them. Place a dime on the table halfway between the coins. Now place the inverted glass upon the quarters (Fig. 5). The problem is to remove the dime from under the glass without touching the quarters, the dime or the glass.

It's easier than you think!

Merlin's Notes

The pictures used to illustrate Merlin's Notes have been contributed by the *Camelot Daily News.* They were made during the puzzle convention which was held last month on the Isle of Merlin.

Picture number 1 shows four puzzlers, an empty bottle and a soda straw. The problem facing these gentlemen is to lift the bottle off the table by using only one hand and the soda straw. You cannot tie the straw around the bottle or make any kind of a loop with the straw. In fact, the straw is not allowed to touch the outside of the bottle. When you try this feat, please use a coke bottle instead of a cut-glass decanter.

Number 2 picture depicts a puzzle that won an award during the puzzle convention. The puzzle took second prize in the Flatland division. The problem looks simple enough: Just duplicate the design of three interlocking squares by drawing one continuous line. The zinger is that at no point may one part of the line cross over any other part of the line.

If you think you are seeing spots before your eyes in photo number 3, then you are wrong. Those are puzzle team buttons. There are seventeen of them, and you are to arrange them into four straight lines, each line containing five buttons. Don't let this puzzle stick you. Ouch!

Our final problem is a noisy one. The drummer is about to hit the drum once for each rectangle depicted in the diagram painted on his drum. How many times will he affront our hearing? Judging by the expression on his face, I'd say we were in for a long ordeal.

rom Merlin's summer castle comes news of an exciting new game called Joust. Everyone, including Merlin, is playing it. Joust is an up-to-date variation of that old game of our childhood called Dots. Merlin's version might be thought of as being "old mead served in a new tankard." The facing page is the layout of the Jousting board. It is made up of nine rows of dots. Each row contains nine dots. Two or more players can play the game. Each player, in turn, must draw a line, horizontally or vertically, from one dot to any adjacent dot (see Fig. 1). No diagonal lines may be drawn. When a player is able to close a square (see Fig. 2), he places his initials inside the square and takes another turn. If he can close another square he initials it and he plays again. The player continues in this fashion until he can no longer close a square, at which point the next player in turn goes. When all the squares have been closed, each player tallies up his score. Empty squares count one point. Squares with shields in them count the number of points printed on the face of the shield. The winner is the Jouster with the highest point total.

Fig. 1   Fig. 2

omeone is flying a puzzle kite from Merlin's castle grounds. It may be that old kite flyer, Captain Kidd. The puzzle depicted by the kite is an easy one. How many squares can you find in the pattern of the kite? See how fast you can calculate the total.

rofessor Hoffmann is back with us again to test our puzzling abilities. The good professor was an outstanding author of the 19th century on the subjects of magic, puzzles and games. His books on magic are considered milestones on the road to modern magical literature. In the realm of puzzles his book, *Puzzles Old and New,* surely ranks as one of the outstanding collections of this genre of entertainment. The next sixteen pages of *Merlin's Puzzler* contain selections from this great work of puzzledom.

The curtain's up professor! You're on!

MAKING THINGS EVEN

Two children were discussing their pocket money. "If you were to give me a penny," said Johnny, "I should have twice as much as you." "That would not be a fair division," said Tommy, "you had better give me a penny, and then we shall be just alike."

How much money had each?

A REJECTED PROPOSAL

A little later Johnny and Tommy met again. "I have now just twice as much as you have," said Johnny, "but if you were to give me a penny I should have three times as much." "No, thank you," said Tommy, "but give me two pennies and we shall be equal."

How much had each boy?

FATHER AND SON

A father aged 45 has a son of 12.

How soon will the father be only three times the age of the son?

THE WALKING MATCH

Four persons, A, B, C, D, start from the same point to walk round a circular piece of ground, whose circumference is one mile. A walks five miles an hour, B four miles, C three miles, and D two miles an hour.

How long will it be before all four again meet at the starting point?

THE THREE LEGACIES

A gentleman, making his will, left legacies to his three servants, of whom the parlourmaid had been with him three times as long as the housemaid, and the cook twice as long as the parlourmaid. He distributed his gifts in the same proportions; and the total amount given was $700.

What was the amount received by each?

THE "ROYAL AQUARIUM" THIRTEEN PUZZLE

This is an adaptation of the "Magic Square" idea, but modified in a very ingenious manner, the ordinary processes for forming a magic square being here quite inapplicable.

The puzzle consists of nine cards, not quite 1½ inches each way, each bearing four numbers, radiating from the centre, after the manner shown below.

The figures shown circled are in the original printed in red. (This puzzle was once procurable at the Royal Aquarium, at Westminster.)

The experimenter is required to arrange the nine cards in a square, the red numbers forming perpendicular lines, and the black numbers horizontal lines, the three figures in each line, whether horizontal or perpendicular, making, when added together, 13.

THE SNAKE AND BIRD

This may be regarded either in the light of a game or of a puzzle, though there is an element of chance about it which to some extent bars its claim to rank as a puzzle proper.

It consists of a cardboard medallion or counter representing a bird, and a snake, of many convolutions, of the same material, chopped up into ten segments, more or less curved, and in length ranging from three to six inches (see Fig. 1).

The "bird" is laid upon the table, and the tail segment of the snake placed hap-hazard a couple of feet or so away from it. The experimenter is then required, beginning from the tail, to.

reconstruct the snake by adding segments one by one, till the head is reached; his object being so to place the head at the finish that the "bird" shall be just within the open jaws. His prospect of effecting this will, of course, depend upon the arrangement of the successive segments, the choice of a wrong segment, or the selection of an upward instead of a downward curl (or vice versa) at a given point, making just the difference between success and failure.

The various segments (which are coloured on both sides, and may therefore be used with either side uppermost) must be so placed as to butt fairly one against another, no overlapping being permissible.

See page 275 for a duplication master for this game.

THE COIN AND CARD PUZZLE

Balance a playing card horizontally on the top of your left forefinger, and on it lay a coin, say a half-dollar or a quarter, so that both shall be in equilibrium. You are now required to remove the card without touching the coin.

Any one not in the secret usually endeavours to draw away the card by slow degrees, when failure is the inevitable result. The proper method is as follows: give the corner of the coin a smart "fillip" (snap) with the second finger of the right hand. If this be done exactly in the plane of the card, the latter will be shot away with a sort of spinning motion, the coin remaining undisturbed.

THE EGG AND CARD PUZZLE

This is similar to "The Coin and Card" puzzle in a slightly altered form. Fill a wineglass half full of water, and over its mouth lay a playing card. On the centre of the card place a wedding ring (or other fairly stout ring of similar dimensions), and with the aid of this balance an egg, small end upwards, upright on the card. You are now required to remove the card, and let the egg fall into the water, without touching egg or ring.

The modus operandi is the same as above described. The card being neatly flicked away with the second finger, the egg and ring will fall into the glass. The water prevents any injury to the egg.

AN EASY CREDITOR

A gentleman being in temporary need of money, a friend lent him sixty dollars, telling him to repay it in such sums as might suit his convenience. Shortly afterwards he made a payment on account. His second payment was half as much as the first; his third three-quarters as much, his fourth one-quarter as much, and his fifth two-fifths as much. It was then found, on striking a balance, that he still owed two dollars.

What was the amount of the first payment?

THE OVER-POLITE GUESTS

Seven gentlemen met to dine at a restaurant, when a question arose as to precedence, no one desiring to take what were regarded as the more honourable seats. To settle the matter, one of them proposed that they should dine together every day until they had respectively occupied all possible positions at the table; and the suggestion was accepted.

How often must they dine together to answer the above conditions?

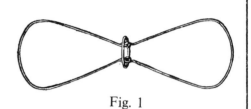

From that emporium of mystery on New Oxford Street, Bland's Magical Palace, Professor Hoffmann has brought us a selection of easily constructed wooden and wire puzzles. These items are, for the most part, unobtainable today. So, put down your pencils and head for the workshop. The professor is putting us to work.

THE DOUBLE BOW AND RING

This is a puzzle of especially simple appearance, consisting merely of two bows of wire united in such manner as to form the shape of an hourglass, with a ring encircling its narrower portion (Fig. 1).

Although so simple in its elements, the usual problem (the removal of the ring) will be found by no means easy of solution until the secret is known.

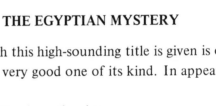

Fig. 1

THE EGYPTIAN MYSTERY

Fig. 2

The puzzle to which this high-sounding title is given is of the same class as the one above, and a very good one of its kind. In appearance it is as depicted in Fig. 2.

The problem is to disengage the ring.

IN THE SOUP

The appliances for this puzzle are a little red earthenware bowl, three inches in diameter by two inches in height (or thereabouts), a glass marble, and a "spoon," consisting of a bit of wire set in a wooden handle, and slightly curved and flattened at the opposite end (Fig. 3).

The bowl is placed on a table or other flat surface, and the puzzle is to get the marble out with no other aid but that of the spoon. It must not be tossed or flirted out, but gently coaxed up the side and over the edge.

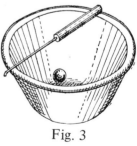

Fig. 3

This is by no means a puzzle of the most difficult kind, but demands a steady hand and a considerable amount of patience, the ball having a provoking way of escaping from the spoon and falling "in the soup" again, just at the very moment when the neophyte thinks that he has at last succeeded. With juveniles it is invariably popular, and affords a good deal of amusement even to older members of the community.

THE STANLEY PUZZLE

The Stanley Puzzle, though not consisting entirely of wire, belongs to this class. We have, in the first place, a little medallion of stamped brass (the reader can substitute cardboard for the brass pieces in this puzzle), bearing the presentment of the celebrated explorer. From this (Fig. 4) depends a wire loop, and from this again another piece of stamped brass, narrow at the top, but widening towards its lower end. Over this hangs a ring, which it is the problem of the puzzle to remove.

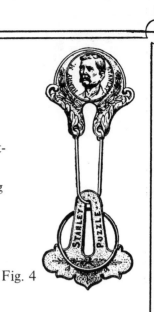

Fig. 4

THE ASHANTEE HORSESHOE

Fig. 5

The requirements for this puzzle are a miniature horseshoe of wood or cardboard, and a couple of pieces of stout brass wire, of the same length as the horseshoe. By the aid of one of these the horseshoe is propped up in a slanting position, as shown in Fig. 5. The horseshoe should have a minute notch or depression on one side, to receive the upper end of the wire, and so prevent slipping.

The experimenter is required (without touching either with the hands) to lift both wire and horseshoe simultaneously with the second piece of wire.

THE LATIN CROSS PUZZLE

This is a very old, and a very good, puzzle of this type.

Given, five pieces of paper or cardboard, one as a, one as b, and three as c (Fig. 6).

Required, of these five segments to form a Latin cross, as Fig. 7.

(see page 276 for scale drawings)

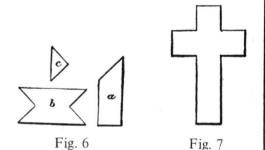

Fig. 6   Fig. 7

THE DIABOLICAL CUBE

The Diabolical Cube is a relatively simple puzzle, but it will, nevertheless, give some trouble to any one attempting it for the first time. It consists of six pieces, shaped as a, b, c, d, e, and f, respectively, in Fig. 8.

Of these six segments the experimenter is required to form a cube. (see page 276 for scale drawings)
The pieces are 1 inch thick.

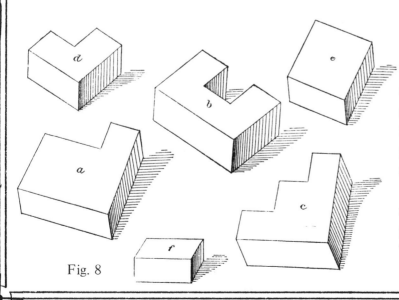

Fig. 8

 ore puzzles from the pen of Professor Hoffmann.

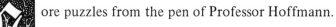

A PUZZLING INSCRIPTION

The following interesting inscription is said to be found in the chancel of a small church in Wales, just over the Ten Commandments. The addition of a single letter, repeated at various intervals, renders it not only intelligible, but appropriate to the situation:

P R S V R Y P R F C T M N

V R K P T H S P R C P T S T N

What is the missing letter?

DROPPED-LETTER PROVERBS

Supply the missing letters, and each of the series following will be found to represent a popular proverb. Each dash represents either a dropped letter or the space between two words. In some of the examples one dash stands for two dropped letters.

1) F-i-t-h-a-t-e-e-w-n-a-r-a-y.
2) B-r-s-f-f-t-r-f-c-t-g-t-r.
3) H-w-o-g-s-b-r-w-g-g-s-s-r-w-g.
4) T-k-c-r-f-h-p-n-n-t-e-p-n-s-w-
l-t-k-c-r-f-t-e-s-l-s.

A PUZZLE WITH COINS

Required, to arrange twelve coins in such manner that they shall count four in a straight line in seven different directions.

A BRIDGE PROBLEM

With three wine glasses and three matches you are to form a bridge between the three wine glasses, using the matches, that will be strong enough to support a fourth wine glass.

Each match must rest on one glass only, and touch such glass only at a single point.

A SQUARE PUZZLE

You are to arrange four and twenty matches on a table so as to form nine squares as in Fig. 1.

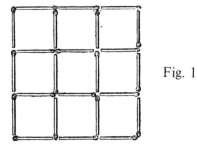

Fig. 1

Required, to take away eight matches and leave two squares only.

SIX INTO THREE

Seventeen matches being laid on the table so as to form six equal squares as in Fig. 1, required, by taking away five matches, to leave three squares only.

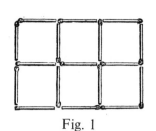

Fig. 1

SIX INTO TWO

Seventeen matches being laid on the table so as to form six equal squares (see Fig. 1), required, by taking away six matches, to leave two squares only.

FIVE INTO THREE

Fifteen matches being laid on the table so as to form five equal squares as in Fig. 2, required, by taking away three matches, to leave three squares only.

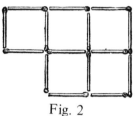

Fig. 2

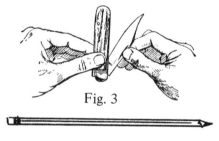

Fig. 3

THE BALANCED PENCIL

Given, a lead pencil, and a penknife (Fig. 3), with which you sharpen the pencil to the finest possible point.

Required, to balance the pencil in an upright, or nearly upright, position on the tip of the forefinger.

THE CUT PLAYING CARD

Given, a playing card or an oblong piece of cardboard of corresponding size.

Required, so to cut it, still keeping it in one piece, that a person of ordinary stature may be able to pass through it.

THE BALANCED QUARTER

The requirements for this puzzle are an ordinary paper clip, a long sharpened pencil, a quarter, and a finger ring, about equal in weight to the quarter.

You are required, by the aid of the other two articles, to balance the quarter on the point of the pencil.

WATER BEWITCHED

Required, to place a glass of water in such a position that the glass cannot be lifted without spilling the whole of the water.

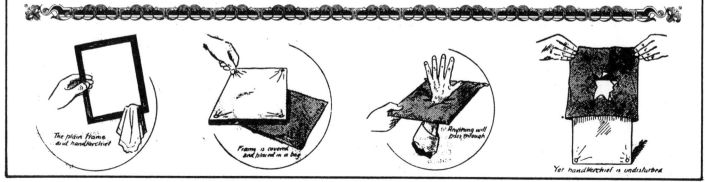

The plain frame and handkerchief

Frame is covered and placed in a bag

Anything will pass through

Yet handkerchief is undisturbed

THE JOHN BULL POLITICAL PUZZLE

The appliances for this puzzle consist of a cardboard puzzle layout on which are described three strongly marked concentric circles, with other lines connecting them (see Figs. 1 & 2), and nine small counters, three white, three red, and three blue. Each group of three bears the letters, C, U, and L, standing for Conservative, Unionist, and Liberal, respectively. Wherever on the board one line intersects with another line, the point of juncture is marked by a circular "spot." These are nine in number, forming straight radial lines of three each. At one corner of the board is a tenth spot connected with the main diagram by a curved line.

The nine counters are to be placed at the outset promiscuously upon the nine spots, the outer one, 10, being unoccupied. The counters are then to be moved, one at a time, along any of the lines, into the spot which happens for the time being to be vacant, until all three colours and all three letters are found in each circle and in each row of spots.

The first move is, as a matter of course, to shift the nearest counter into the 10 spot, thereby giving room to manipulate the others. The last move will be to replace this counter in its original position, leaving the 10 vacant as at first.

We have provided you with a playing board (see next page).

Fig. 1

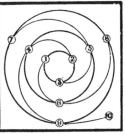

Fig. 2

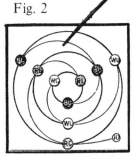

THE JOHN BULL POLITICAL PUZZLE

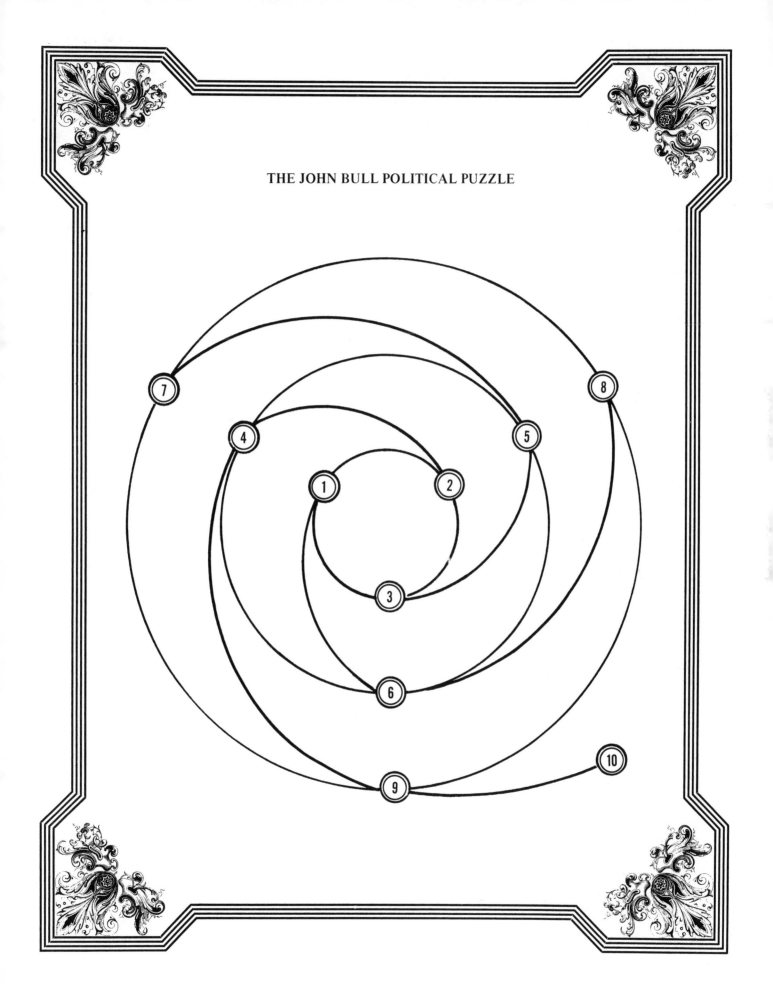

Still more puzzles by Professor Hoffmann!

THE BRAHMIN'S PUZZLE

This very clever puzzle is professedly based on a Hindu legend, to the following effect:

At the beginning of the world, Brahma set up in the great Temple of Benares three diamond pyramids. Round the first of them he hung sixty-four rings, made of purest gold, and arranged in regular order, the largest ring encircling the foot of the pyramid and the smallest its top. And Brahma said unto the priests, "Transfer these sixty-four rings from the first pyramid to the third, transposing one ring at a time only, and putting it either on a vacant pyramid or on a larger ring. By the time you have executed this task the end of the world will be near."

As few persons would care to attempt a puzzle which professedly takes some thousands of years to solve, it has been found necessary to modify the conditions of the problem, the number of rings to be transposed being reduced from sixty-four to eight. Instead of gold, they are in this case discs of cardboard, colored alternately orange and black. The three diamond cones are represented by three little wooden

slabs (Fig. 1), each with a cylindrical peg standing up in its center. The method of transposition is the same as laid down in the legend.

Fig. 1

TO BALANCE AN EGG ON THE POINT OF A CANE

In this case the difficulty of the feat of balancing an egg on end is enhanced by the fact that the egg is to be balanced on the end of a walking stick.

The articles employed are an egg, a cork, and a couple of dinner forks.

Required, to balance the egg, by the aid of the other three articles, on the smaller end of the stick.

SILKEN FETTERS

This is a puzzle for two persons, preferably a lady and gentleman. Two pieces of ribbon, each, say, a yard and a half in length, are required. One end of the first ribbon is to be tied round each of the lady's wrists, and the second ribbon is then in like manner secured to the gentleman's

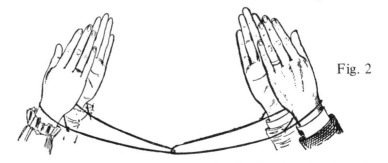

Fig. 2

wrists, one end of it however, being first passed inside the lady's ribbon, so that the pair are held captive, after the manner illustrated in Fig. 2. The puzzle is to disconnect them, but without untying either of the knots. How is it to be done?

THE THREE FOUNTAINS

A,B,C,D (Fig. 1) represents a walled space; E,F, and G, three houses, and H,I,K, three fountains. It is required to lay pipes in such manner as to bring water from I to G, from H to F, and from K to E; but the pipes must not cross each other, nor must they pass outside the enclosure. How is it to be done?

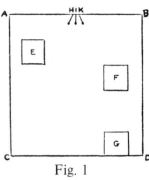
Fig. 1

THE PENETRATIVE QUARTER

In a piece of stout paper cut a circular hole the size of a nickel. Invite any one to pass a quarter through the hole without touching the coin or tearing the paper. He will naturally tell you that it can't be done, the diameter of the quarter being so much greater than that of the hole. And yet the thing can be done — easily done; and the reader is invited to find out how to do it.

THE SINGULAR QUARTER

A handkerchief being spread out squarely upon the table, and a quarter laid on its center, required, so to pick up the handkerchief, by any two corners, as to bring it into a vertical position, the quarter still remaining in the center, supported by the handkerchief only.

THE BALANCED QUARTER

It would stagger most people to be invited to balance a quarter on edge on the point of a needle, and yet, if you know how to do it, the feat is not only possible, but easy.

The requirements for the trick are to be found in any household. They are a corked wine bottle, a second cork of somewhat smaller size, a needle, and a couple of dessert forks of equal size and weight. Last, but not least in importance, the quarter.

Having provided himself with these aids, the reader is invited to try whether he can solve the puzzle.

THE THREE PEANUTS

This is propounded in the shape of a conjuring trick, usually after two or three bona fide tricks have been performed. You place three peanuts on the table, and cover each with a borrowed hat. You make a great point of having nothing concealed in your hands, and profess your willingness to allow the audience, if they please, to mark the three articles, so that there can be no question of substitution.

You then take up each hat in succession, pick up the peanut beneath it, and gravely eat it, replacing the hat mouth downward on the table. Any one is at liberty to see that there is nothing left under either hat. You then undertake to bring the three peanuts under whichever of the three hats the company may select; and the choice being made, you at once do so. How is it to be done?

uibble" or "Catch" Puzzles from Professor Hoffmann.

THE MYSTERIOUS OBSTACLE

You undertake to clasp a person's hands in such manner that he cannot leave the room without unclasping them. How is it to be done?

THE PORTRAIT

A portrait hung in a gentleman's library. He was asked whom it represented. He replied:
"Uncles and brothers have I none, But that man's father is my father's son."
What relation was the subject of the portrait to the speaker?

THE EGG AND THE CANNON BALL

Exhibiting an egg and a cannon ball (you can use a basketball), you hold forth learnedly on the extraordinary strength of a perfect arch, and, still more, of a perfect dome, remarking that few people know how strong even the shell of an egg is, if it is placed in a proper position. In proof of your assertion, you undertake to place the egg, without covering it in any way, in such a position that no one present can break it with the cannon ball.

How can that be?

A CURIOUS WINDOW

A window in a certain house has recently been made twice its original size, but without increasing either its height or width.

How can that be?

ARITHMETICAL ENIGMA

From a number that's odd, drop the first letter,
    It then will even be;
Its tail, I pray, next take away,
    And the mother of us all you'll see.

NECESSITY THE MOTHER OF INVENTION

I have a bottle of wine, corked in the ordinary way. Unfortunately, I have no corkscrew.

How can I get the wine out, without breaking the glass, or making a hole in the cork?

EASY, WHEN YOU KNOW IT

What two numbers multiplied together will produce seven?

118

MORE "QUIBBLE"
AND "CATCH"
QUESTIONS BY
PROFESSOR
HOFFMANN

A SINGULAR SUBTRACTION

From six take nine, from nine take ten, from forty take fifty, and yet have six left.

How is it to be done?

A VANISHING NUMBER

There is a number of three figures, in value not very far short of a thousand, but when halved its value is nothing.

What is it?

AN INTERESTING QUESTION

Twice ten are six of us,
Six are but three of us,
Nine are but four of us;
    What can we possibly be?
Would you know more of us,
Twelve are but six of us,
    Five are but four, do you see?

THE MOUSE

A mouse found in a box a number of ears of corn, and set to work to carry them off to his hole. He brought out with him three ears at each journey, and it took him nine journeys to remove the whole.

How many ears of corn were there in the box?

A REVERSIBLE FRACTION

Required, to find a fraction whose numerator is less than its denominator, but which, reversed, shall remain of the same value.

THE THREE COUNTERS

Three counters are laid in a row on the table.

Required, to take the middle one away from the middle without touching it.

MAGIC MADE EASY

Borrow a quarter and a penny, and hold them one in each hand, with the hands open, in front of you, the hands being about two feet apart. Now close the hands, and announce that you will make the coins change places without again opening your hands, which you proceed to do accordingly.

How is it done?

THE ENDLESS CHAIN PUZZLE

A piece of cardboard, six inches square, and bearing the representation (in gold, on a blue ground) of an endless chain, is cut into eighteen pieces, of various sizes, and such pieces are placed hap-hazard, as shown in Fig. 1. The puzzle is to rearrange them so as to re-form the endless chain, with each link in proper connection.

A large-size drawing of this puzzle, ready for mounting, will be found on page 277.

Fig. 1

THE "SPOTS" PUZZLE

This puzzle is very much more difficult than it looks. It consists (see Fig. 2) of a wooden cube, not quite three inches each way, cut into nine bars, of equal size. (This should be a fairly easy puzzle for the reader to make in his puzzle work-shop.) Each of these is decorated with one or more "spots," half an inch in diameter; and the experimenter is required to put together these bars in such manner that the resulting cube shall represent an enlarged model of the die familiar to the backgammon player (see Fig. 3), with all its spots in proper position. These, it may be mentioned for the benefit of the uninitiated, are arranged as follows: The "ace" point is on the opposite side to the "six"; the two on the opposite side to the "five," and the "three" on the opposite side to the "four," the total of each pair of opposite sides being always seven. A die which does not answer these conditions is regarded as fraudulent.

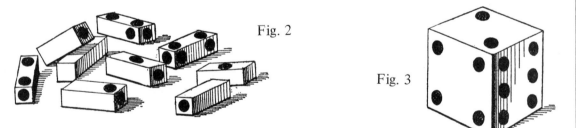

Fig. 2

Fig. 3

FIXING THE RING

This is described, with a touch of poetry, as a "matrimonial" puzzle. It is, in fact, a puzzle for two persons, who, to give it the proper touch of sentiment should be a lady and a gentleman.

The appliances consist of a silken cord and a plain gold ring. The lady holds the cord, and the gentleman the ring, and they are required, by their joint efforts, to tie the cord in a knot round the ring, each using *one hand only*.

THE THIRTY-SIX PUZZLE

his is the last puzzle from Professor Hoffmann for this volume of *Merlin's Puzzler,* so give it a good try.

Thirty-six counters are arranged in the form of a square, six rows of six each.

Required, to remove six counters in such manner that the remaining counters shall still have an even number in each row, horizontal and vertical.

L'ENVOI

In the manner of Professor Hoffmann we would like to leave the readers with a short postscript. The Professor has once again reached across the borders of time and has entertained the readers of today with the charm and ingenuity of the puzzles of yesterday. For us, these puzzles are truly old wine in new bottles.

Thank you, Professor, for a most pleasant interlude. We look forward to seeing you again in the next volume of *Merlin's Puzzler.*

Goodbye until later!

Your Editor.

PROFESSOR HOFFMANN

I say, Pamela, I have a wizard of a riddle for you. Can you guess what I am holding behind my back? It is red and white on the outside and gray on the inside.

Really Cedric, how droll. My nanny told me that one years and years ago. The answer is . . . .

PUFF'S PUZZLE

Mr. Puff has an interesting little puzzle for us. Lay out twelve coins in the form of a square, four coins to a side. Now rearrange the twelve coins so that there are five coins on each side of the square.
(Editor's note: Please don't ask me who Mr. Puff is. When I arrived in the morning, there was a note on my desk, "Use this puzzle." I think he's one of Merlin's relatives.)

The Rhino's Riddle

Rupert has been having a great time stumping everyone at Merlin's court with a new math puzzle.

The puzzler is required to arrange the four numbers 2, 3, 4 and 5, along with a plus sign and an equal sign, into a valid mathematical equation.

(1) White to move and win.

(2) Black to move and win.

(3) White to move and win.

(4) Black to move and win.

Have you tried your hand at solving a good old-fashioned checker problem lately? If not, then you are in for a treat. Herr Kempelen has just activated his famous Automaton Chess Player and he has instructed the machine to pose four checker problems for your entertainment. Please step up to the board, it is your move.

THE SPHINX

One of Merlin's favorite puzzle practitioners is Professor Stodare's marvelous illusion called The Talking Sphinx. Where it came from only the professor knows, but its knowledge of puzzles is truly immense. Professor, the curtain is up!

1. On which side of church does a cypress tree grow?

2. What kind of hen lays the longest?

3. What does no man want yet no man wants to lose?

4. What is the only thing you break when you say its name?

5. Who was the first electrician?

6. When do 2 and 2 not make 4?

7. What is the unluckiest vegetable to have on board a ship?

8. What is worse than raining cats and dogs?

9. Who was the most popular actor in the Bible?

10. Is there a word in the English language that contains all the vowels?

11. What has two heads, six feet, one tail and four ears?

12. When is an elevator not an elevator?

13. What is the hardest thing about learning to ride a bicycle?

14. What musical instrument never tells the truth?

15. What is the shortest month in the year?

16. What is worse than biting into an apple and finding a worm?

17. What three words which read the same backwards and forwards did Adam use when he first met Eve?

18. Where do fish wash their faces?

ld dictionaries are always fun to browse through. I have made up a sample page from an old 1915 edition of Funk and Wagnalls dictionary, but I have left out the descriptive words for each of the illustrations. Below the page are eighteen words. Can you match up twelve of the words with the pictures on the page?

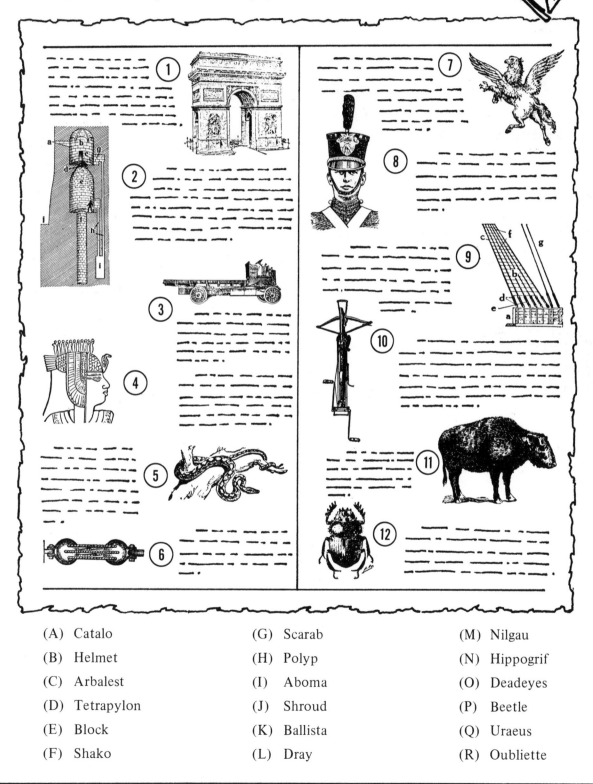

(A) Catalo
(B) Helmet
(C) Arbalest
(D) Tetrapylon
(E) Block
(F) Shako

(G) Scarab
(H) Polyp
(I) Aboma
(J) Shroud
(K) Ballista
(L) Dray

(M) Nilgau
(N) Hippogrif
(O) Deadeyes
(P) Beetle
(Q) Uraeus
(R) Oubliette

ards and conjuring have always gone together, as have cards and puzzles. Merlin has requested the prestidigitator above to entertain us with some puzzles and pasteboard statistics.

"Ladies and gentlemen, please take note that this innocent pack of playing cards that I hold in my hand is in reality a most ingenious form of calendar. Please note the following similarities:

(1) There are 52 playing cards and 52 weeks in the year.

(2) There are 13 cards in each suit and 13 weeks in each season.

(3) There are 4 suits and 4 seasons.

(4) There are 12 court (face) cards and 12 months in the year.

(5) The Red cards stand for day and the Black cards for night.

(6) If you total up the values of all the cards, counting Jacks as 11, Queens as 12, and Kings as 13, the sum will be 364. Add 1 to this for the Joker and you have the number of days in a year.

(7) Also of interest is the fact that if you add up all the letters in all the names of the cards, to wit: one, two, three, four, five, six, seven, eight, nine, ten, Jack, Queen, and King, you will get a total of 52, the number of cards in a deck of playing cards.

"Do you find these statistics a bit strange and disturbing? Is it mere coincidence, or is there something to the old admonition that a deck of cards is the Devil's picture book?"

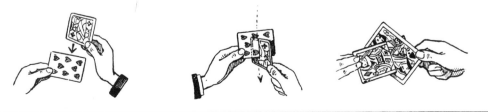

THE ELEVEN TRICK

Tell your friends that you are about to show them a trick based on lightning calculation on your part. Discarding all of the face cards from the pack, take the remaining cards and start laying them down on the table in groups of three. Explain to your audience that each group of three cards forms a three-digit number that can be exactly divided by 11 without leaving a remainder. You form these three-digit numbers as fast as you can lay the cards down.

In our example we have formed the number 231. Eleven goes into this number exactly 21 times.

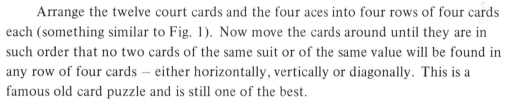

The explanation as to how the trick is performed is very simple. Just make sure that the total of the first card plus the third card adds up to the value of the middle card.

Simple . . . . . . but very, very good!

NO TWO IN THE SAME ROW

Fig. 1

Arrange the twelve court cards and the four aces into four rows of four cards each (something similar to Fig. 1). Now move the cards around until they are in such order that no two cards of the same suit or of the same value will be found in any row of four cards — either horizontally, vertically or diagonally. This is a famous old card puzzle and is still one of the best.

THINGS ARE LOOKING UP!

Lay three cards on the table, two cards face-down and one card face-up (see Fig. 2). Now, in three moves, turning over two cards during each move, end up with all three cards facing upwards on the table.

This trick is sometimes performed with water glasses or coins, the answer being the same in all cases.

Fig. 2

THE FIVE PAIRS PUZZLE

Lay out a row of ten cards on the table. Starting with any card, pick it up and move it left or right over the next two cards in the row and place it on top of the third card. You now have a pair. Next, pick up another single card and pass it left or right over the next two cards in the row (a pair counts as one card), and place it on the third single card. You are to continue in this manner until you have five pairs upon the table.

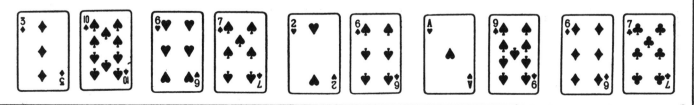

127

erlin has released some more pictures from last month's puzzle convention. These pictures illustrate four prizewinning puzzles which I think you will find quite challenging. If you missed the convention, then this is your opportunity to get in on the fun.

rofessor Pepper exhibited at the convention his latest invention, The Automation Puzzle Generator. (I'm sure you all remember Pepper's Ghost, his most famous illusion to date.) Just turn the crank at the base of the generator, and the figure dressed like a clown will draw a different puzzle for you every time. The puzzle for picture number 1 is simply to calculate the number of triangles in the star drawing. Be careful, though, you get only one try at it.

he beautiful young lady in picture number 2 stole the hearts of the judges with her dancing and second prize for her most perplexing problem, entitled "The Magic Pyramid." The puzzle is to rearrange the numbers 1 through 9 that are printed around the three sides of the pyramid so that the total of the four numbers along any one side will be 17. The numbers at the corners will, of course, be included in the totals of the adjacent sides.

ow, in picture number 3 we have an interesting puzzle entry. The soup tureen is not valued at $700, but rather it contains $700. The money is all in silver and it is divided into quarters, half-dollars, and dollars, there being an equal number of each. How many of each are there?

ur last problem was brought to us by a mystic from far-off India. When he arrived at the convention, he promptly levitated himself and refused to come down until our experts had solved his puzzle. In the picture you will note four circles enclosing signs of the Zodiac. You are to draw a perfect square in such a position that each one of the circles will be on one of the four lines of the square.

rom Merlin's personal library of puzzle lore comes this very old and very excellent problem of checker transposition. I asked Merlin to furnish us with one of these delightful amusements, one that was not too hard, and yet one that would still offer a challenge to our readers. Merlin also commissioned the royal engraver to create a puzzle board for us to use, and we have reproduced it on the next page.

Enough said, let us get on to the business at hand. To set up the puzzle, place three red checkers on the squares marked 1, 2 and 3. Next, place three black checkers on the squares marked 5, 6 and 7. The object of the puzzle is to make the red and black checkers change places. To do this, a checker may be moved to an adjacent empty square, or you may jump a checker over an adjacent checker to a vacant square beyond. You do not remove any checker that you happen to jump. All movement must be in a horizontal or vertical direction. No diagonal moves are allowed. The solution we give at the back of the book uses just fifteen moves. Try to do it in less.

Alright now, the board is set up and the move is yours. Merlin thinks you can solve it in 10 minutes . . . or a little more.

After solving the above problem I think that you are ready for an easy puzzle. At the left is a magic square, but the numbers seem to be placed in the wrong squares. The numbers are to add up to six in every horizontal, diagonal, and vertical line, but whoever was working it seems to have given up and left the puzzle unfinished. Can you arrange the numbers correctly to satisfy the requirements of the puzzle? I give you three minutes on this one.

erlin's Seaport is alive with activity, for the four-masted clipper ship, *The Camelot*, has just dropped anchor. I was talking to some of the lads from the ship and they bring news of a new game they learned in the South Seas. You'll need a bit of cardboard, say twelve inches square, divided into twelve squares. Two mates play the game, one getting four red checkers and the other four black checkers. One player places a checker on an empty square. Then the other one places one of his checkers on an empty square. They go back and forth in this fashion until all the checkers are on the board. Now, if any player has been able to place his four checkers in a row, up, down, or diagonally (see Fig. 1), then he is the winner. If not, the players, in turn, begin to move their checkers. One checker may be moved at a time to any adjacent empty square. All moves must be in a horizontal or vertical direction. The first one to move his four checkers into a straight line is declared the winner. Jumping one checker over another is not allowed.

When you have played the game a while and have begun to master it, for I can see that you are a bright lad and quicker than most, you might try making the board bigger and using more checkers (twenty-five squares and ten checkers). Also, you might allow the checkers to be moved diagonally during play.

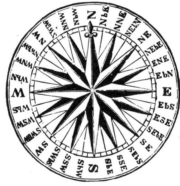

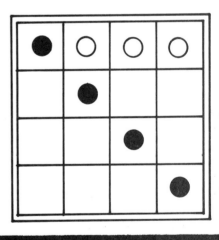

hat we are looking at is truly a frightening picture from the past. The palace is that of Sennacherib at Kouyunjik. An evil Jinn is materializing behind the palace, and it will soon command Sennacherib to solve the Pyramid Puzzle of Ur or face destruction. To work this puzzle, you must first place fourteen coins on all the circles of the pyramid except circle 6. Then jumping one coin over another, as you would in checkers and removing the jumped checker, you try to remove every coin from the board except one. You can only jump along the diagonal lines and the lines across the bottom row.

Can you save the palace from certain destruction? Hurry, there is not much more time to save them!

133

Treasure Island

**M**any years ago a ship was sent out from Merlin's Isle to discover if any plunder still remained buried on Treasure Island. We all know now of the fabulous hoard of riches that was brought back by these hardy adventurers. What hasn't been told until now is the extent of the dangers and hardships to which they were exposed. Treasure Island was surrounded by seven obstacles. To reach the island and return, they had to face great storms, pirates, the hungry maw of a maelstrom, sea monsters, doldrums, treacherous rocks, and an unfriendly fortress. If the captain had not been a great puzzler, the voyage would have ended in ruin, for there was only one way through this maze of misfortune. Our ship and its brave crew were strong enough to meet and overcome one of these hazards during one voyage, but if they had been forced to face a second, their ship would have been lost with all hands aboard.

It is now time for you to take the helm and lay a course for your ship to sail to Treasure Island and back.

START

END

135

The Chess Master

 empelen's famous Automaton Chess Player is with us once again to challenge our wits with a checker problem that makes use of a portion of his chess board. The section we will use is five squares wide and five squares long. Place seventeen checkers (it doesn't matter whether they are red or black) on the seventeen numbered squares indicated in Fig. 1. The object of the puzzle is to remove sixteen of the checkers from the board by jumping one checker over another and then removing the jumped checker from the board. At the end of your solution the last remaining checker must be on square 9. Every move must be a jump. When, during a move, you can jump more than one checker it will still be considered one move (as in checkers when you have a double or triple jump). The first move of the game will be by the checker on square 9. You should be able to solve this problem using no more than four moves. That is according to the Automaton, and machines do not lie (?).

THE HINDU BANGLE TRICK

From the fabled regions of the Indian subcontinent comes this mysterious feat of magic. The Hindu Bangle Trick, Merlin calls it. It is truly puzzling when performed well. Follow closely the details of its presentation.

The performer has someone come forward from the audience. He hands him a stout length of rope, about two and a half feet in length, and has him tie both ends of the rope to the magician's wrists (see Fig. 1). The knots should be very tight and even sealed with tape to heighten the effect. Next, hand him a plastic ring some four inches in diameter. He may pass it among the audience to verify that it is whole and not gimmicked in any way. Returning the ring to the magician, he is instructed to drape a three-foot square cloth over the magician's hands and arms. Have him step back and slowly count to five. At the count of five, the magician lets the cloth slip to the floor and the audience sees that the ring is now threaded on the rope. On examination, your wrists are found to be securely bound (see Fig. 2). Have the assistant cut you free and step back to acknowledge the thunderous applause (?).

How is it done? When you go to the magic store (Woolworth's of course), buy two matching bangles. When presenting the trick, the second one is already on your arm halfway up your sleeve. Under cover of the cloth, slip your other hand up your sleeve and bring the bangle down. Hold this bangle with one hand while the other hand slips the first bangle (the one you showed to the audience) onto a hook inside your coat. Or, slip the ring back up the sleeve of your coat and get rid of it as soon as possible. A little ingenuity and practice will win the day.

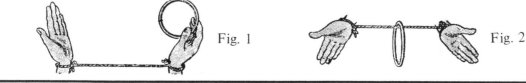

Fig. 1   Fig. 2

A

B

① ②

ollowing the recent puzzle convention, Merlin gave a great banquet to honor the winners. The court artist, Ector Pendragon, overindulged, and when he awoke the next day he found that he had created a puzzle collage before retiring the previous night (see page 138). When Merlin saw it he immediately named it Mead Madness and had it hung in the Puzzle Gallery. Pendragon included several puzzles in his picture. Let us see if you can solve them.

The first puzzle concerns the two lines which converge on the horizon. Is line A shorter or longer than line <u>B</u>?

The second problem is with the marble monument decorated with the head of Medusa. You are to divide this mitred monument into four parts, all of the same shape and size.

The third puzzle concerns the triangle of keys. By rearranging the position of three of the keys, cause the triangle to point downwards instead of upwards.

The fourth puzzle is about a block of wood. If a carved piece of wood looks like picture (1) when seen from the front and looks like picture (2) when seen from the top, what does it look like when seen from the side?

The last question is about the figure at the bottom of the collage. Is it a young girl looking at the picture, or an old woman looking away from the picture?

Another picture by Ector Pendragon is seen below in this view of the Puzzle Gallery. The picture puzzle is called Tri-Square-1. How many squares can you find in the painting? How many triangles?

TRI-SQUARE-1

Greetings from Merlin go out to the United States Post Office for the valiant Airmail Service they have provided for over 50 years now. To honor them Merlin has designed a special game board using famous stamps that have carried the mail to all parts of the globe.

The game is played by two people. One player places four black checkers on the four stamps along the top row, and his opponent places four red checkers on the four stamps along the bottom row. The players, in turn, move one checker at a time along the lines to an adjacent empty stamp. A player can move his checkers backwards and forwards, side to side. The object of the game is to remove all of your opponents checkers. You can remove an opponent's checker by jumping one of your own checkers over another of your own checkers and then landing on one of your opponent's checkers. You then remove his checker from the board. At the time of the jump, all three checkers must be in a straight line, horizontally or vertically. You can also win the game if you can block all of your opponent's checkers in such a way that there is no vacant stamp to which he can move.

I hope that you have fun playing this game. I am sure that the pilots in the Postal Balloon shown here could use a good game to while away the hours as they go about their appointed rounds of delivering our fourth-class mail.

The Rhino's Riddle

Rupert The Rhino has come up with a new puzzle involving numbers. He claims he can arrange four 4's in such a way that they will equal any number from zero thru nine. To show you how it is done, here is the way Rupert makes a zero:

$$0 = 4 + 4 - 4 - 4$$

This is easy, you say! O.K. puzzlers, show Rupert how easy it is and give him the answers for the numbers one thru nine.

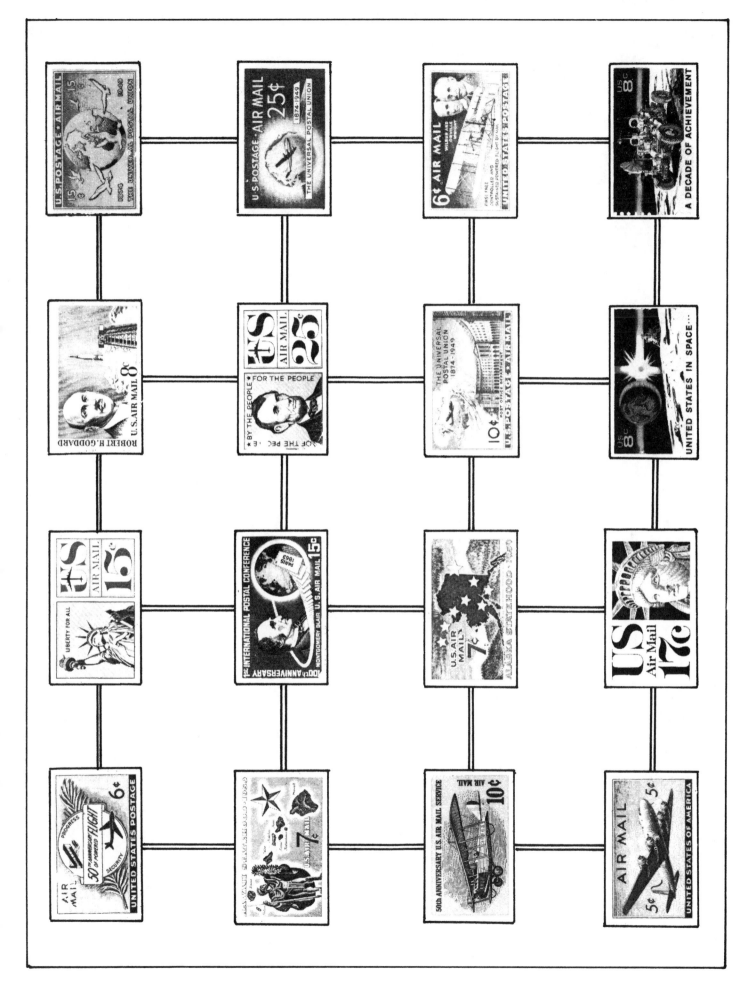

The Word Professor

lright, students, please step forward and meet your new teacher, Mr. Willard Wordsworth, "The Word Professor."

"Thank you, sir, and good-day to you, students. Let us start off with a few "change-the-word" puzzles. In all of these puzzles, see if you can change the first word into the last word in just four moves. Change one letter in the word with each move. (For example: You can change the word POUR into the word FAIL using the following four moves — POUR, FOUR, FOUL, FOIL, FAIL). Use the boxes for writing in the words from top to bottom."

W	A	R	M
C	O	L	D

B	O	A	T
C	A	S	H

S	T	A	R
F	E	E	T

M	O	R	E
L	E	S	S

F	I	S	H
M	E	A	T

Instead of a spelling bee, we are now going to have a "rearranging bee." Each set of letters below, when rearranged, will spell out the name of a country. I expect everyone to score a hundred on this test.

A. A D E K M R N   B. G R B A A I L U
C. H P E I T I A O   D. D A U R O H N S
E. U A N M A R I   F. G L E D A N N
     G. S H I N I N E C L T E E T
     H. H F N N A A S T G A I
     I. S W E Y N G A R M T E
     J. S A T N K P I A

Since you did so well with the "rearranging bee," I think that I will give you an "insect bee" instead of a spelling bee. In the boxes in Fig. 1 we have sixteen letters. The pesty problem that you have is to make at least ten insect names from them. Please don't get stung on this test.

Fig. 1

O	I	M	G
N	C	S	L
F	P	T	Y
H	E	W	A

For the alphabet soup kids I have a Super change-the-word puzzle. They must try to change the word SOUP to FISH.

One more question, students, and class is dismissed. Can you think of an English word of four letters meaning "water" which becomes a word meaning "land" by the changing of one letter?

S	O	U	P
F	I	S	H

Your car is ready, so please hurry along, we don't want to be late. Merlin is giving a party tonight and he has hired England's home of mystery, Maskelyne's famous Egyptian Hall in Piccadilly, for the evening's entertainment. Merlin informs me that he has summoned many of the outstanding magicians and practitioners of mystery to perform tonight.

The theme of the evening is "Mysteries of The Early Conjurors." We should be seeing such personages as Houdini, Professor Hoffmann, DeKolta, Will Goldston, Kellar, Charles Bertram, Professor Pepper, etc. Also, puzzles will no doubt be presented by Maskelyne and Cooke's two automatons, Psycho and Zoe. Professor Stodare is also on hand and he will once again be exhibiting his illusion, The Sphinx.

There's the theater up ahead. Driver, please pull over and let us out here. By the look of things I believe we arrived just in time.

Now, here is someone I would like you to meet. Hello, Professor, it is good to see you again. Allow me to introduce to you Professor Kunze, 'The Christmas Conjuror.' Professor, my friend and I are both interested in magic. I wonder if you would show us how to perform the card trick you fooled us with the other night at my wife's birthday party?"

"I would be delighted to, gentlemen, please be seated. Here are two fresh decks of playing cards, one for you and one for me. Now then, follow me closely. First, we both shuffle our decks and then we exchange them. Very good; here is your deck. Now, we place them on the table in front of us, so. We then cut our decks into three piles. You look at the top card of your middle pile, note it and place it back on the top of the pile. I will do the same with my middle pile. We both now put our decks back together, square them up and exchange them once again. Now you shuffle your deck and I will shuffle mine. Good. Now look through your deck and find the card that you looked at before and place it face down on the table. I will do the same and find the card that I looked at. Alright now, on the count of three turn over the cards, one, two, three, they are both the same.

"How I did it, gentlemen, is simplicity itself. In the beginning when I shuffled and exchanged decks with you I noted the bottom card of the deck I gave to you. Then, when you cut the deck you cut it left to right. After you had looked at the top card of the middle pile I reached across and restacked the piles for you, once again going left to right. This put the stack, whose bottom card I knew, on top of the card you had looked at. After that, we exchanged decks and shuffled them. I, of course, false-shuffled mine by merely cutting it three or four times which does not alter the arrangement of the cards. When you looked through your deck you found the card you had chosen and placed it on the table. I then looked through my deck until I found the previously noted bottom card. The next card was your card. Easy, wasn't it!"

ome over here and see what's on this table. Merlin has provided his guests with souvenir booklets and tricks to mark this occasion. Take some of these books; there are plenty. Now, here is a trick I think you will like, I know my children will. It is called The Card With Many Sides, four sides to be exact. Watch while I demonstrate. When I show you Side 1, you see one spot upon the card (Fig. 1). When I turn the card over, you see four spots (Fig. 2). When I turn it over once again, there are three spots on it (Fig. 3), and finally, when I turn it over for the last time, you see six spots. One card with four sides, incredible.

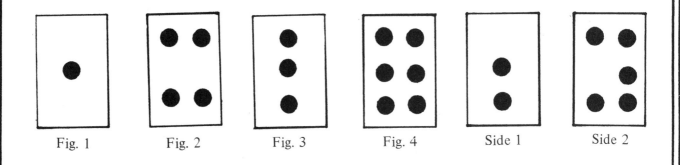

The truth of the matter, though, is that you only think that you see the full number of spots on each side of the card each time I turn it over. The card really looks like this: Side 1 has only two spots on it (Side 1), and Side 2 has only five spots on it (Side 2). The first time I held the card up I covered up the bottom spot of Side 1 (Fig. 5). When I turned the card over I covered up the middle spot on Side 2 (Fig. 6). The third time I covered up the end of Side 1 (Fig. 7), and on the last turn I covered the middle blank spot of Side 2 (Fig. 8).

(The reader will find a duplication master for this card trick on page 278. Copy the page and glue to a piece of cardboard.)

uick, come over here and see this. Mr. Cooke is exhibiting his automaton, Psycho, and he has programmed him to play a game with the audience. Our turn is next. In the dish in front of him are fifteen gold sovereigns, which are used as counters to play the game. Each player, in turn, must remove one, two, or three coins from the dish. When it is Psycho's turn, he shows a card with a number on it to indicate the number of coins he wants removed from the dish. The object of the game is to avoid being the player that has to remove the last coin from the dish. The first person to beat Psycho will win the fifteen sovereigns. Well, he just beat the chap in front of us. Let us see if those gold coins are ours!

You, too, can play against Psycho. Place fifteen coins on the table and make your move. You will find Psycho's answering move by looking below at the card that is under the circle with the number that indicates how many coins remain on the table. If you want Psycho to go first, start him off with the card under the circle with 15 in it.

(15)	(14)	(13)	(12)	(11)	(10)	(9)	(8)
2	1	1	3	2	1	1	2

(7)	(6)	(5)	(4)	(3)	(2)	(1)
1	1	1	3	2	1	LOSE

ook at this now, Maskelyne and Cooke's "Wonder Of The Age," an electronic computer that solves forever that mathematical mystery, the Magic Square. It goes on to say that the "MAC" computer, which is locked in the basement vault of the Egyptian Hall, is connected by wires to the typewriter on this table. This is all very hard to believe, you know, even if it is 1890. Let's see now; it says that Mr. Cooke, who is at the table, can communicate with MAC by using that telegraph key in front of him. He will relay any number that you give him, say between 40 and 100, and the computer will immediately calculate the square and print it out on the Columbia Typewriter for you. This I have got to see! "Mr. Cooke, I challenge that infernal machine of yours to construct a square using my age, 47, as the magic number."

"I assure you, sir, that if your age were 147 or a biblical 1047, MAC would not fail. Stand back and witness the wonder of this or any other age, big MAC."

Well, bless my soul, look at that. The typewriter has come alive, and look, it is printing a Magic Square. Why, I don't believe my eyes, it seems to total 47 in every direction. Now how did they do it, man, how did they do it?

THE SECRET MATHEMATICAL FORMULA

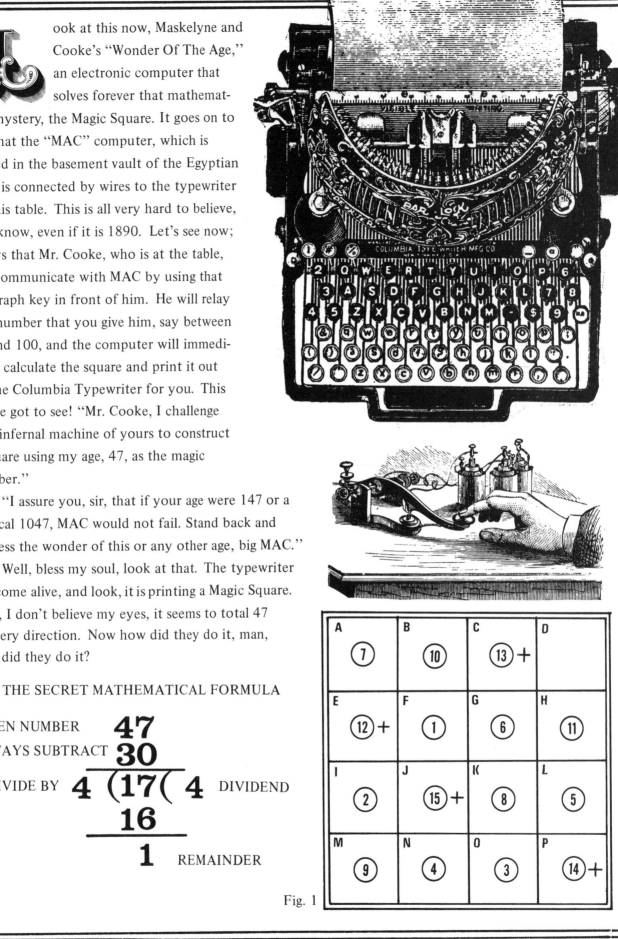

GIVEN NUMBER **47**

ALWAYS SUBTRACT **30**

DIVIDE BY $4 \overline{)17(}\ 4$ DIVIDEND

16

1 REMAINDER

A	B	C	D
⑦	⑩	⑬ +	
E	F	G	H
⑫ +	①	⑥	⑪
I	J	K	L
②	⑮ +	⑧	⑤
M	N	O	P
⑨	④	③	⑭ +

Fig. 1

Mr. Cooke has graciously consented to let the readers of *Merlin's Puzzler* in on the secret of creating a Magic Square. At the bottom of page 148 you will find the secret mathematical formula needed to work this puzzle out. Follow closely: Take the number 47 (remember that you can do this with any number greater than 40); subtract 30 from it; divide the difference (17) by 4. This will leave you with a dividend of 4 and a remainder of 1. Next, look at Fig. 1 on page 50. In each one of the squares you will find a number in a circle (except for square D). This is the initial value of the square. You must add the dividend (4) to this value to get the final value for the square. For square D you must enter only the value of the dividend, (4). In the four squares that have a plus sign (+) next to the circled initial amount (squares E, J, P), you must also add the remainder (1) from your calculation to get the final value for the square. Our sample square would be: (A) 7+4=11, (B) 10+4=14, (C) 13+4+1=18, (D) 0+4=4, (E) 12+4+1 = 17, (F) 1+4=5, (G) 6+4=10, (H) 11+4=15, (I) 2+4=6, (J) 15+4+1=20, (K) 8+4=12, (L) 5+4=9, (M) 9+4=13, (N) 4+4=8, (O) 3+4=7, (P) 14+4+1=19.

You can make up squares for very large numbers, say the year you were born. With a little practice, and some memorizing, you can actually learn to do this in your head. Why, you might even bill yourself as "The Eighth Wonder of the World, the Walking Computer."

THIS HISTORICAL MATHEMATICAL PUZZLE IS KNOWN AS A MAGIC SQUARE

THIS MAGIC SQUARE HAS BEEN ELECTRONICALLY COMPUTED BY THE MAC COMPUTER TO TOTAL 47 WHEN ADDED IN ANY DIRECTION. THE COMBINATIONS ARE:

A, B, C, D   E, F, G, H

I, J, K, L   M, N, O, P

A, F, K, P   M, J, G, D

A, D, M, P   F, G, J, K

I, J, M, N   A, B, E, F

C, D, G, H   K, L, O, P

E, I, H, L   B, C, N, O

A, E, I, M   B, F, J, N

C, G, K, O   D, H, L, P

A	B	C	D
11	**14**	**18**	**4**
E	F	G	H
17	**5**	**10**	**15**
I	J	K	L
6	**20**	**12**	**9**
M	N	O	P
13	**8**	**7**	**19**

PROGRAM PROBLEMS

ere are our seats. Let us settle down and peruse the program before the curtain goes up. Look at this, they have a puzzle section in the program. I think I'll try a few, since we have several minutes to go before show time.

Now, the first puzzle is an interesting one. It seems that a farmer owned twenty-one cows. He was very protective towards them and wished to enclose them in four fenced-in pastures. For some unknown reason he stipulated to the fence builder that each enclosure must hold an odd number of cows. Now, how in the world was he to do that?

Problem number 2 is one of those delightful area divisional problems. It stipulates that the square in the picture must be divided into six perfect squares. This is to be accomplished by drawing four straight lines across the square. An interesting puzzle!

Ah ha, here is an old favorite of mine. In puzzle number 3 you must place the four white counters and the four black counters in the sixteen squares of the diagram in such a way that no two counters of the same color will be in the same row, horizontally, vertically, or diagonally. Try this one, it's not as easy as it looks.

Here is a problem from Merlin. He states that to test the quickness of mind of three candidates for knighthood he had them solve the following problem. First, he showed them five helmets. Three of the helmets were white and the other two were gray. Next, he instructed them to close their eyes. Once they had done this, he placed a gray helmet on one man and a white helmet on each of the other two men. He then told them to open their eyes, look at each other, and then state what color helmet they were wearing and how they knew the color. You have just enough time to solve this one before the curtain goes up.

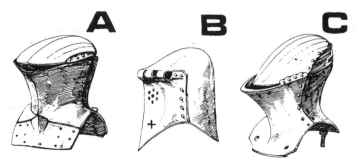

A B C

Charles Bertram

The first act is Charles Bertram, the famous Edwardian magician. Known as "The Royal Conjurer," he has appeared many times at the Egyptian Hall. A great manipulative artist, he will show many of his famous card tricks tonight. He has contributed to this book an interesting rope trick called Here, There, Everywhere. The magician picks up a piece of rope and shows it to the audience. There are three knots tied in the rope. On one of the end knots there hangs a solid metal ring (Fig. 3). He passes the rope behind his back and the ring jumps to the knot at the other end of the rope (Fig. 4). He once again passes the rope behind his back and the ring jumps back to the other end (Fig. 3). The third time he does this, the ring is found to have jumped to the middle knot (Fig. 5). The magician immediately hands the rope, with the ring still tied to the middle knot, out for inspection.

Fig. 1

The secret lies in the fact that there is a fourth knot tied in the rope. This knot is hidden by the performer's hand, which covers the knot when he holds the rope (Fig. 2). Also, the bottom knot on the rope is a slip knot (Fig. 1 and Fig. 2).

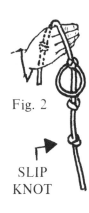

Fig. 2

To perform: The performer picks up the rope with his right hand concealing the extra knot (Fig. 2) and holds it up to the audience (Fig. 3). When he passes the rope behind his back, the left hand takes the end with the extra knot and covers it. The rope is brought out and shown (Fig. 4). The previous action is reversed for the next pass. During the final pass behind your back, you pull the rope tight so that the slip knot will come apart and disappear. When you bring the rope out now, you do not cover the extra knot. The ring will be on the middle knot. Another miracle!

SLIP
KNOT

Fig. 3

Fig. 4

Fig. 5

THE STAGE AT THE EGYPTIAN HALL

Harry Houdini

arry Houdini, the greatest magic showman of all time, is performing tonight. He will present a program of magic, escapes and spiritual manifestations. For Merlin's souvenir program he has contributed an escape and spirit seance trick that anyone can master. The materials needed for the trick are four six-foot-long lengths of rope, a card table, a slate, a bell, a wooden straight-back chair, and a three-sided screen made of cardboard that can stand upright by itself on the card table. The screen must be high enough to conceal all but the top of the performer's head when he is seated behind the table.

The performer states that he will give a spirit seance under the most rigid of conditions. He sets up the card table a few feet from the audience and places a large cloth over it, one that will hang down to the floor on all sides. Next, he places the wooden chair behind the table facing the audience. On the table he places the slate, the bell, and other objects for the spirits to play with. The performer now steps forward and asks someone to act as his assistant. The assistant is asked to tie securely a rope around the performer's left wrist and then tie another rope around his right wrist. The performer then folds his arms in front of him, turns around and instructs the assistant to tie the ends of the two ropes tightly behind his back so that he cannot move his arms. Once this has been done, he then sits down on the wooden chair and instructs the assistant to tie the ends of the rope to the middle bar of the back of the chair. Also, he has him tie each leg to a leg of the chair. The screen is then placed in front of the objects on the table. Although it is obvious that the performer cannot use his hands or feet and that the top of his head is visible at all times, the bell begins to ring, objects are thrown over the screen, and any number called for is written on the slate. When the screen is removed the magician is found to be still securely bound to the chair. Shades of Daniel D. Home! How is a thing like this possible? How could *you* do this trick?

The secret, as in all good feats of magic, is simplicity itself. After the ropes have been tied to your wrists you start to fold your arms and turn your back so that the audience can see the ropes being tied behind your back. In the act of folding your arms, your right hand grasps the rope tied to your left wrist and your left hand grasps the rope tied to your right wrist (see Fig. 1). When you have completed the folding of your arms, it will appear

from the back that each hand is holding the rope that is tied to that wrist. After the two ropes have been tied together you sit down and have the ends tied to the center bar of the back of the chair. Although you appear to be fairly tied you can, in reality, unfold your arms and reach any item in front of you on the table. The spirit manifestations that you perform I leave to your own imagination. The beauty of this spirit tie is that it looks genuine, and it would be genuine if you had not reversed the ropes as you turned around.

Remember, the best trick in the world is only a puzzle with a little showmanship to entertain your audience. The key word here is *entertain.* So, think before you act, and practice, practice, practice before you perform.

(Who is that in Figure 2? Has Mr. Home returned to guide us?)

Mr. Daniel Home in a
levitating mood.

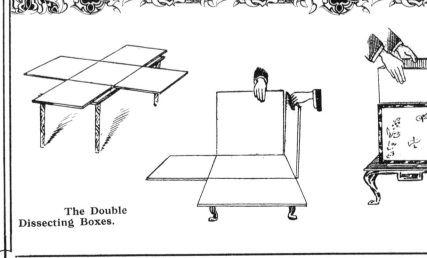

Fig. 2

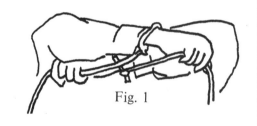

Fig. 1

The Double
Dissecting Boxes.

Professor Hoffmann

I n a surprise move the legendary Professor Hoffmann is to perform the show tonight that he last presented in 1883 at the Tolmers Square Institute, London. The trick you find in your program is from his first great book, entitled *Modern Magic.* I will let the Professor take it from here.

"TO PLACE THE FOUR KINGS IN DIFFERENT PARTS OF THE PACK, AND TO BRING THEM TOGETHER BY A SIMPLE CUT: Take the four kings (or any other four cards at pleasure), and exhibit them fan-wise (see Fig. 1), but secretly place behind the second one (the king of diamonds in the figure) two other court cards of any description, which, being thus hidden behind the king, will not be visible. The audience being satisfied that the four cards are really the four kings, and none other, fold them together, and place them at the top of the pack. Draw attention to the fact that you are about to distribute these four kings in different parts of the pack. Take up the top card, which, being really a king, you may exhibit without apparent intention, and place it at the bottom. Take the next card, which the spectators

suppose to be also a king, and place it about half way down the pack, and the next, in like manner, a little higher. Take the fourth card, which, being actually a king, you may show carelessly, and replace it on the top of the pack. You have now really three kings at the top and one at the bottom, though the audience imagine that they have seen them distributed in different parts of the pack, and are proportionately surprised, when the cards are cut, to find that all the kings are again together.

"It is best to use knaves or queens for the two extra cards, as being less distinguishable from the kings, should a spectator catch a glimpse of their faces."

PROGRAM PROBLEMS

hat was some first act. During the intermission let's do some more of the puzzles in the program and then go outside and see Professor Stodare's Sphinx, or The Talking Head illusion that's to be on exhibition. It looks as though we have three coin puzzles to contend with.

The first puzzle uses three matches and a coin. Well look at this, for a coin they are using a palming coin minted for the old Holden's magic store of New York City. I remember my dad taking me there when I was a small boy. I bought my first magic book there. Anyhow, the puzzle, as stated, is to place the coin in the glass by rearranging two of the four matches that are used here to represent a long stemmed glass. You work on that one for a while. I think I will try number 2 first.

It states here that, in puzzle 2, each of these ancient Greek coins is worth one dollar. The problem is to make change for one of the coins, using exactly fifty coins in doing so. You can use pennies, nickels, dimes, quarters, and half-dollars. That should be easy.

The third puzzle looks like a really tough one. First, you place a small plate in the middle of the table. Then you put a dime down in the middle of the plate. Now, without touching the table, the plate or the dime, you are to remove the dime from the plate. Well, that sounds impossible, but I am sure there must be an answer.

Here are a couple of extra puzzles.

Can you write the number 24 using three equal digits. The catch is that none of the digits can be an 8.

Another problem the Word Professor would love is as follows: What word means "exist" when read forwards and "wicked" when read backwards?

THE WONDERBOWL.

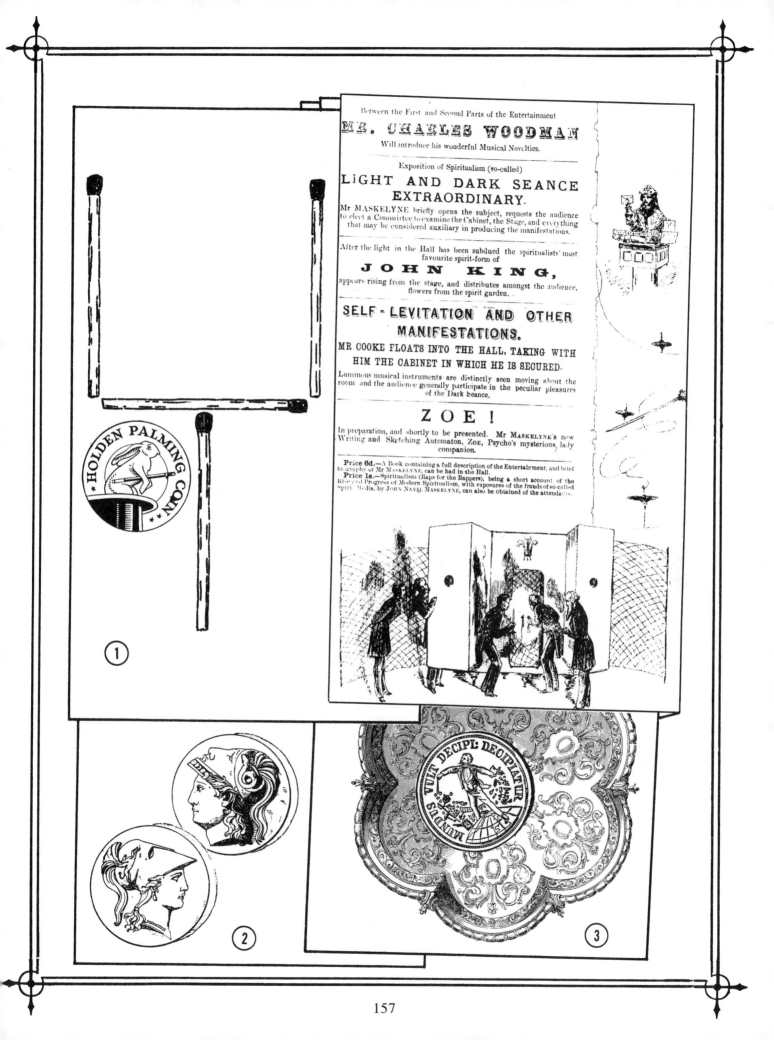

Between the First and Second Parts of the Entertainment

MR. CHARLES WOODMAN

Will introduce his wonderful Musical Novelties.

Exposition of Spiritualism (so-called)

LIGHT AND DARK SEANCE EXTRAORDINARY.

Mr MASKELYNE briefly opens the subject, requests the audience to elect a Committee to examine the Cabinet, the Stage, and everything that may be considered auxiliary in producing the manifestations.

After the light in the Hall has been subdued the spiritualists' most favourite spirit-form of

JOHN KING,

appears rising from the stage, and distributes amongst the audience, flowers from the spirit garden.

SELF - LEVITATION AND OTHER MANIFESTATIONS.

MR COOKE FLOATS INTO THE HALL, TAKING WITH HIM THE CABINET IN WHICH HE IS SECURED.

Luminous musical instruments are distinctly seen moving about the room and the audience generally participate in the peculiar pleasures of the Dark Seance.

ZOE !

In preparation, and shortly to be presented. Mr MASKELYNE'S new Writing and Sketching Automaton, ZOE, Psycho's mysterious lady companion.

Price 6d.—A Book containing a full description of the Entertainment, and brief biography of Mr MASKELYNE, can be had in the Hall.
Price 1s.—Spiritualism (Raps for the Rappers), being a short account of the Rise and Progress of Modern Spiritualism, with exposures of the frauds of so-called Spirit Media, by JOHN NEVIL MASKELYNE, can also be obtained of the attendants.

HOLDEN PALMING CORN

MUNDUS VULT DECIPI: DECIPIATUR

① ② ③

The Black Widow

rofessor Stodare was unable to make it to Merlin's party tonight. Mr. Maskelyne, however, was able to get Professor Pepper to exhibit his famous illusion, The Black Widow. Like Professor Stodare's Sphinx illusion, The Black Widow also propounds riddles and puzzles for the audience to solve. Don't step too close there, young man, you might get caught in the web!

(1) How long did Cain hate his brother?

(2) What's best when it's cracked?

(3) How are a clock and a river alike?

(4) What kind of iron is in the blood of a prize fighter?

(5) What key is the hardest to turn?

(6) Arrange six 6's so that they total 37.

(7) How many times can you subtract 5 from 135?

(8) How many cubic feet of dirt are there in a hole 3 feet wide, 3 feet long and 2½ feet deep?

(9) Write the number 20 using four 9's.

(10) When is it that 8 plus 6 equals 2?

(11) Why is the letter D like a bad boy?

(12) Why does an Indian wear feathers in his hair?

(13) Why is a caterpillar like a hot biscuit?

(14) What table has no legs?

(15) Where can you always find happiness?

(16) How many peas go into one pot?

The Man In The Iron Mask

 hen the three musketeers broke into the dungeon beneath the Bastille, they found not one man in an iron mask but five. Which one was the true king of France? By asking the guard some quick questions they learned the fourteen facts I have listed below. Coupled with the knowledge that the true king of France drank only wine, they were able to discover which prisoner to free. Can you do it, too? Hurry up, I hear more guards coming.

(1) The man in the red mask has a cell with a stone door.

(2) The man in the green mask wears sandals.

(3) Tea is drunk in the cell with the oak door.

(4) The man in the blue mask drinks water.

(5) The cell with the oak door is to the right (your right) of the cell with the barred door.

(6) The man who eats chicken wears boots.

(7) Beef is eaten in the cell with the iron door.

(8) Beer is drunk in the middle cell.

(9) The man in the black mask has the first cell on the left.

(10) The man who eats fish lives next to the man who wears shoes.

(11) Beef is eaten in the cell next to the man who wears only socks.

(12) The man who eats pies drinks milk.

(13) The man in the yellow mask eats grapes.

(14) The man in the black mask is in the cell next to the one with the paneled door.

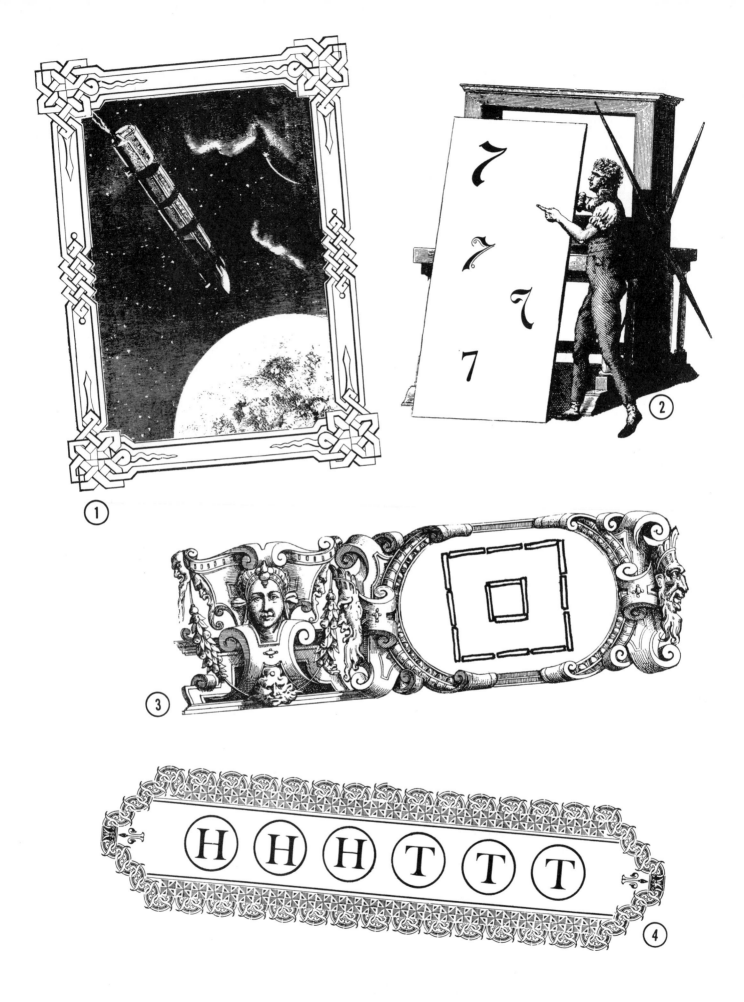

Merlin's Notes

Merlin starts out his notes with a humdinger of a problem. On the opposite page you will find a picture showing a spaceship from the Earth speeding towards a landing on the Moon. This is the Star Ship, *Merlin 1.* Now, if you will look at Fig. 1 on this page, you will see the floor plan of the command deck of the forward module. Every hour the officer of the deck had to make his rounds. He had devised a route that would take him down every corridor that was designated by the letters <u>A</u> through <u>M</u>, once and only once. The outer corridor, <u>N</u>, could be entered any number of times. The four command centers (1, 2, 3, and 4) could also be entered any number of times. He always ended up his tour of inspection in command center 1. See if you can lay out the route that he took.

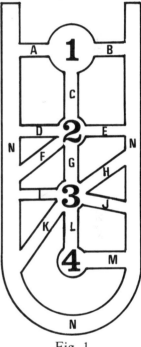

Fig. 1

Problem number 2 comes from the royal printer, Mr. Phineas Fenwick. Mr. Fenwick challenges the reader to arrange four 7's in such a manner that they shall total exactly 100.

Here is a puzzle that Merlin highly recommends. Arrange sixteen matches into two squares, one with three matches to a side, and inside of it, one with one match to a side. By moving just four of the matches you are to reform the squares so that you now have three squares (see Fig. 3). If you solve this one in five minutes you're doing very well.

Our last entry in these selections from Merlin's notebook is an old problem employing coins. Lay six coins out in a row on the table, the first three being heads up, and the last three being tails up (Fig. 4). Now, by turning over any two adjacent coins at a time, in three moves you are to end up with the head/tail arrangement illustrated below. Good luck on this one.

A Game of Poker

I would like to introduce you to a Mr. J. Wellington Moneybags and his associate, Mr. Monk. Mr. Monk is the one poking his nose into the picture. More about Mr. Monk later. J. Wellington is quite rich, as you can tell from his appearance. He came by his wealth at the gaming tables where he is extremely clever at playing a card game called Poker Solitaire. The game is very easy to play. You can play it by yourself, or two or more players can participate. Each player has his own deck and must shuffle and cut it before starting. During play each player will lay out twenty-five cards in the form of a card square (Fig. 2). This allows you to build ten poker hands: five horizontally, and five vertically. You begin by turning over the top card of your deck and placing it anywhere in front of you.

From then on, each subsequent card that you turn over must be placed so that it is next to the side of a card already played, or end-to-end with a card played, or corner-to-corner to a card on the board (Fig. 1). Once a card has been put down it cannot be moved. When all twenty-five cards have been played, you then find the best poker hand, horizontally, or vertically, in your square. If it is higher than your opponent's best hand, then you win. Skill enters the picture during play when you have to decide where to place each card. You can vary the game by moving the cards around, or by placing them down without regard to the cards that are already on the board.

One last word. If you run into J. Wellington and lose to him at this game, please pay up promptly, Mr. Monk is his debt collector.

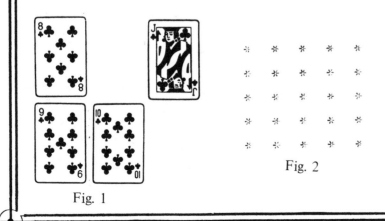

Fig. 1

Fig. 2

The Word Professor

 ecess is over, students. Mr. Willard Wordsworth, "The Word Professor," is back with some more of his change-the-word puzzles. Remember that to solve these puzzles, you must change the top word into the bottom word in four moves, changing one letter in the previous word in each of the moves. Use the boxes for writing in the words. Everyone should score a hundred on this test.

R	O	A	D
C	O	I	L

B	E	L	L
S	I	F	T

C	A	L	L
M	U	T	E

F	I	R	E
C	O	L	D

R	A	F	T
W	I	N	G

SUPER CHECKERS

uper Checkers, as defined by Merlin, is a variation of the regular game of checkers. It is an attempt to increase the pleasures to be derived from this truly great game by enlarging the size of the board, increasing the number of checkers used by both sides, and by testing various methods of play. The present board being used for Super Checkers on Merlin's Isle has a total of 144 squares, there being 12 squares to a side. Instructions for constructing such a board are to be found on the opposite page. A total of 30 red checkers and 30 black checkers are used by the two players. Each player places his 30 checkers on the red squares in the first five rows on his side of the board. Play proceeds as in regular checkers and ends when the winner has removed all of his opponent's checkers. Because each side has so many more pieces to play with, a player has a better chance to recover from a mistake he might make in the early stages of the game.

In super checkers you are not limited to a board that is 12 inches by 12 inches. You can make your board 16 by 16 or 20 by 20, or shoot for the Guinness book of records, whatever that might be. Just use your imagination. The size and shape (you can make it a rectangular board if you want to) is up to you.

Besides the regular mode of playing checkers there are some interesting variations of the game you might like to try.

GIVEAWAY CHECKERS. Here the object of the game is the reverse of regular checkers in that the winner is the player who manages to lose all of his checkers first. The rules of play are the same as in regular checkers.

KINGS. Each side starts the game with eighteen kings set up on the first three rows on each side of the board. The rules of play are the same for the kings as in regular checkers.

The Rhino's Riddle

upert has a nifty puzzle for you. Using a set of colored pencils, and the nine squares in the drawing, color three squares blue, three squares green, and three squares orange in such a way that no two adjacent squares will be of the same color.

A Super Checkerboard is easily made. The materials you will need are:

1. A sheetrock knife.
2. 3 inexpensive checkerboards.
3. Glue.
4. A large sheet of heavy cardboard (try art store).

With the knife trim two edges from the full checkerboard (Section 3) and glue to cardboard. Next, cut second checkerboard into two pieces and trim so you will have the Section 2 pieces. Glue (Section 2) pieces to cardboard. Finally, cut the quarter segment (Section 1) from the third checkerboard, trim and glue to the cardboard.

Now, wasn't that easy?

(You will also need three boxes of checkers.)

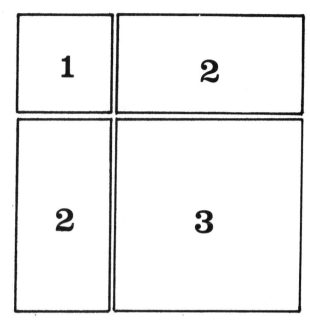

Millard Oglethorpe

A Tale Of Woe

Millard Oglethorpe, a poor but honest medical student, was working his way through college when he found himself in financial difficulties one day. He had fallen behind in his room rent. "Oglethorpe, pay up or get out," ordered his landlord. "You owe me 7 weeks rent, at $13 per week."

Oglethorpe never thought faster in his life than he did at that moment. He removed $28 from his wallet and handed it to the landlord saying, "Here is your money, sir! Paid in full."

"Twenty-eight dollars," thundered the landlord, "You owe me a sight more than that, young man!"

"If I can prove that this is the correct sum, using the New Math, will you accept it as payment in full?"

"Alright," sneered the landlord, "Let's see your New Math prove it by addition."

Oglethorpe wrote down a column of seven 13's and drew a line under them (Fig. 1). He totaled up the right-hand column of 3's, and then the left-hand column of 1's and added the totals together getting an answer of 28.

"Well, it may add up to 28," said the landlord, "but it doesn't look right to me. Prove it with multiplication."

"Nothing could be easier," replied Oglethorpe. He wrote down the number 13 and then placed a 7 beneath it. He then proceeded to carry out the multiplication according to his version of the New Math (Fig. 2). When he was done the result was still 28.

"I don't believe this," cried the landlord, "something is very wrong here. Prove it one more way. Divide 7 into 28, and if you come up with 13 for your answer then I'll take the $28 as payment in full."

A smiling Millard Oglethorpe set up the mathematical expression and started dividing.

"The 7 won't go into this 2 but it will go into the 8, so we will start here," he said. So saying, he wrote a 1 above the line and placed a 7 under the 8. He subtracted the 7 from the 8 giving 1.

"Now, we drop down the 2 that the 7 couldn't go into and place it in front of the 1. That gives us 21, and 7 goes into that number exactly 3 times."

Oglethorpe wrote a 3 above the line and handed the paper to his landlord saying, "I think that from now on I'll pay my rent every 7 weeks."

"You may call that an example of your New Math, Mr. Oglethorpe," groaned the landlord, "but I call it the old flim flam. Now, if we had tried subtracting 13 from 28 seven times . . ."

Wretched Landlord

```
 13
 13
 13
 13        13         13
 13         7    7    28
 13        21         7
 13         7        21
 __        __         __
 28        28         21
Fig. 1   Fig. 2    Fig. 3
```

The Great Nesselrode was a conjuror who really knew how to pack them in. He had a large, sophisticated show, as you can judge for yourself by studying the picture to the left. Besides performing magic and juggling, he also doubled as a dentist. Here we see him shooting a tooth out of his own mouth. His dentistry, if not painless, was at least quick. He also had a shooting gallery concession. You got three shots for a shilling, and if you knocked down three birds whose numbers added up to exactly 50 you won a prize. What was the prize? One tooth pulled absolutely free. Now, who's first, you over there hiding behind Rupert?

| 25 | 27 | 3 | 12 | 9 |
| 15 | 6 | 30 | 21 | 19 |

The Rhino's Riddle

O,T,T,F,F,S,S,E,...

upert was swapping puzzles with Merlin the other day when Ector Pendragon came rushing in with a new puzzle he had made up. He wrote the letters "O, T, T, F, F, S, S, E, ..." out in a row and challenged them to find the logical sequence in their order and to write down the next letter in line. Merlin said that the puzzle might be new to Pendragon but it was as old as the Pillars of Hercules, and he left Rupert there to figure it out. Why don't you give him a hand!

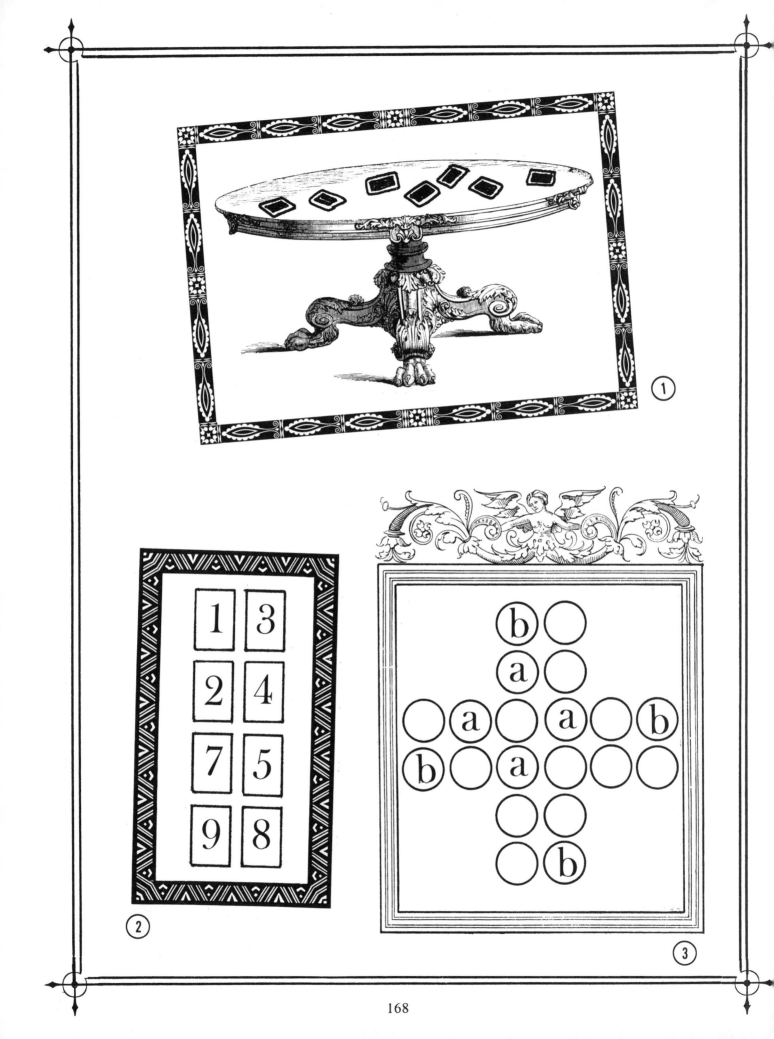

1

2

3

Merlin's Notes

roblem one from Merlin's Notes is both a puzzle and a game for two players. All you need to play is a table and two packs of playing cards. Each player has a pack, and play alternates with each player placing one card at a time down on the table. When a card is placed on the table, no part of the card can overlap any part of a card that is already on the table. The person who is able to place the last card down on the table is the winner. There is a way that a person can always be sure of winning. Can you puzzle out the secret?

ounds, but that is a good puzzle," exclaimed The Word Professor, "even if it only contains numbers." The problem that has so delighted Willard Wordsworth is illustrated in Figure 2. You are to rearrange the eight numbered cards into two columns, each column containing four cards. The numeric total of one column should be the same as the sum of the other column. You, too, are entitled to shout "Zounds" when you have found the correct answer to this "simple" puzzle.

e have twenty circles arranged in the form of a cross (Fig. 3). How many perfect squares can you see in this cross when you consider any four circles as being the corners of the square. Look at the diagram and you will see what I mean. The four squares, which contain the letter <u>a</u>, form the corners of one square. Also, the four circles containing the letter <u>b</u> form another square. This should keep you busy for a while.

One other little puzzle you might try, when you have solved the aforegoing, is to remove six of the circles from the cross so that it is impossible to form any squares from the remaining circles.

A Movie Detective Quiz

etective story fans gather near for I have a challenging quiz for you. Below is a list of twenty-six fictional detectives and villains that have appeared in the movies over the last forty years. Next to this list is another list of the actors who portrayed them on the screen. Your job is to match up detective (or villain) and actor. Twenty right would be a good score.

Detectives and Villains	Movie Actors
(A) Lew Archer	(1) William Powell
(B) Charlie Chan	(2) Tom Conway
(C) James Bond	(3) Ralph Bellamy
(D) Boston Blackie	(4) Robert Montgomery
(E) Father Brown	(5) Basil Rathbone
(F) Nick Charles (The Thin Man)	(6) Humphrey Bogart
(G) Simon Templar (The Saint)	(7) Paul Newman
(H) Harry Palmer	(8) Sean Connery
(I) The Falcon	(9) Henry Daniell
(J) Dr. Fu Manchu	(10) Tony Randall
(K) Matt Helm	(11) Lloyd Nolan
(L) Sherlock Holmes	(12) Jack Hawkins
(M) Professor Moriarty	(13) Chester Morris
(N) Inspector Maigret	(14) Warner Baxter
(O) Philip Marlow	(15) Sidney Poitier
(P) Mr. Moto	(16) Edward Arnold
(Q) Hercule Poirot	(17) Boris Karloff
(R) Ellery Queen	(18) Ian Carmichael
(S) Raffles	(19) Warner Oland
(T) Michael Shayne	(20) Alec Guinness
(U) Sam Spade	(21) Michael Caine
(V) Virgil Tibbs	(22) David Niven
(W) Lord Peter Wimsey	(23) Jean Gabin
(X) Nero Wolfe	(24) Peter Lorre
(Y) The Crime Doctor	(25) Warner Baxter
(Z) Gideon of Scotland Yard	(26) George Sanders

The Royal Feast

"I'm Henry the Eighth I am, I am, I'm Henry the Eighth I am," sang that king of noble girth. "Fetch me my Lord Chamberlain, for there will be a wedding on the morrow and I want to know how things progress."

"You there, victualer, step forward. Have you procured the beasts and birds for the feast?"

"Beggin' your pardon, me lord, but I'm still not sure of the number of each that you desire, sire!"

"Gadzooks, man do you have ears that heareth not? Come closer and listen well to this ditty, lest you end up on the spit instead of yonder boar."

"One hundred-eighty head of bird and beast,
     You'll need to cook for my great feast.
Five hundred feet they have to stand on,
     The number of each, now, you must land on."

"Now get thee hence and victual, Mitchell."

Mitchell had better hightail it down to the village market and use the royal credit card. The only trouble is that Mitchell can't figure out how many birds he should buy and how many beasts. Now according to the song, there are 180 heads between them and 500 feet all told. Can you help Mitchell out?

The Rhino's Riddle

In Vol. 1 of *Merlin's Puzzler*, Rupert presented a puzzle wherein the puzzler was required to arrange eight 8's so that when they are added up they will total 1,000.

The answer we gave is printed here. One of our valued readers, after pondering and solving

$$
\begin{array}{r}
8 \\
8 \\
8 \\
88 \\
888 \\
\hline
1,000
\end{array}
$$

this problem, has come forward with two more solutions to this problem. This time we want two mathematical expressions, using eight 8's, that equal 1,000.

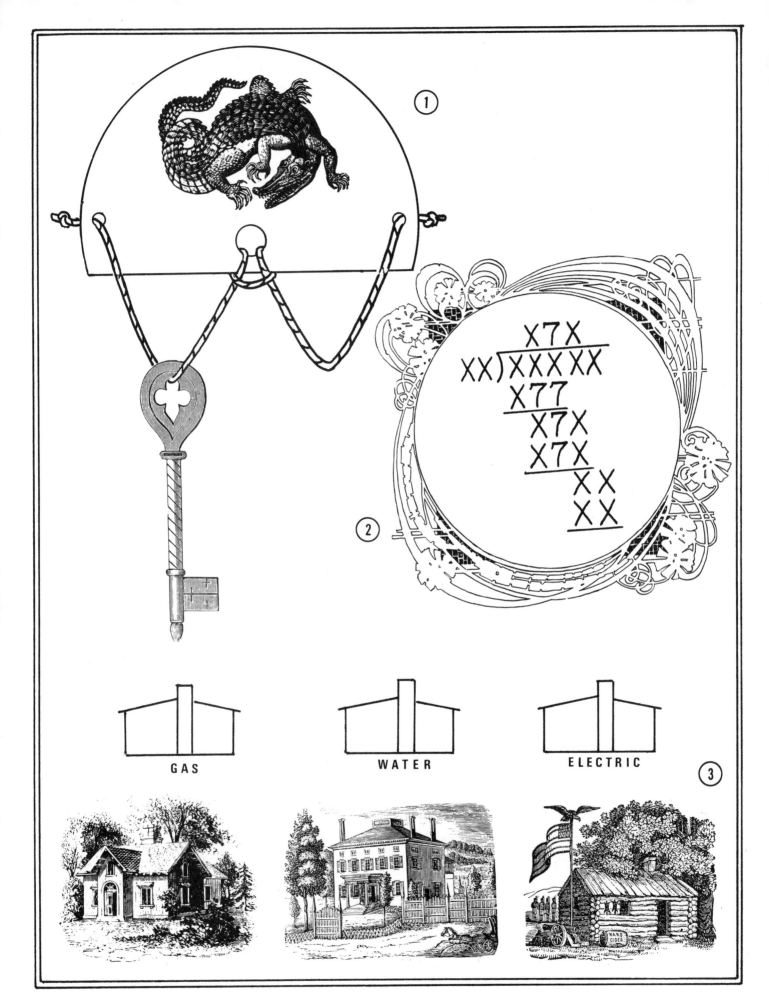

①

② X7X
XX)XXXXXX
X77
X7X
X7X
XX
XX

③ GAS   WATER   ELECTRIC

Merlin's Notes

riar Tuck's Key Holder Puzzle is the name of puzzle number 1. This is a simple puzzle to make. The materials needed are a piece of cardboard, some string, and an old key or ring. Cut the cardboard to roughly the shape and size of the one in the diagram. Make two small holes on either side of it just large enough to poke the ends of the string through. Make a larger hole in the middle of the cardboard. The hole must be too small for the key to pass through. Cut off a piece of string about twelve inches long, thread it through the key and the holes in the cardboard and knot the two ends. You should have no difficulty duplicating the setup in the diagram. The puzzle is to transfer the key from the left-hand loop to the right-hand loop. This puzzle is very old, but still very good. Friar Tuck can testify to this as he has won many a pint with it over the years.

traordinary," exclaimed Merlin. "Rupert, you do come up with some amazing puzzles to tax our wits. Now, let me see if I have this right. We have here a simple case of division, but you have gone and substituted X's for all of the numbers in the expression except an occasional 7 here or there, and it is our job to reason out what these numbers were and to write them back into the expression? This is an interesting problem, Rupert, now let me see, if I were to divide by . . . . " (see Fig. 2)

utside of town, in the new housing development called Arthur's Acres, they completed three more houses over the weekend. Today the waterworks, the power station and the gasworks are going to start laying pipe, from each of the utilities, to each new house. Their only problem is that according to the town ordinances they are prohibited from having one pipe cross over another pipe. How can they manage to comply with the law?

(see Fig. 3)

t Merlin's zoo, in anticipation of the arrival of a new shipment of animals, they started construction on a series of pens. Their intention was to construct six pens of equal size, using thirteen sections of straight fencing (see illustration). When they inventoried their supplies on hand, they found out to their dismay that they had only twelve sections of fencing. Walter Snaretrap, the park commissioner, thought that this problem was similar to a puzzle that he had once seen in Merlin's Puzzle Museum. He called up the museum and explained his predicament. He was right, he was told. This was very much like an old match puzzle, where the puzzler had to take twelve matches and outline six equal-size enclosures. The matches could not be broken or laid one on top of another. His informant then went on to explain the method to him over the telephone. Could you have arranged those twelve sections of fencing to create six pens of equal size?

The Wizard

The Wizard has gone to his vast library and found a mental mystery which you can use to astound your friends. Make a copy of the card below. When you present this trick, pass the card out and request that someone call out one of the circled numbers. You immediately tell him what the seven-digit number below it is. You can do the whole card if they can stand it. The secret is very simple. Now listen carefully!

A) Take the number they give you, say 25, and add 11 to it (giving us 36 for this example).

B) Reverse the result. This gives you the first two digits of your answer (63).

C) From this point on you will always add the previous two numbers as you construct your number. The third digit will be 9 (6 plus 3 = 9).

D) For the fourth digit we add 3 and 9, getting 12. When the sum gives you a double digit answer, drop the 10's position and use the units position. Our digit is 2.

E) The fifth digit is 1 (9 plus 2 = 11, drop the 10's position, use the units position, 1).

F) The sixth digit is 3 (2 plus 1 = 3).

G) The seventh and final digit is 4 (1 plus 3 = 4).

Our final answer for the number 25 is 6392134.

Now, go forth and mystify the world, oh mighty master of mathematical marvels and miscellaneous meanderings.

(23)	(39)	(18)	(22)	(4)	(38)
4370774	0550550	9213471	3369549	5167303	9437077
(2)	(45)	(30)	(34)	(25)	(6)
3145943	6516730	1459437	5493257	6392134	7189763
(9)	(37)	(46)	(3)	(1)	(17)
0224606	8426842	7527965	4156178	2134718	8202246
(21)	(5)	(44)	(11)	(41)	(19)
2358314	6178538	5505505	2246066	2572910	0336954
(29)	(12)	(33)	(13)	(43)	(7)
0448202	3257291	4482022	4268426	4594370	8190998

Mr. Sherlock Holmes

think Moriarty should be asleep by now, Watson. These steps here lead down to the outer door of the basement."

"Quickly now, shine your torch onto the map that young Fernwhistle gave to us before he died. This door is marked with an *a* on the map and the room that Lestrade is being held a prisoner in is on the other side of the cellar behind the door marked *b*." Fernwhistle said that the lock on the door is electrically operated. To open it, you must turn on sixteen switches that are located throughout the cellar in a particular sequence. There is one switch located in each of the sixteen rooms. The one clue that we have as to the order in which they are to be turned on is the fact that you must enter every room once and only once. You cannot retrace your steps and go through a room twice."

"You said back at Baker Street that you had discovered a route through the cellar that would satisfy those conditions," replied Watson.

"I know, old friend, but suppose that I am wrong. What diabolical trap might be sprung if we were to turn them on in the wrong order?"

"It's too late to turn back now. Lead on Holmes!"

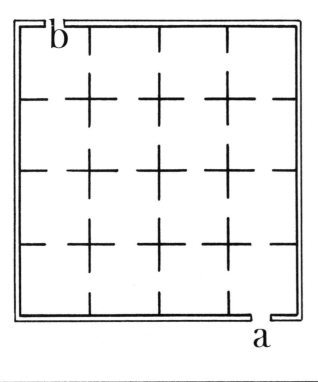

Egyptian Hall Mysteries

erlin sent over two more puzzles from the Egyptian Hall. The first one uses a puzzle board which I have reproduced below. Place four black checkers on squares 1, 2, 6, and 7, and four red checkers on squares 4, 5, 9, and 10. You are to make them change places in just ten moves. To play, you can move a checker into an empty square next to the one the checker is on, or you can jump one checker over one or two other checkers to an empty square beyond. Our second problem is illustrated in Fig. 1. You are to cut this square into five pieces that can be rearranged to form a perfect Greek Cross. (A Greek Cross has four arms all of the same length. If you tell me that the way to make a Greek Cross is to step on his foot, I'll make the answer disappear!)

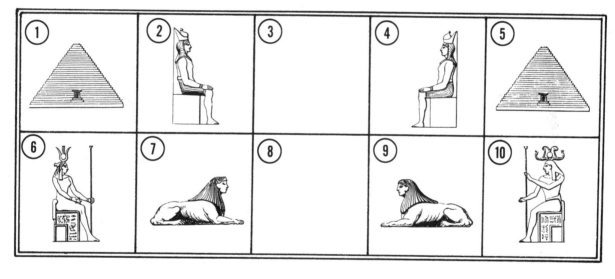

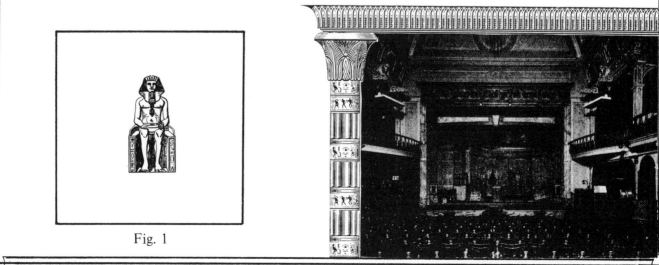

Fig. 1

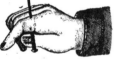

From the proprietor of the magic department of Gamage's, the famous old Victorian department store in London, comes this interesting game of solitaire. On a sheet of paper, draw up a sixteen-square puzzle board. Then place ten checkers in the squares as indicated in the illustration below. This is the setup before play begins. The puzzle is to remove all of the checkers from the board save one. You do this by jumping one checker over another and then removing the jumped checker. You are not allowed to jump diagonally, only horizontally or vertically. As there is no jump possible in the starting setup, you are allowed to move one checker out to a vacant square. All moves from then on must be jump moves.

he society magician pictured above seems to have an appreciative audience. Professor Hoffmann has an interesting sleight with cards which he thinks would be of help to you in winning approval from your audience. Professor, if you please!

"To Throw A Card — This sleight also belongs rather to the ornamental than to the practical part of conjuring, but it is by no means to be despised. It is a decided addition to a card trick for the performer to be able to say, 'You observe, ladies and gentlemen, that the cards I use are all of a perfectly ordinary character,' and by way of offering them for examination, to send half-a-dozen in succession flying into the remotest corners of the hall or theatre.

"The card should be held lightly between the first and second fingers, in the position shown in Fig. 1. The hand should be curved inward toward the wrist, and then straightened with a sudden jerk, the arm being at the same time shot sharply forward. The effect of this movement is that the card, as it leaves the hand, revolves in the plane of its surface in the direction indicated by the dotted line, and during the rest of its course maintains such revolution. This spinning motion gives the flight of the card a strength and directness which it would seem impossible to impart to so small and light an object.

"A skilled performer will propel cards in this way to a distance of sixty or eighty feet, each card travelling with the precision, and wellnigh the speed, of an arrow shot from a bow. The movement, though perfectly simple in theory, is by no means easy to acquire in practice. Indeed, we know no sleight which, as a rule, gives more trouble at the outset; but, after a certain amount of labour with little or no result, the student suddenly acquires the desired knack, and thenceforward finds no difficulty in the matter." Professor Hoffmann wrote these words nearly 100 years ago in his monumental book, *Modern Magic.* The great American magician, Howard Thurston, was reputed to have been able to scale cards from the street to the roofs of four-story buildings.

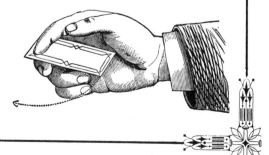

Merlin's Notes

erlin insists on presenting the first puzzle himself. Coin tricks and puzzles are among Merlin's favorite types of diversions, and he claims that this one is at least 700 years old. In the picture, Merlin is pointing to four English pennies. You can, of course, use four quarters or half-dollars. You are required to arrange the four coins in such a way that each coin is equidistant from every other coin. This puzzle sounds easy, but many have found it extremely difficult.

n the old American West, if a card player was caught in an attempt to tilt the odds of poker in his favor during his DEAL with the pasteboards, it often came to pass that he would end up being SHOT or run out of town on a rail. Our second puzzle gives you the opportunity to solve the problem of changing DEAL to SHOT without getting caught along the way. It is a simple (?) change-the-word puzzle, and if you have forgotten how to do them go back to page 142 of this book for instructions.

t first glance this looks like an example of Babylonian arithmetic (Fig. 3). This, of course, is not the case, for this is an extremely interesting type of puzzle. You can make this mathematical expression correct by adding two minus signs (−) and one plus sign (+) to it between certain numbers. (Example: $12+34-567-89 = 100$) Our example above is wrong, but there is a correct one for this puzzle and it is your problem to find it.

ur final problem is an artistic one. Inside the mouth of Sid the Ogre is a geometrical design that the puzzler must duplicate. It is to be drawn with one continuous line without lifting the pencil from the paper. No part of the line can cross over any other part of the line.

The Game Of Yacht

acht, which has absolutely nothing to do with ships of any kind, is one of the best games you can play. It has been around for a good many years which, in this case anyway, is an indication of how good it really is.

To play the game you will need five dice and a score sheet. (Duplicate the one on page 183.) Any number can play. You should also have a dice cup. The object of the game is to score the most points. To start the play, everyone rolls the five dice once, and the highest roller goes first. Play then continues to the left around the table. Game play is as follows:

There are twelve rounds of play in the game. During each round every player gets a chance to roll the dice. A player may cast the dice three times during his turn. He may stop after the first cast or after the second cast if he is satisfied with the dice values, or he may set aside some of the dice after a cast and recast the remaining dice. After he has finished throwing the dice, he picks one of the twelve categories on the score sheet and enters his score there. You cannot choose a category that you used on a previous round. After the player has entered his score, he passes the dice to the next player. After twelve complete rounds have been played, each player's score is totaled up and the winner is declared.

Scoring, by category, is as follows:

1) Yacht: Any five of a kind scores 50 points.

2) Big Straight: This is 1-2-3-4-5 or 2-3-4-5-6 on the five dice. Score 30 points.

3) Little Straight: This is 1-2-3-4 or 2-3-4-5 or 3-4-5-6 on four of the dice. Score 15 points.

4) Four-of-a-Kind: Any four of a kind scores the <u>total</u> spots on all of the <u>five dice</u>. (Example: four 3's and a 1 would score thirteen.)

5) Full House: This is any three-of-a-kind and a pair. Scores the total number of spots on the five dice.

6) Choice: This is a free play, and it scores the total number of spots on the five dice. (Example: Suppose that you roll four 6's and an ace and you have already used the four-of-a-kind category in another round of play, you can use choice and enter a score of 25 in the category.)

Players	C a t.	①	②	③	④	⑤	⑥
Yacht	**1**						
Big Straight	**2**						
Little Straight	**3**						
Four of a Kind	**4**						
Full House	**5**						
Choice	**6**						
Sixes	**7**						
Fives	**8**						
Fours	**9**						
Threes	**10**						
Deuces	**11**						
Aces	**12**						
Total							

7–12) The remaining categories, 7 through 12, score the total number of spots on those numbers cast in the selected category (Example: If you chose category 8, which is 5's, and you have two 5's showing, then you would enter a score of 10 for that category).

Winning strategy: The higher scoring categories (1 through 8) are the ones you will be trying for during your turn of play. If you miss making one of these categories, you should "waste" one of the lower scoring categories, such as aces or deuces, and enter any score you can, even if it is only a zero. This preserves for you the opportunity, during later rounds, to go after these high scoring rounds.

That about covers the rules for the game of Yacht. I hope you enjoy playing it. This is one of the best dice games around and it is great fun for the family.

ictionary quizzes have proved to be quite popular with our readers, so I have made up another one to test your wits. Try to match up the pictures in the sample page with the correct words listed below.

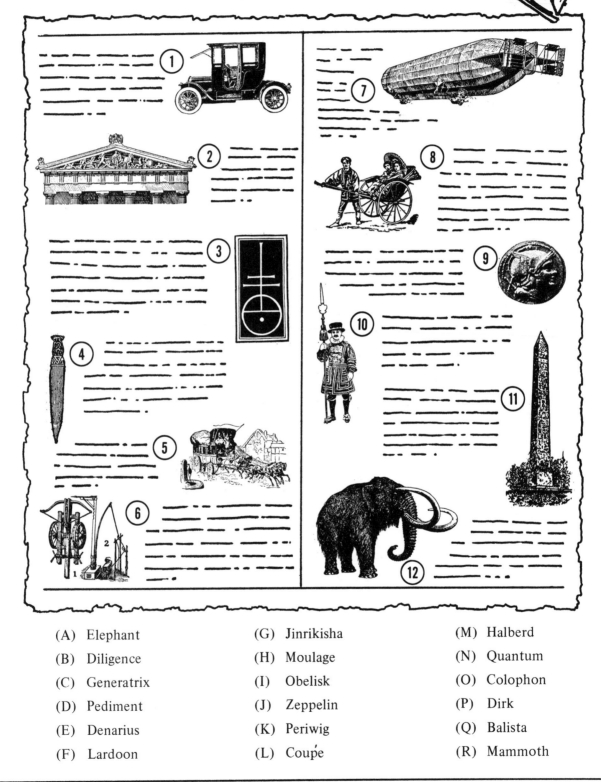

(A) Elephant	(G) Jinrikisha	(M) Halberd
(B) Diligence	(H) Moulage	(N) Quantum
(C) Generatrix	(I) Obelisk	(O) Colophon
(D) Pediment	(J) Zeppelin	(P) Dirk
(E) Denarius	(K) Periwig	(Q) Balista
(F) Lardoon	(L) Coupé	(R) Mammoth

veryone on Merlin's Isle is nervously looking over his shoulders these days. It is rumored that the dreaded Chicken-man has come down out of the mountains from the Forest of No Return. Industrial pollution is said to be the cause of breaking the spell which had kept him locked within the Tree of 10,000 Thorns. It seems that the thorns all fell off the tree, setting this fearsome ogre free after 700 years of prickly imprisonment. To say that he is a bit irritable would be putting it mildly.

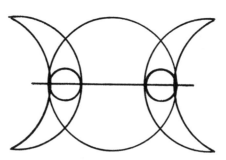

So, if you chance to meet up with him you had better take up a stick and make the sign of the Double-Horned Zat on the ground and stand in the middle of it until he flies away. (see Fig. 1). When drawing the sign you must do it with one continuous line. Also, no part of the line may cross over any other part of the line.

Now, practice well, you never know when you may hear the flap, flap, flap of giant chicken wings.

A surveyor stopped by the Grits-N-Bits coffee shop the other day and told about a job he had just finished. Two farmers had bought five square acres of land that had divided their farms and had asked him to lay out a straight fence that would divide their purchase into two equal parcels of land. After much thought, the surveyor came up with the answer. The only trouble is that he left town before telling anyone how he did it. Can you tell the folks at the Grits-N-Bits how it was done?

The Idle Hours
Country Club

t the Idle Hours Country Club the players are out early this morning. Come over here on the veranda for a moment, I want to show you something. Over there is our tennis area. There seems to be a lively game in progress. You'll notice that the chalk lines outlining the court are getting rather thin. As soon as the game is over Mr. Rakencut, our grounds keeper, will rechalk them with a new machine the club has bought from Professor Pepper called the Steam Man. All you have to do is to fire up his boiler and program him to do any job around the club. The Steam Man uses one of the roller-type markers. Once he puts it down he can't pick it up again without making a mess of the job. We have worked out a route for him to take so that he can mark off the court using one continuous line. It is impossible, of course, to do this without going over some of the lines twice. The route we worked out is the shortest possible one, one that goes over the least number of lines twice. Here is a sketch of the court with the lengths of the lines in feet (Fig. 1). See if you can discover the route that the Steam Man will take.

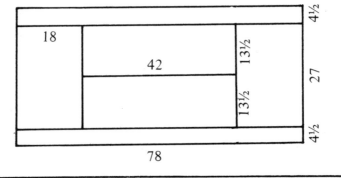

ashing Dan the Duffer has become the most talked about player at our club. It seems that after years of scooping divots out of the fairways and slicing golf balls over and through the club house, Dan has finally gotten his game together. The strange thing about it is that no matter what wood or iron he hits the golf ball with, it travels only one of two distances. Dan has worked it out so that by combining these two shots, sometimes hitting two long shots and one short shot as an example, he can play the front nine of our course in twenty-six strokes.

Now Dan always plays in a straight line from tee to cup, his hooks and slices being a thing of the past. Also, he sometimes will hit the ball past the green and have to hit back to the green to hole out. It makes no difference to him, he is always able to sink the ball by hitting it one of two distances. Our problem is to try and calculate what the two distances are that Dan uses in hitting his way to fame and fortune. The yardage for the first nine holes on our course is 150 yards, 300 yards, 250 yards, 325 yards, 275 yards, 350 yards, 225 yards, 400 yards, and 425 yards.

If you want to beat Dan at his own game, then you had better hurry up with the answer. Our group is on the tee next.

ver here is our Archery range. Those two lovely ladies warming up for the competition are the Hood sisters. They usually compete as a team. They are extremely good; so good in fact that no one knows which one is the better archer. Why, just last week in competition they scored exactly the same. They both put each of their three arrows in the same circles of the target and came up with a combined score of 96 points. If you were not there it makes a nice little puzzle to try and figure out which of the circles the arrows ended up in. Would you care to give it a try?

Merlin's Notes

erlin has come up with three very interesting problems. The first puzzle is quite unique in that it doesn't fall into any of the regular categories of puzzledom. Pictured in Fig. 1 is a square board with a hole in the upper left-hand corner. The problem is to figure out the least number of pieces the board would have to be cut up into so that when you reassembled the pieces the hole would now be in the center of the square board.

ur second problem is from the brush of Merlin's court artist, Ector Pendragon. He calls it Pendragon's Perplexing Pyramid Puzzle. It is not a very hard puzzle as puzzles go, but you are given only one opportunity to answer it correctly; no second chances please. You are to add up all the equilateral triangles you can find in the painting. Be careful, it's easy to miss one or two.

lright folks, step right up and try your luck at solving the Jumbo Puzzle. No shoving now, there is plenty of room in the puzzle tent. It only costs a dime, one-tenth of a dollar to play. All you have to do is solve the puzzle depicted on Jumbo's back and you will win the biggest prize in the world. What is this puzzle, you say? In the picture are six large spots. You are to change the position of one of these spots so that there are now four rows of spots with three spots in each row. Some of the spots can be in more than one row. Stop pushing there, little man! What's that you say? You want to know what the prize is! Let me put it this way, my good man, the prize comes with a year's supply of peanuts!"

The Jumbo Puzzle

If you are planning on going for a trip soon, here is a solitaire game you might like to take along. Using the board pictured above, place sixteen coins on the numbered squares. The puzzle is to remove all of the coins but one by jumping one coin over another to an empty space beyond. When one coin jumps over another one, the coin that was jumped over is removed. You can jump horizontally or vertically, but not diagonally. Multiple jumps by one coin count as one move (like a triple-jump in checkers). The puzzle can be solved in seven moves.

9	10	11	12	13	14	15	16
1	2	3	4	5	6	7	8

 or the puzzlers who enjoy word puzzles, we present our old dictionary quiz. Below is a special page, made up by Merlin, featuring illustrations from very old dictionaries. Below the page are eighteen words. You are to match up twelve of these words with the appropriate pictures in the sample page. If you can get all twelve correct then you will be two-up on Willard Wordsworth, the Word Professor.

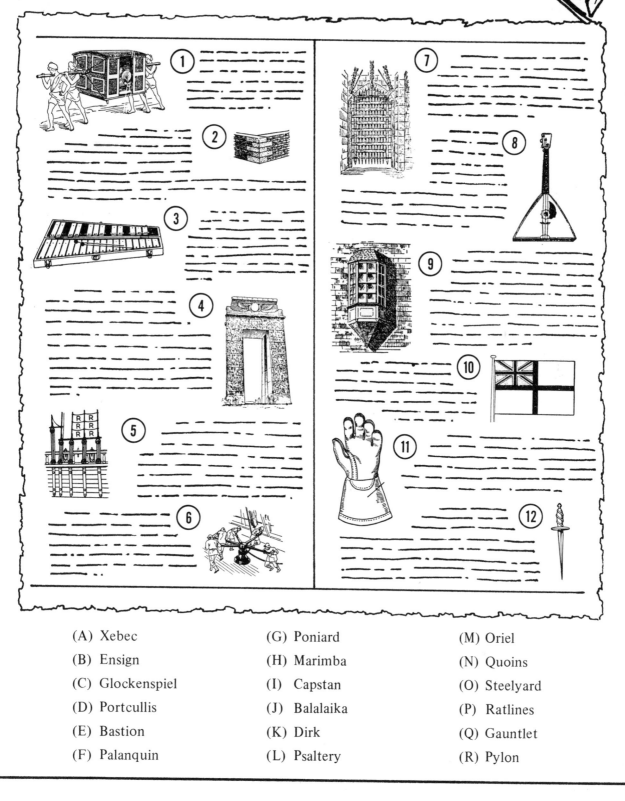

(A) Xebec

(B) Ensign

(C) Glockenspiel

(D) Portcullis

(E) Bastion

(F) Palanquin

(G) Poniard

(H) Marimba

(I) Capstan

(J) Balalaika

(K) Dirk

(L) Psaltery

(M) Oriel

(N) Quoins

(O) Steelyard

(P) Ratlines

(Q) Gauntlet

(R) Pylon

rofessor Hoffmann is back again with us in this, the third volume of *Merlin's Puzzler.* The Professor has his usual mixed bag of puzzles from the past to perplex the reader of today. The puzzles that will be presented in the next sixteen pages are all from the Professor's great nineteenth-century work, *Puzzles Old and New.* This is your editor's favorite work dealing with puzzles of the past. I am sure you will be entertained by the Professor's charm and wit and puzzled by the ingenuity of the problems he is about to present.

Ladies and Gentlemen, adjust your thinking caps, please, for the Professor is about to take the floor.

olitaire, though commonly referred to as a game, belongs rather to the category of puzzles, the problems which it affords being numerous and interesting. It is played with a circular board, as shown in Figs. 1 and 2, with thirty-seven hemispherical depressions, in each of which rests a small marble or glass ball. One of these being removed from the board, another is moved into the vacant space thus created, but in so doing it must pass (jump) over one intervening ball lying in a straight line (not diagonally) between it and the hole. This intervening ball is removed from the board (just as a man is "taken" in checkers), and another jump is then made after the same fashion into one or another of the holes now left vacant, a fresh man being removed from the board at each move.

For the third move there will be *three* holes vacant, for the next – *four*, and so on, one ball being removed from the board at each move. The puzzle, in its simplest form, is to remove all the balls save one, which last cannot be removed, inasmuch as it has no second ball to jump over.

Sometimes it is left optional in what part of the board such last ball shall remain. In more elaborate forms of the puzzle the player is required to leave one or more balls in a previously determined hole or holes.

Each alteration of the starting point makes a fresh problem. We have selected three examples, viz.:

1. Starting with No. 1 as the vacant hole, to leave the last ball in No. 37.

2. Starting with No. 19 (the center hole) vacant, to leave all the outer holes (1, 2, 3, 8, 15, 22, and so on) occupied, and the last ball in the center hole. (This is sometimes known as the Curate and his Flock.) To be done in nineteen moves.

3. The Triplets. Starting with the center hole vacant, to leave holes 1, 3, 6, 9, 12, 15, 17, 18, 20, 21, 23, 26, 29, 32, 35 and 37 occupied, forming a geometrical figure. (To be done in 20 moves)

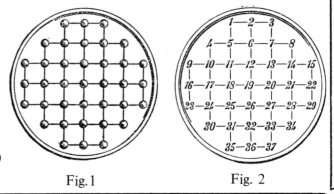

Fig. 1   Fig. 2

By devising other geometrical figures and endeavoring to produce them according to the conditions laid down, a very interesting series of puzzles may be produced. (A similar puzzle called The Lion was presented in *Merlin's Puzzler,* Vol. 1. The board in The Lion was made without the four corner holes — 4, 8, 30, and 34 of the Eagle board layout on the previous page. When using either of these board layouts you will use coins or some other small counters.)

his is a puzzle of a very novel and ingenious kind; indeed, we believe it to be unique. At any rate, we have come across no other upon precisely the same principle.

It consists of a cardboard box, four inches square, with the top and bottom of glass. The intermediate space is occupied by a metal plate divided by upright partitions (just high enough to touch the glass) into a number of different compartments, somewhat after the fashion of a maze (see Fig. 1). On turning the box over, we find that the underside of the plate is divided after a similar fashion, but that the shape of the compartments is in this case different, the partitions on this side running in different directions. There is no direct communication between the compartments of the top or between those of the bottom, each being fully enclosed on all sides; but the intermediate "floor" is perforated with a number of holes (in most cases two to each compartment) which form a means of communication between the upper and the lower compartments, and therefore indirectly between compartments on the same side.

Fig. 1

In the front of the box (see Fig. 1) will be seen a small round hole. A little leaden ball, *a*, is introduced at this point and allowed to drop through the hole immediately in front of the opening. It is then to be made to travel up one hole and down another, from compartment to compartment, till it comes out again at the hole to the right of the opening, the box being turned over at each stage so as to enable it to fall in the desired direction. On the next page are two illustrations, Figures 1 and 2, the first representing the upper, and the second the underside of the puzzle, which show the course the ball must travel in order to fulfill the conditions of the puzzle. The letter <u>A</u> indicates the point of entrance and exit, and the numbers show the order in which the various holes are to be passed.

A <u>dot</u> beneath a number indicates that the ball (relative to the side represented by the diagram) passes <u>downward</u> through the hole in question. A <u>cross</u>, that the ball is to be brought <u>through that hole from the opposite side</u>.

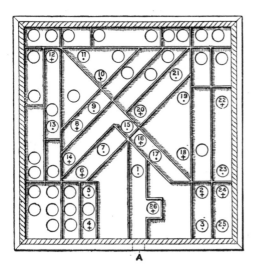
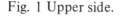

Fig. 1 Upper side.

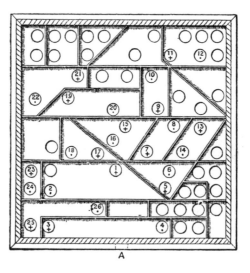

Fig. 2 Underside.

(We realize that it is quite impossible for the average reader to build this puzzle for himself. We have, however, come up with an idea that will allow the puzzler to enjoy this problem. On Page 282 you will find enlarged copies of Figures 1 and 2. Cut them out and glue them to opposite sides of a piece of cardboard of the same size. Be sure that the <u>A</u> edge of each figure is along the bottom edge on both sides. You will notice that each circle [holes] has been numbered so that when you turn the card back and forth you can keep track of each hole while you are plotting a course through this maze. A little effort will reward the reader with a truly unique puzzle from the past.)

THE WOLF, THE GOAT AND THE CABBAGES

A boatman has to ferry across a stream a wolf, a goat and a basket of cabbages. His boat is so small that only one of the three, besides himself, can be contained in it. How is he to manage so that the wolf shall have no opportunity of killing the goat, or the goat of eating up the cabbages?

PASSING THE GATE

It was the rule in a certain continental town that anyone passing through either of the four city gates, whether going out or coming in, should pay a penny. A stranger arrived one day at the town, paid his penny and passed through the first gate. He spent in the town one-half of the money he had left and then went out again by the same gate, again paying a penny. The next day he did the like, entering and passing out by the second gate and meanwhile spending half his available cash in the town. On the following two days he did the same, entering and leaving by the third and fourth gates respectively. When he left the town for the fourth time he had only one penny left.

How much had he at first?

A FEAT OF DIVINATION

A couple of dice are thrown. The thrower is invited to double the points of one of the dice (whichever he pleases), add 5 to the result, multiply by 5 and add the points of the second die. He states the total, at which point anyone knowing the secret can instantly name the points of the two dice.

How is it done?

HIDDEN PROVERBS

The apparent jumble of letters in the figure below contains five well-known proverbs arranged in a systematic order. When the clue is once discovered, the proverbs can be read without difficulty.

PUZZLE: To find the five proverbs.

```
R E N O W N E D T H A N W
S Y O U R C A K E A N D A
S T E T O B E F E A R H R
E A R K S S P O I L E A F
L E O O H E R S N T D V O
O T M O T L I N O H T E U
N O S C A L A G M E H I R
S N I Y G O R S O B A T S
E N G N E N O T S R N P A
I A O A M O O T S O A E W
R C D E V I L A H T D A S
O U O Y N O I L D A E C A
T C I V R E H H T A H E Z
```

THE "ANCHOR" PUZZLE

This consists of a square piece of cardboard divided into seven segments of the shapes shown in Fig. 1 (viz.: two large triangles, a, a; a smaller one, b; and two still smaller, c, c; a square, d; and a rhomboid, e). In Fig. 1 we see these pieces arranged in a square. Even the rearrangement of these pieces back into a square, when once fairly mixed, will be found a matter of some little difficulty, but this is the smallest of the problems presented by the puzzle. (An enlargement of Fig. 1 will be found on Page 277. Once duplicated you can paste it on a sheet of cardboard and cut out the pieces needed to work this puzzle.) Below you will find some of the different designs which may be formed by combining these pieces in different ways. It is to be noted that the whole seven pieces must be employed in the formation of each design, and it is a curious fact that some of those designs which are simplest in appearance are the most difficult to work out. No more aggravating, and at the same time fascinating, puzzles have come under our notice than this series.

Fig. 1

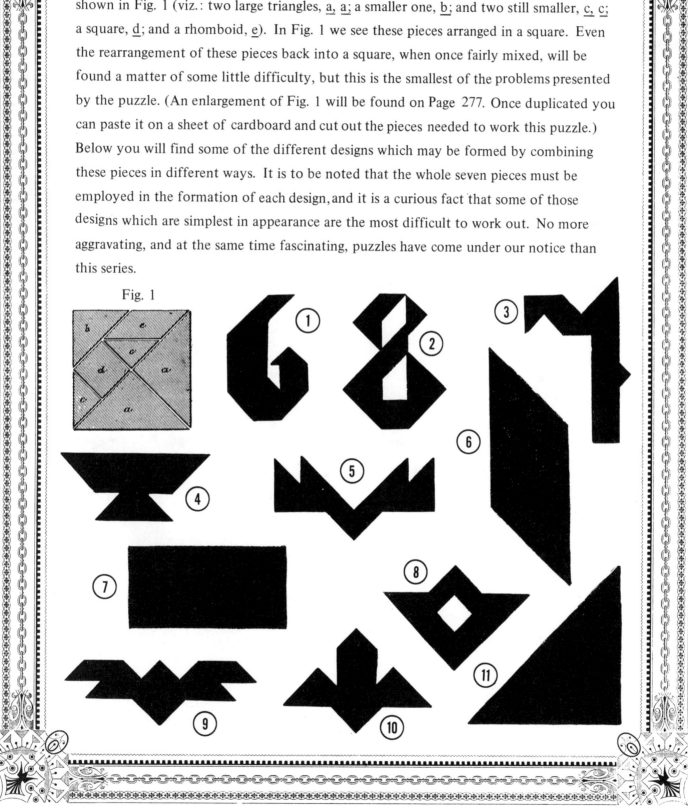

THE "FIVE AND FIVE" PUZZLE

Rule on cardboard a rectangular figure divided into twelve squares, as Fig. 1, and in the first ten spaces, beginning from the left hand, dispose ten counters, red and black alternately.

Fig. 1

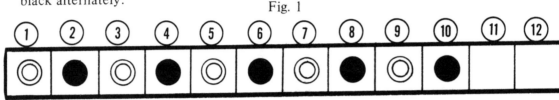

The puzzle is to move *two adjacent counters at a time* so that the five red and the five black counters are grouped, each color together without any interval, and this must be done *in five moves only.* At the close of the operation the ten counters should be as shown in Fig. 2.

Fig. 2

They are then to be worked back again, after the same fashion, to their original positions.

THE "SIX AND SIX" PUZZLE

This is again the same problem as the last puzzle, but with twelve counters, six of each color, the transposition to be effected in *six* moves. The board, in this case, should be divided into 14 squares.

HOW TO DIVIDE TWELVE AMONG THIRTEEN

A gentleman has a sum of twelve dollars to be distributed in charity, a dollar to each approved candidate. On the day of distribution, thirteen claimants appear. The donor has reason to believe that one of them is a less deserving object than the rest and desires to leave him out, but without showing any apparent favoritism. He directs the claimants to stand in a circle and announces that every ninth man, as he counts round and round, shall step out of the circle and receive his gift till the fund is exhausted, the last man receiving nothing.

Where must the distributor begin to count in order to exclude the candidate he desires to reject?

A LONG FAMILY

A farmer and his wife have fifteen children born at regular intervals, there being a difference in each case of a year and a half. The eldest is eight times the age of the youngest. How old must the latter be?

THE THREE JEALOUS HUSBANDS

Three jealous husbands traveling with their wives find it necessary to cross a stream in a boat which only holds two persons. Each of the husbands has a great objection to his wife crossing with either of the other male members of the party unless he himself is also present.

How is the passage to be arranged?

THE FOUR JEALOUS HUSBANDS

Arithmeticians have racked their brains to devise a means of transit for four husbands and four wives under the same conditions stated in the previous puzzle, but, with a boat holding two persons only, the problem is insoluble. If we suppose, however, that the boat contains three persons, it may be solved.

How is this passage to be arranged?

A LOAN AND A PRESENT

This puzzle is usually presented in the shape of a conjuring trick. The operator requests some one to think of a given number of dimes, large or small, as he pleases. He is then in imagination to borrow the same amount from some member of the company and add it to the original number. "Now please suppose," says the operator, "that I make you a present of fourteen dimes, and add that also. Now give half the total amount to the poor; then return the borrowed money and tell the company how much you have remaining. I know already what it is; in fact, I hold in my hand the precise amount." "Seven," is the reply. The operator opens his hand and shows that it contains exactly seven dimes.

How is the amount ascertained?

"Confound it Professor, how did you know it was seven?"

THE SHEPHERDESS AND HER SHEEP

A shepherdess had the care of a number of sheep in four different folds. In the second were twice as many as the first, in the third twice as many as the second, and in the fourth twice as many as the third. The total number was 105.

How many sheep were there in each fold?

ore puzzles by Professor Hoffmann!

LOCKED OUT

ount Bettsalot, a well-known gambler in the betting spas of Europe, returned to his villa late one night to discover that he had been robbed. Now, the Count's villa contained many great works of art and literature, and to help in the safeguarding of these treasures, he had commissioned a deep moat to be dug around the house with a small drawbridge to afford passage in and out. It seems that while the

Count was away gaming, four thieves had broken into his villa and had made away with the painting. On leaving they had destroyed the drawbridge so that the Count's servants could not pursue them. The only parts of the bridge remaining were two boards, each 14 feet 11 inches in length. As the moat was 15 feet wide on all sides, and the Count had nothing with which to bind the two boards together, it looked as though he would have to spend the night out in the cold. As he nudged one of the boards with the tip of his boot, a flash of inspiration showed the Count how he could use the boards to cross the moat. In 30 seconds he was across the moat and racing up the steps of the villa.

How did the Count manage to cross the moat?

APPLES AND ORANGES

A paterfamilias brought home a quantity of apples and oranges, the same number of each, and distributed them among his children. After each child had received twelve apples, there were forty-eight left over, and after each child had received fifteen oranges, there were fifteen left over.

How many were there of each kind of fruit, and among how many children were they divided?

THE DEVIL'S BRIDGE

To perform this experiment you will need four table knives and five water glasses. Place four of the glasses in the form of a square on the table. The rims of each of the glasses should be of a distance from each other 1/4 inch longer than each of the knives. The problem is to construct a bridge between the four glasses, using just the four knives, that will be strong enough to support the fifth glass.

THE CARPENTER'S PUZZLE

A carpenter's apprentice has a board 3 feet in length by 1 foot in width. With this he is required to fill up a space 2 feet in length by 18 inches in width, but he is not to cut the board into more than two pieces.

How can he manage it?

THE EXTENDED SQUARE

Required, so to cut a cardboard square, as <u>a</u> in the diagram (Fig. 1), into two portions, in such a manner that by successive shiftings of their relative positions, they may form

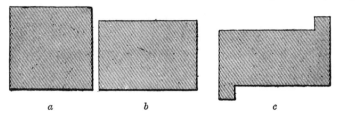

Fig. 1

a   b   c

the parallelogram <u>b</u> and the eccentric figure <u>c</u> in the same diagram.

THE TWO SQUARES

Given, a piece of paper or cardboard of the shape depicted in Fig. 2, being that of a small square in juxtaposition with one four times its size. Required, by two cuts (each in a straight line) so to divide the piece of cardboard that the resulting segments shall, differently arranged, form one perfect square.

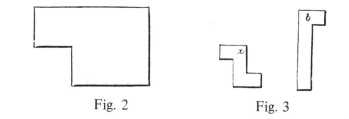

Fig. 2   Fig. 3

ANOTHER CROSS PUZZLE

In this puzzle you are given five pieces of wood or card-board, three shaped as <u>a</u> (Fig. 3), and two shaped as <u>b</u>.

Required, so to arrange them as to form a Latin cross.

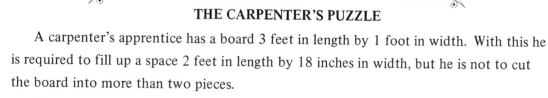

uibble" or "Catch" Puzzles from Professor Hoffmann.

A REMARKABLE DIVISION

A gentlemen divided six dollars between two fathers and two sons, each father and each son receiving two dollars. How did he manage it;

A DISTINCTION AND A DIFFERENCE

What is the difference between twice twenty-five and twice five and twenty?

A SUM IN SUBTRACTION

What is the difference in capacity between twenty four-quart bottles and four-and-twenty quart bottles?

MULTIPLICATION EXTRAORDINARY

What three figures multipled by five will make six?

A QUESTION IN NOTATION

How would you write in figures, twelve thousand twelve hundred and twelve?

A SINGULAR SUBTRACTION

Required, to take ten from ten so that ten shall remain.

THE FLYING HALF-DOLLAR

A half-dollar being placed in each hand and the arms extended shoulder-high, required, to bring both coins into one hand without allowing the arms to approach each other.

THE DRAPER'S PUZZLE

A draper dividing a piece of cloth into yard lengths found that he cut off one yard per second. The piece of cloth was 60 yards in length.

How long did it take him to cut up the whole?

THE CHARMED CIRCLE

You invite a gentleman to stand in the middle of the room. Taking a piece of chalk, you undertake to draw round him a circle which he cannot jump out of.

How is it to be done?

ARITHMETICAL ENIGMA

Write down a zero, prefix fifty, to the right place five, and to the whole add one-fifth of eight. The result will give you the most important factor in human happiness.

THE ABBOT'S PUZZLE

In this problem you are given a square that is divided into nine smaller squares. The puzzler is required to arrange counters in the eight outer squares in such a manner that there shall always be nine on each side of the square, though the total be repeatedly varied, being twenty-four, twenty, twenty-eight, thirty-two and thirty-six in succession.

This is a very ancient problem. It is usually propounded after the fashion following: A blind abbot was at the head of a monastery of twenty-four monks who were domiciled three in a cell in eight cells occupying the four sides of a square, while the abbot himself occupied a cell in the center. To assure himself that all were duly housed for the night, he was in the habit of visiting the cells at frequent intervals and counting the occupants, reckoning that if he found nine monks in each row of three cells (see Fig. 1), the tally was complete.

But the bretheren succeeded in eluding his vigilance. First four of them absented themselves (reducing the number to twenty), but still the abbot counted and found nine in a row. Then these four returned, bringing four friends with them, thus making twenty-eight persons, and yet the normal nine in a row was not increased. Presently four more outsiders came in, making thirty-two. The result was the same. Again, four more visitors arrived, making a total of thirty-six, but the abbot, going his rounds, found nine persons in each row as before.

How was this managed?

3	3	3
3	A	3
3	3	3

Fig. 1

A COMPLICATED TRANSACTION

William gives Thomas as many quarters as Thomas has. Thomas then gives William as many quarters as William has left. This done, William has thirty-six quarters, and Thomas has forty-two quarters.

How much had each at first?

A GEOMETRIC PROBLEM

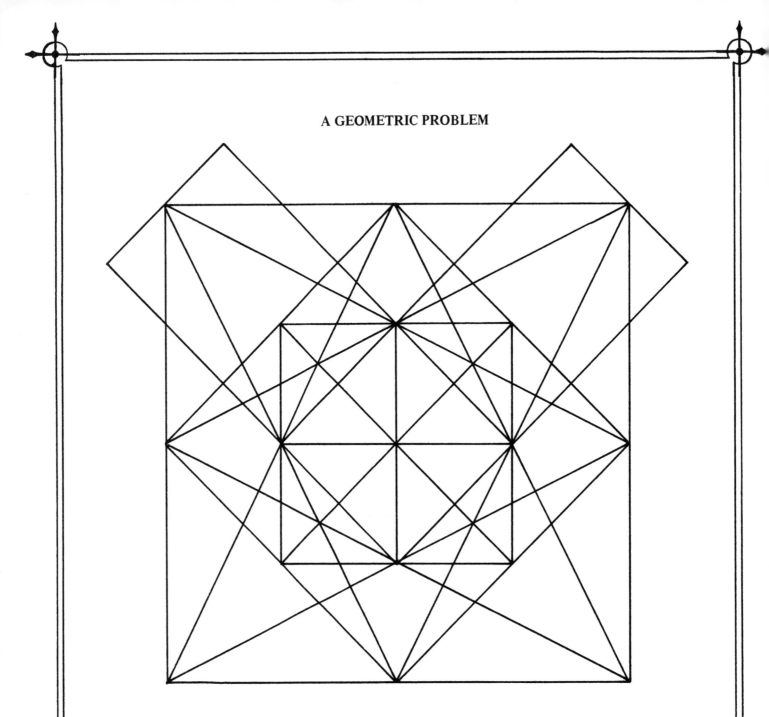

The puzzler is required to place at the intersections of the geometric design above twenty-one counters (small coins or buttons) in such a manner as to form thirty rows of three counters each, each group of three being united by one of the lines in the design.

THE CAPTAIN AND HIS COMPANY

In the course of his day's march, the captain of a company of soldiers comes to a river which must be crossed. The only means of transit is a boat wherein two children are paddling about and which is so small that it will only hold the two children or one grown person.

How is the transit to be effected?

THE PEN AND WHEEL

The Pen and Wheel is an ingenious type of puzzle. It consists of a little iron wheel (which the reader can make out of cardboard) with six spokes and a hole in the center (Fig. 1). A double cord, about twenty inches in total length, is looped over one of the spokes, then laced in and out between the remaining spokes and finally brought through the hole in the center. It is then passed through a bit of stamped brass (cardboard again) in the form of a pen (penpoint) and secured by a double knot on the opposite side (see Fig. 1).

The puzzle is to detach the cord and pen from the wheel without unfastening the knot.

THE CHINESE ZIGZAG

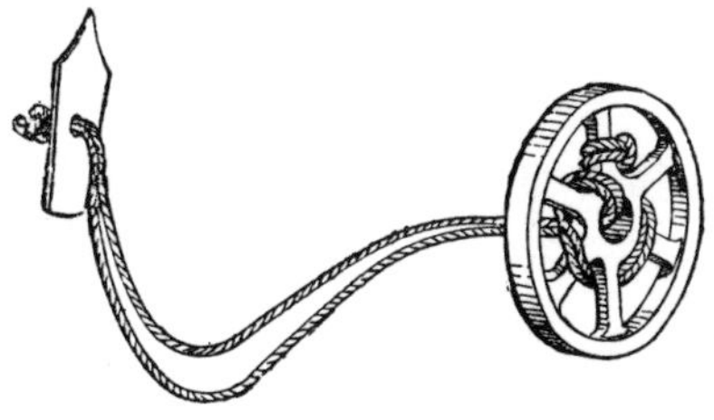

The reader is probably familiar with the ordinary zigzag puzzle, a thin flat piece of mahogany or other hardwood out of which portions have been cut in wavy lines by a jigsaw, the general effect being that of a dissected map of more than ordinary complication. The piecing together of such a puzzle is, however, a mere

Fig. 1

work of patience, involving no more intellectual effort than the comparison of a given space and a given segment. The Chinese Zigzag is a much more ambitious affair and will give some trouble even to the most experienced puzzle amateur. It consists (see Fig. 2) of a block of wood, three inches in length by two in width and depth, cut into sixteen pieces after the manner following. It is first cut vertically into four segments after the zigzag fashion already described. The block is then laid on its side and without any displacement of its parts is cut into four horizontal segments after the same manner. From the peculiar fashion of the cutting, the sixteen pieces still remain locked together, though loosely. To take them apart, one layer (either horizontal or vertical) is removed at a time. Once removed, such layer promptly falls to pieces, the resulting segments being of the most eccentric shapes. The puzzle is to reconstruct the block as at first. (This puzzle is available in the better toy stores today. If the reader has access to a jigsaw he will have very little difficulty in making this puzzle himself out of soft pine.)

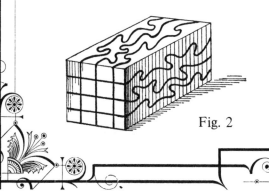

Fig. 2

Editor's note: If it should prove to be impossible for the reader to obtain or construct a copy of the Chinese Zigzag puzzle, there is still an intellectual problem here for him to solve. What would be the most logical way to go about putting the pieces back together? Give this a try before looking at the answer.

TRANSFORMATIONS

This is a form of word-puzzle that deserves to be better known, as it may be made productive of considerable amusement. It consists in taking a word of a given number of letters and trying in the fewest possible "moves" or transpositions, altering only one letter each time, to transform it into some other prearranged word of the like number of letters but of different or opposite meaning; as Light into Heavy, Rose into Lily, Hard into Easy, or the like. Each step of the process must be a known word. We will take the last-named pair as an example. Five moves will in this case suffice:

Hard - (1) card, (2) cart, (3) cast, (4) east, (5) Easy.

This, however, is a more than usually favorable specimen, one of the letters, a, being common to both words and therefore requiring no change. A considerably larger number of moves will usually be found necessary.

Unless one or more letters are common to both words, the number of moves cannot possibly be *less* than the number of letters in each word.

Where several persons take part, this may be made a very amusing game. Certain pairs of words having been agreed upon, each takes the list and tries in the fewest moves he can to effect the required transformations, the player with the smallest total winning the game.

The reader is invited to transform:

Hand into Foot — in six moves.
Sin into Woe — in three moves.
Hate into Love — in three moves.
Black into White — in eight moves.
Wood into Coal — in three moves.
Blue into Pink — in four moves.
Cat into Dog — in three moves.
More into Less — in four moves.
Rose into Lily — in five moves.
Shoe into Boot — in three moves.

A DIFFICULT PLACEMENT

In this problem you are required to place ten counters in such a manner that they shall count four in a row in eight different directions.

THE TWO CORKS

ake two wine-bottle corks and hold them as shown in Fig. 1, viz.: each laid transversely across the fork of the thumb. Now with the thumb and second finger of the *right* hand (one on each end) take hold of the cork in the *left* hand and at the same time. with the thumb and second finger of the *left* take hold of the cork in the *right* hand and draw them apart.

The above sounds simple enough, but the neophyte will find that the corks are brought crosswise, as shown in Fig. 2. The puzzle is to avoid this and enable them to part freely.

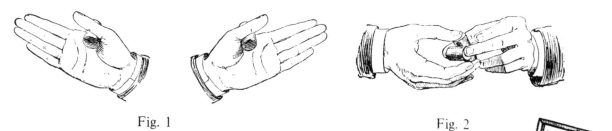

Fig. 1   Fig. 2

L'ENVOI

Thank you Professor Hoffmann for a most enjoyable visit. Your puzzles, as always, were most ingenious and baffling. Many of the items that you presented have not been seen in print for many, many years. It is a pleasure to try our hand at solving these Victorian puzzles from your famous book, *Puzzles Old and New*.

Once again, thank you Professor, we had a lot of fun and we look forward to seeing you again in the next volume of *Merlin's Puzzler*.

Goodbye until later!

Your Editor.

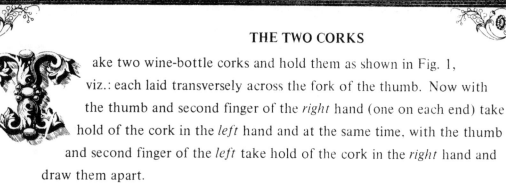

PROFESSOR HOFFMANN

WILL GOLDSTON Ltd.

ALADDIN HOUSE, 14 GREEN STREET, LEICESTER SQUARE, LONDON, W.C.2

JUGGLING AND BALANCING APPARATUS

No. 499. Cigar Box and Bottle.

No. 486. The Perfect Juggling Hoops.

No. 481. Billiard Balls and Cue Balance.

No. 480. Juggling Daggers.

Juggling Clubs.

No. 510. Swinging a Glass of Water and Hoop.

No. 477. The Egg on Straw Balance.

MANAGER & BUYER WILL GOLDSTON.

Over fifty years ago Mr. Will Goldston wrote a book called *Juggling Secrets.* In it he detailed many simple feats which the novice juggler could master and that would convey the impression of great skill and dexterity to the uninitiated. Merlin has selected four of these feats for presentation in this volume. You would be well advised to start off using plastic plates.

ne of the most effective juggles with a plate is that in which the plate apparently revolves between the two hands. When the trick is done smartly, the plate seems to be running round the hands. Of course, a good deal of practice will be required before this effect is produced, and the learner should practice with an enamel plate unless he is content to go through all his rehearsals while standing over a bed.

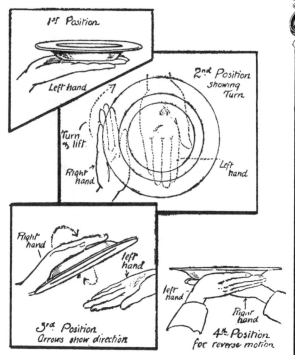

The directions for turning the plate must be followed very carefully, or it will be impossible to perform the feat with any certainty. The practice should be done very slowly at first, until the correct movements have been learned by heart and the learner is not obliged to stop to look at the directions and the accompanying illustrations.

The learner begins by holding out his left hand with the palm uppermost and placing the plate on that hand. He then puts his right hand underneath the plate and on the side nearest to him and turns the plate by putting the little finger of the right hand against it. The plate thus turns on the left hand. When it is turned right round so that it is resting on the palm of the right hand, the left hand goes under it and turns it by raising it with the little finger. The plate thus turns on the right hand until it is brought back to the original position on the left hand, when the right hand at once begins its work once more.

At first progress with this trick will be very slow, but with a little practice the feat will be made very effective. The great thing to remember is to raise the plate with the little fingers. The positions of the hands will seem unnatural at first, but if they are held in any other way the plate will probably fall.

n amusing little piece of byplay with a plate consists in dropping it and catching it – apparently without an effort – just before it touches the ground. The trick is very showy, but it is not at all difficult.

Bend the right arm and, holding it close to the body, rest the plate on the arm, just above the cuff. Now, if the arm be moved downwards the plate will fall, but the right hand will be exactly behind it. Extend the arm so that the right hand travels downwards behind the plate, the back of the hand being towards the back of the plate. When the plate has almost reached the ground, lift the right hand slightly, and the fingers will be in such a position that they can easily grasp the edge of the plate. The juggler appears to the audience to stoop down exactly at the critical moment and to take hold of the plate just before it touches the ground; another second, apparently, and he would have been too late. The audience does not realize that the juggler's hand has traveled down behind the center of the plate, and that when he wants to grasp the plate, all he has to do is to lift his right hand a few inches. In other words, what the juggler does is really much easier than the feat which the audience believes he performs.

Fig. 1   Fig. 2   Fig. 3   Fig. 4

Our last two juggling feats will require for props six half-dollars and the performer's own anatomy. Three coins are placed one behind the other on the back of the right hand. These are then thrown up into the air and are caught, one by one as they descend, by the hand on which they originally rested. The essence of the trick is in the way the coins are thrown up. They should be thrown so that they go up one after the other, the force of the throw being in the coin marked $\underline{C}$ in sketch Fig. 5, which should be the highest thrown and the last to come down. $\underline{A}$ should have the least force, and $\underline{B}$ a little more. $\underline{A}$ will then be the first to descend, and $\underline{B}$ the second, and should be caught in the order named, i.e.; $\underline{A}$, $\underline{B}$, and $\underline{C}$. The same coins can be used for the next trick. Lay the three coins on the right elbow about half an inch between each coin. Jerk the elbow well up and bring the right hand down, catching the coins as they descend. The sudden jerk will cause them to come close together, and thus be easily caught. Again pile the coins one on top of the other on the tip of the elbow, throw up as before and catch them as they fall. With skill and practice, some twenty coins can be manipulated in this manner. Care should always to taken to keep the knuckles of the hand uppermost and to bring the hand well down sharply before closing it. Fig. 5, sketch $\underline{D}$, shows this trick in progress.

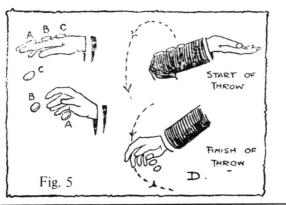

Fig. 5

Charlie Chin, the great Oriental Juggler

uring the recent explorational trip to Mars by the Star Ship *Merlin 1*, the crew amused themselves by playing a three-dimensional version of that venerable old game, Tic-Tac-Toe. Merlin would like to make this game available to all of you earthbound puzzlers, so he commissioned Ector Pendragon to draw up the gameboard that you see on this page. The only additional items that you will need to play this game are 26 small pokerchips, 13 red and 13 white (or you can use pennies and dimes). The play is the same as in regular Tic-Tac-Toe in that the winner is the first one to place 3 of his counters in a straight line horizontally, vertically or diagonally. This can be done by placing a counter on each of the three gameboards. Neither player is ever allowed to place a counter in a square number 14, and no three-in-a-row can be scored using square number 14. Some examples of winning 3-in-a-row combinations are: (1-2-3), (1-4-7), (1-5-9), (7-16-25), (7-17-27), (3-15-27), (19-23-27), (12-15-18). An interesting variation of this game is to have play continue until each player has placed all of his counters on the board. The winner in this case is the player that has made the most 3-in-a-rows during play.

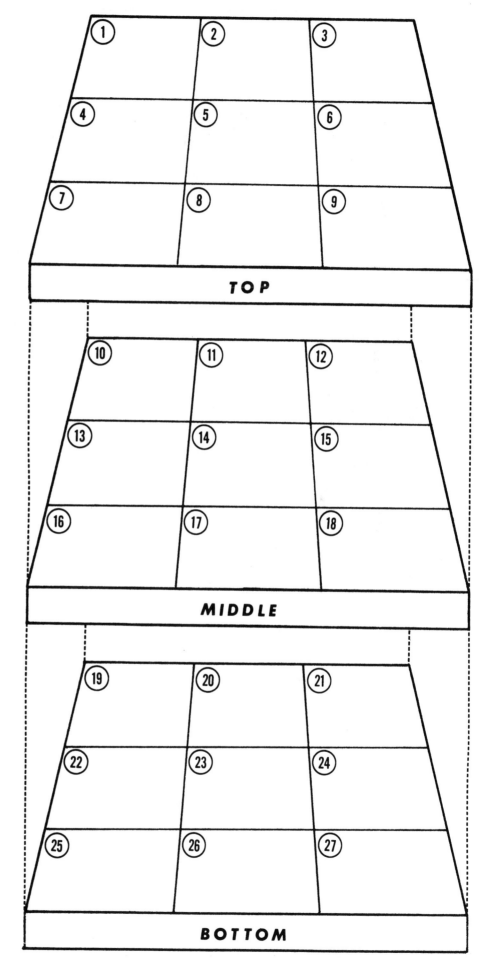

211

All right, Bertie, try this riddle on for size: What is it (you may not ask whether it is an animal, a bird or a reptile) that has this peculiarity — one leg cannot be raised from the ground without raising two or more legs?

That is a rum riddle, Clive, I'm dashed if I have the foggiest!

"A SQUARE DEAL FOR MR. BANG"

Mr. Bang thinks that he got a "raw deal," not a "square deal." His puzzle was to take eight equal squares of cardboard, divide four of the pieces diagonally (corner to corner), and rearrange the twelve pieces to form a perfect square. Obviously, Mr. Bang has failed to do this and he is now on the war path. I am sure that you will do much better than Mr. Bang; after all, you have control of your temper . . . or do you?

All right, quiet down over there. The Meeting of the Merlin Chapter of the Baker Street Irregulars is now in session. The first order of business is a new test that we have devised for evaluating the observational qualities of all new candidates for membership. I have here a detailed floor plan of Mr. Sherlock Holmes's flat in Baker Street. The applicant will be required to study this plan and then be quizzed on what he can remember about it." On the next page is a copy of the floor plan. Study it for five minutes, turn the page and see if you qualify for membership.

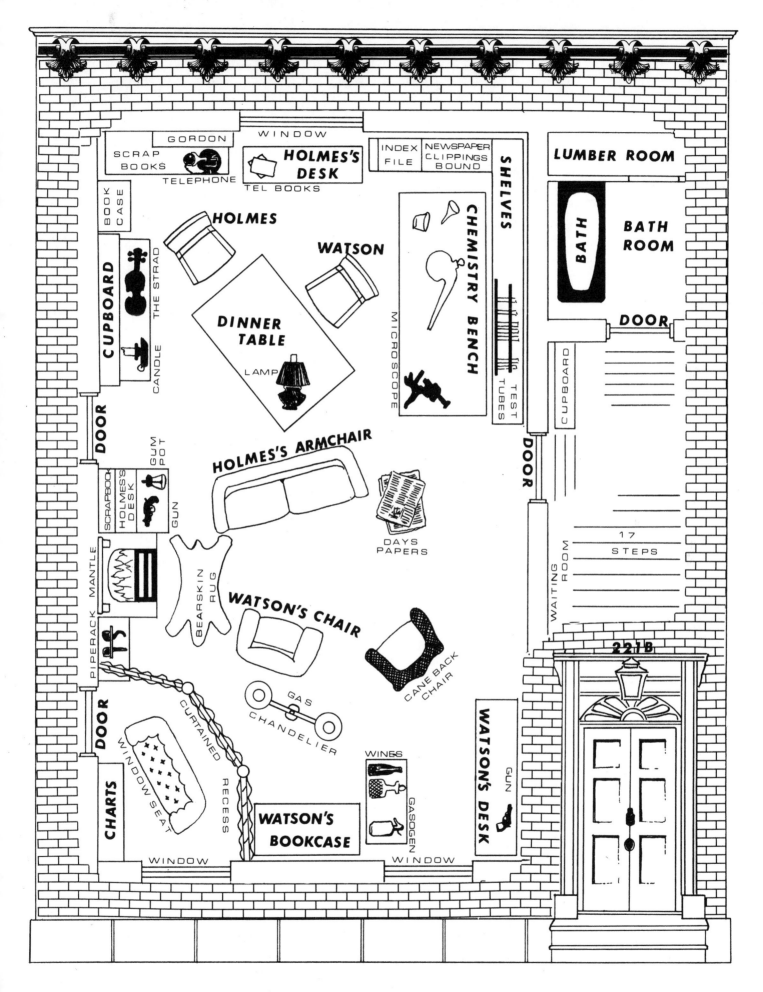

THE SHERLOCK HOLMES OBSERVATIONAL TEST

Use the diagram on the right to write in your answers. Check answers on Page 213.

(1) Where is Holmes's gun? Watson's gun?
(2) Where is the lumber room?
(3) Draw in Holmes's armchair.
(4) Where is the Stradivarius?
(5) Draw in the window seat.
(6) What is on the dinner table?
(7) Where is the microscope?
(8) Where is the telephone?
(9) Where is the index file?
(10) Where are the day's papers?
(11) Where is the gasogen?
(12) Where is the cupboard?
(13) How many steps are there up to Holmes's door?
(14) Where is the piperack?
(15) Where are the charts kept?
(16) Where is Watson's desk?
(17) Where is the gum pot?
(18) Draw in Watson's chair.
(19) Where are the scrapbooks? (two places)
(20) Where is the candle?
(21) Where is the bookcase?
(22) Where are the wine bottles?
(23) Draw in the gas chandelier.
(24) Where are the test tubes?
(25) What is on the floor in front of the fireplace?
(26) Where are the telephone books?
(27) Where is Watson's bookcase?
(28) Where is Holmes's dinner table chair?
(29) Draw in the caneback chair.
(30) Where are the bound newspaper clippings?
(31) Where is General Gordon's picture hung?
(32) Where is the chemistry bench?

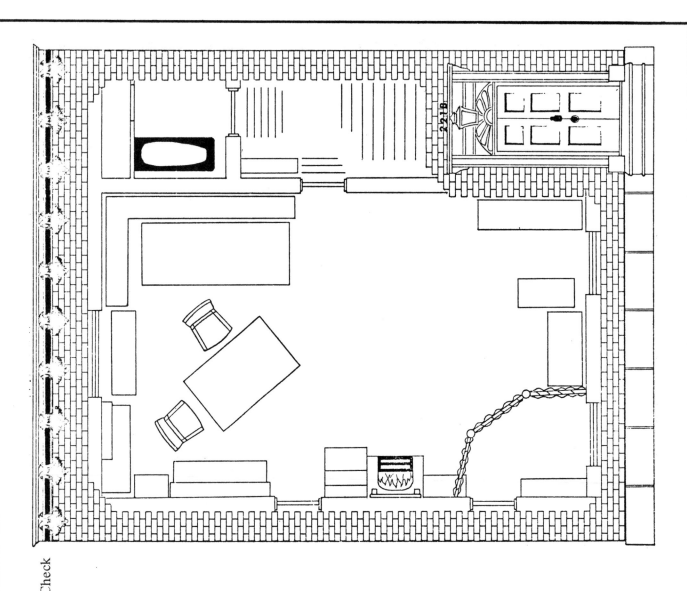

PuzzleRock

On the left is a picture that Merlin found the other day while cleaning out his desk. It shows your Editor in his salad days, sitting on top of Puzzle Rock in the gardens behind Merlin's castle. Puzzle Rock is the only place on the island where you are actually encouraged to write graffiti, just as long as it's a puzzle that you are writing on it. Every few months the High School kids come over and clean it up so that fresh puzzles can be presented in this unusual manner.

The puzzle that we can see in the picture has to do with the colorful language employed in the roadside diners of days gone by. When a customer would order eggs-on-toast, Hash House Harriet would yell out to the cook, "Adam and Eve on a raft." Well, we've taken that discription and made an addition problem out of it. If you replace each letter with a number, using the same number for the same letter wherever it appears, you can make a correct mathematical expression. Since there are several answers to this puzzle you must come up with the answer that will give you the highest possible total.

▼▼▼▼▼▼▼▼▼▼▼▼▼▼▼▼▼▼▼▼▼▼▼▼▼▼▼▼

Another puzzle painted on Puzzle Rock that day went something like this: "Take the digits 1 through 9 and arrange them in such a manner that when they are added up the total will be 99,999.

1 2 3 4 5 6 7 8 9

▼▼▼▼▼▼▼▼▼▼▼▼▼▼▼▼▼▼▼▼▼▼▼▼▼▼▼▼

Our last problem is a match puzzle. Move one of the matches to a new position so that the equation is correct.

VI = II

ell, here we are at last, inside Merlin's Crystal Palace looking down the south transept. There must be a thousand exhibits under this glass roof to choose from. Let's try this one over here. This exhibit is sponsored by a paper manufacturer. I suppose they are here because there are so many good puzzles and tricks that employ paper in their performance. The company's representative, Pierre DeForester, is presenting some paper problems now. Let's listen!

HEAVEN AND HELL

"I once heard a story concerning Greed that I would like to pass on to you. It seems that two souls confronted St. Peter at the gates of Heaven and asked to come in. St. Peter told them that there was but room for one of them and that they must therefore draw lots to see who was the worthiest. St. Peter then took a sheet of paper and folded it once, then once again, and finally a third time. (See Figures 1, 2, 3, and 4.) He then tore the folded sheet of paper into two unequal protions (Fig. 5) and was about to speak when one of the two souls knocked the other aside and reached out and grabbed the larger portion of paper. 'I have the bigger piece,' he shouted. 'I won, let me in!' 'Quiet,' commanded St. Peter, 'let us see what these lots tell us. The smaller piece belongs to this gentleman who has yet to speak. If we open it up we find that it is in the shape of a cross (Fig. 6). Now, let me have the piece that you took from me. Before we open it up we will tear it down the middle (Fig. 7). Now, open up the pieces and see what they have to tell you.' When he did so the poor man found that the pieces formed the word HELL (Fig. 8). Seeing his fate clearly written before him the man turned to go, but St. Peter bade him enter along with the other man saying, 'There is always room for one more up here and I can see from this lesson that greed has been driven out of your heart for good.' I'd say that's a pretty good lesson for all of us."

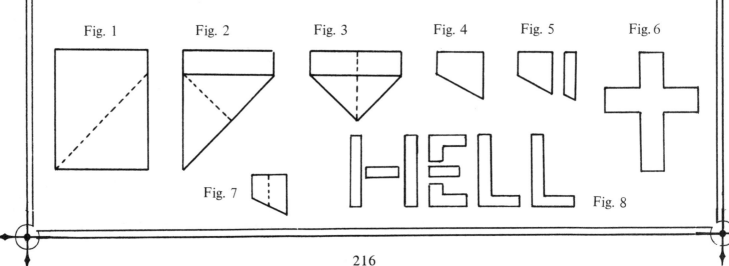

Fig. 1   Fig. 2   Fig. 3   Fig. 4   Fig. 5   Fig. 6

Fig. 7

Fig. 8

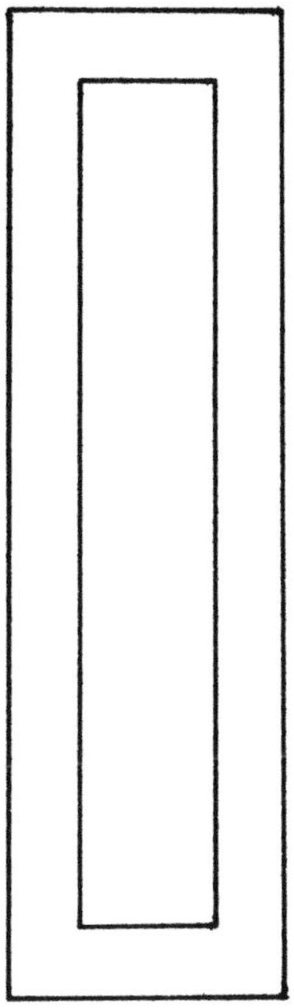

TINTINNABULATION

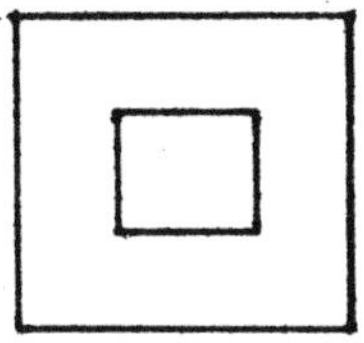

Ladies and Gentlemen, this is certainly one of the finest tintinnabulous puzzles that I have ever seen. Step a little closer, please, so that you can examine the paper puzzle that I am holding in my hand. (See Fig. 1.) It is constructed of three fairly stiff pieces of paper. The puzzle, Ladies and Gentlemen, is to discover just how they were put together without tearing or mutilating any of the fragile pieces. Please note that the paper bell is firmly locked onto the large paper link by the smaller paper link. The hole in the small link, however, is far too small for either side of the bell to pass through it. How was it done? A ringing solution from one of you is needed. Now! Who would like to try it first? (Note: The three pieces to the puzzle are shown in Figures 2, 3, and 4. They are drawn in the correct proportions for the working of this puzzle.)

Fig. 1

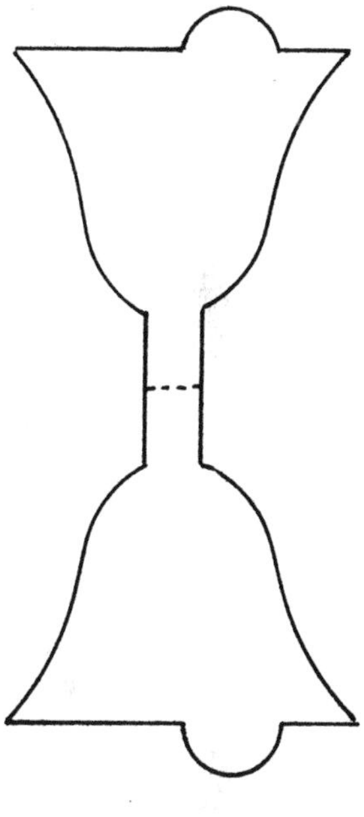

Fig. 2

Fig. 3

Fig. 4

BELLZEBUB

Your friends will think that this is a Devil of a trick if you do it well. Pass a length of rope and a stiff piece of paper in the shape of a bell to your audience for examination. Next, have someone thread the bell onto the rope and then have him tie each end of the rope to your wrists. (See Fig. 5). You can even have him seal the knots with tape. Lastly, have him drape a large cloth over your arms so that your hands, the rope and the bell are out of sight. In ten seconds flat you drop the cloth and show that the paper bell has been removed undamaged from the rope and that your hands are still securely tied. The rope and bell may once more be examined. How are you to do this masterful magical feat of matter through matter? You must have *two* identical paper bells. (How else?) The second paper bell is in the inside pocket of your jacket. Raise your arms chest high. Under cover of the cloth, tear the bell off of the rope, crumple it up, and slip it into your inside jacket pocket. Remove the other paper bell and the trick is done. You might also try secreting the second bell up the sleeve of your jacket instead of in your coat.

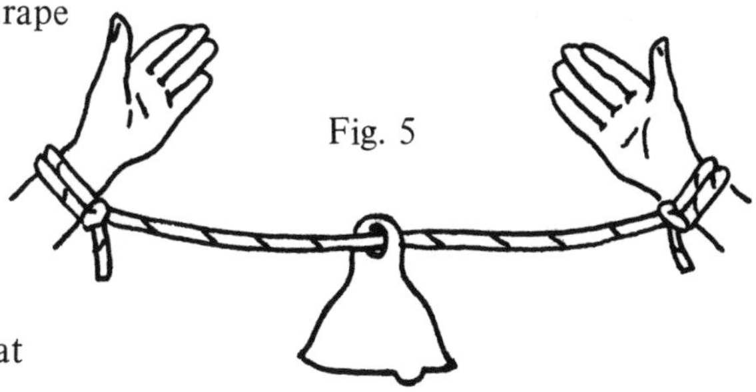

Fig. 5

"Mr. DeForester, these feats are amazing! Please show us some more!"

THE FANTASTIC FIR TREE

For our next event we will build a tree up instead of chopping a tree down. From several double-sheets of newspaper cut four or five strips 12 inches or so in width. Take one of the strips and start rolling it up into a cylinder. When you get to the last 5 inches of the strip, overlap another sheet (Fig. 1) and keep on rolling. Do this with each of the remaining sheets until the tube is complete. Snap a rubber band around the tube near the bottom. Flatten out the tube and tear the tube down the center. Stop around two-thirds of the way down (Fig. 2). Flatten out the tube the other way and tear again the same way (Fig. 3). Bend the four sections of strips down along the sides of the tube (Fig. 4). Take hold of the tube with one hand and with the other reach into the center of the tube and take hold of a few of the strips. Gently pull them up and out of the tube. Keep pulling and working the strips upward (Fig. 5). You will end up with a paper fir tree four, five or six feet high, depending on how many strips of paper you used to make the tube.

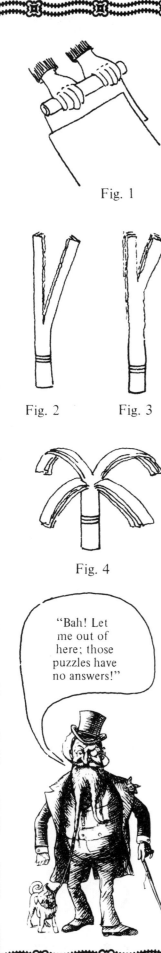

Fig. 1

Fig. 2   Fig. 3

Fig. 4

"Bah! Let me out of here; those puzzles have no answers!"

Fig. 5

THE MAN WITH THE X-RAY EYES

Yes, I am the man with the X-Ray eyes. I can see through walls, drive a car down Broadway while blindfolded and read sealed letters from across the room. What's that? You say you don't believe me! Step forward, please, and I'll prove it to you. While my back is turned, place a half-dollar on the table, date side up. Now, take the piece of paper in the shape of a bell and place it on top of the coin. Make sure that no part of the coin is showing (Fig. 6). All right, now I shall turn around and, without lifting or moving the paper off the coin, I will tell you the date of the coin. If I succeed I get to keep the coin, if I fail you get to keep it. (Editor's note: Can you figure out how DeForester did it?)

Fig. 6

A CUTTING PROBLEM

Here is a simple (?) problem. Take an irregular-shaped piece of cardboard (Fig. 7) and cut it into three sections, using two straight cuts, and rearrange the three sections to form a perfect square.

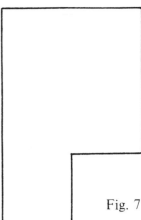

Fig. 7

A PAPER MAGNET?

Yes, Ladies and Gentlemen, you heard me correctly; a paper magnet is both a possibility and a fact! Watch closely while I demonstrate this new wonder of science to you. First, I take this pencil and I draw a picture of a magnet on this small piece of cardboard (Fig. 2). Next, I cut a 2-inch piece from this paper straw and place it on the table. Now, to magnetize the paper magnet I rub it vigorously back and forth on my sweater to build up a charge of static electricity. I now place the magnet on the table just in front of the paper straw. Now, watch this: As I move the magnet away from the straw, the straw follows it. Did you see that? Would you like to be able to make a paper magnet like this one? Well, listen closely and I will let you in on the secret. The card isn't really magnetized. When I bend over the table and draw the card away from the straw I open my lips slightly and gently blow a stream of air down on to the table just behind the straw (Fig. 1). A little practice will show you just how easy it is to make the piece of paper straw appear to be following the card across the table. It is really all quite easy when you know the secret!

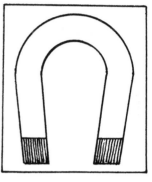

Fig. 1

Fig. 2

THE PUZZLING PAPER PUFF BALL

My last item is an amusing novelty that is both a puzzle and a game. It is a paper ball that, once put together, can be handed out with the challenge to take it apart and put it back together again without ripping the paper parts. This is a very difficult puzzle to do. It should be constructed of light cardboard. Cut out three circles, each _3_ inches in diameter (Figs. 3, 4, and 5). Slits must then be cut in each circle as indicated by the dotted lines. Fold the two sides marked _A, A,_ in Fig. 3 and pass the upper half of Fig. 3 through the center slit in Fig. 4. Open up Fig. 3 and you will have a construction like that in Fig. 6. Now, fold the four upper halves marked _A, A, A, A,_ Fig. 6, together and pass through the star slit in Fig. 5. When it is half-way through open up the folds and you will have Fig. 7, a Paper Puff Ball. An amusing game is played using several of these paper balls. Mark each ball with a number and give each contestant a paper straw. Line the puff balls up along one side of a table and have a race, seeing which player can force his puff ball along, by blowing through the straw, to the opposite end of the table first. Children will also find these puff balls are a lot of fun to throw around and they are not likely to injure anyone.

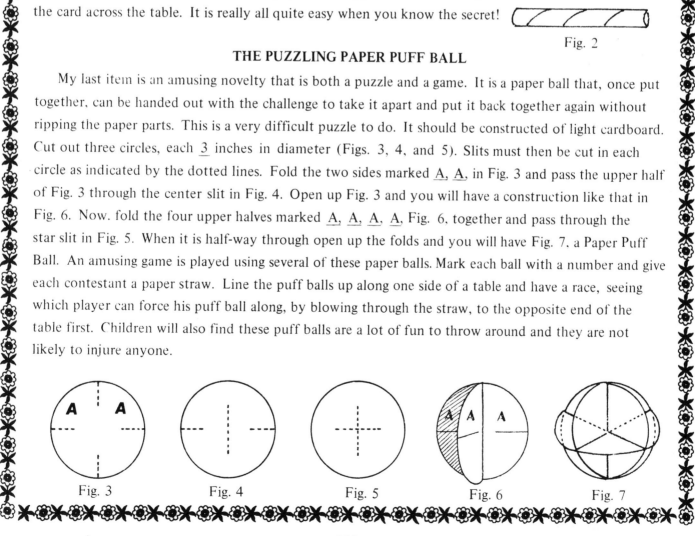

Fig. 3   Fig. 4   Fig. 5   Fig. 6   Fig. 7

Sam Loyd

am Loyd was America's genius puzzle-maker of the nineteenth century. His lifetime output was prodigious, and one of his books, *Sam Loyd's Cyclopedia of 5,000 Puzzles*, is surely one of the biggest and most fascinating collections of puzzles ever written. Over here at this booth they are displaying some of Sam Loyd's work. Let's see what is being offered."

Here, Ladies and Gentlemen, is Sam Loyd's greatest puzzle, called Get Off The Earth. The puzzle is printed on two pieces of cardboard, one of which is a circle depicting the earth. This piece is attached to the other piece of cardboard by a pin through the center. Thirteen Chinese warriors are arranged around the earth (Fig. 1). When the center disc is rotated to the left, from position <u>NE</u> to <u>NW</u>, one of the Chinamen disappears. There are now only twelve to be seen (Fig. 2). Your problem is to explain where the thirteenth Chinaman has gone to. (See Page 281 for a full-size duplicating master of this puzzle.)

◆◆◆◆◆◆◆

Our next Sam Loyd entry is a board puzzle he called The Fore And Aft Puzzle. The playing board is made up of seventeen squares on which are placed eight white counters and eight black counters. (The illustration on the next page shows how the counters are positioned at the beginning of play.) This is a transpositional type of puzzle where you must make the white and black counters change positions in the fewest possible moves. A counter can be moved from one square to an adjacent vacant square. It may also jump over an adjacent counter of either color to an empty square beyond. All moves must be either horizontal or vertical, no diagonal moves please!

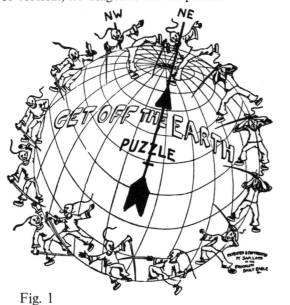

Fig. 1

Fig. 2

Reverend I.N. Spire has purchased a new bell for his church, and somehow, he was able to talk the Durango Kid into helping him hang it. The interesting thing is that the bell and the Kid weigh exactly the same. When the Kid started hauling on the rope a surprising thing happened. See if you can guess. (1) Did the bell go up while the Kid stayed down? (2) Did the Kid go up while the bell stayed down? (3) Did the Kid and the bell go up together?

SCRAPS FROM MY NOTE BOOK

ook who's on next, it's our old friend, Professor Hoffmann. The Professor is going to show us a few small tricks from his *Note Book.* Those of you in the back will be able to follow his moves by watching the large television monitors on either side of the stage. Here he comes now!

"Good afternoon, my friends, it's so good to see you all here and having such a fine time. My first trick is called The Three-Card Trick. This is more of a sharper's than a conjurer's trick, but it is a frequent experience with any one who is known to dabble in sleight of hand to be asked, 'Can you do a three-card trick?' It is humiliating to be obliged to reply, 'No, I can't,' and moreover the trick, neatly performed, may be made the occasion of a good deal of fun.

"The effect of the trick is as follows: – Three cards are used, one of them being a court card, the two others plain or low cards. We will suppose for the sake of illustration that the cards used are the king of hearts, the seven of spades, and the nine of diamonds. The performer takes one of the low cards, say the nine of diamonds, in his left hand facedown, between the tips of the second finger and thumb. The other two cards are held in the right hand in like manner one above the other, about an inch apart; but the uppermost card, which we will suppose to be the seven, is held between the thumb and the tip of the first finger, while the undermost (the king) is supported between the thumb and the second finger (see Fig. 1). The performer now throws the three cards in succession facedown upon a table or on the ground before him (in the latter case kneeling to do his work), shuffles them about with more or less rapidity, and then invites the spectators to guess (or, in the cardsharping form of the trick, to bet) which is the court card. This would seem to be a perfectly easy matter. The spectators have observed where the king originally fell; and the subsequent shifting of the cards has not made it much more difficult to keep note of its position, but if the trick has been skillfully performed they will be much more often wrong than right.

"The main secret lies in the position of the cards in the right hand, coupled with a dexterity acquired by much practice. The performer professedly throws down the <u>undermost</u> of the two

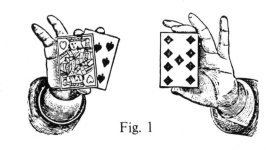

Fig. 1

cards in the right hand first, and this card has been seen to be the king. As a matter of fact, however, he can at pleasure let the uppermost card fall first, the first finger, which supported it, taking the place of the middle finger at the top of the second card. The change is so subtle that even the keenest eye cannot detect whether it has or has not been made, and this makes practically two chances to one against the person guessing.

"This would seem to be pretty good odds, but they are not enough for the cardsharper, and in the swindling form of the trick as practiced on racecourses, etc., a new deception is introduced. The player works in conjunction with two or three confederates, each suitably disguised; say as a parson, a farmer, or a country yokel. These gentlemen start the betting, and, as might be expected, pick out the right card each time, the performer at the outset making no attempt to disguise its identity. Presently one of them takes an opportunity, while the performer's attention is professedly taken up in pushing back bystanders who are crowding him, or the like, to turn up the king, show it to the company, and in replacing it slightly to bend up one corner. The operator, good innocent man, takes up the cards again, little thinking (of course) of the trick that has been played him, and begins to shuffle them about once more. Move them as he will, that telltale corner marks the king, and presently some bystander, whose greed is greater than his honesty, ventures a bet that he will pick out the card. Others follow the example, only too glad to bet on a supposed certainty, and not deeply concerned with the morality of the proceeding. When no more bets are to be procured, one of the victims turns up the supposed king, and finds instead – the seven of spades, the fact being that the performer, in throwing down the cards for the last time, had with the point of the finger deftly straightened the bent corner of the king, and made a corresponding dog's ear on the low card.

"The moral of this little apologue is obvious. Don't try to take a mean advantage of a poor cardsharper, and if you don't want *him* to take advantage of *you, don't bet on the three-card trick*, or any other."

<hr />

"I call this one The Alternate Card Trick. Arrange thirteen cards of any given suit in the following order, taking the first card in your hand faceup and placing the others on this in like manner:

Seven, ace, queen, two, eight, three, jack, four, nine, five, king, six, ten.

"You are now ready to show the trick. Take the thirteen cards facedown in your left hand, place the first card underneath the pack and turn up the next (which will be the ace) on the table. Place the third card below the packet and turn up the fourth, which will be the two, and so on, the turned-up cards appearing in regular order.

"This can be presented as a puzzle where, after showing the trick, you challenge anyone to take the thirteen cards and see if they can figure out the arrangement you used. The chances are mighty slim that anyone will be able to.

"Another trick very similar to the last one is called The Spelling Trick. In this trick, the performer begins by saying 'o-n-e, one' (passing one card underneath for each letter), and turning up the fourth, which proves to be the ace. He then spells 't-w-o, two' (passing one card under for each letter), and produces the

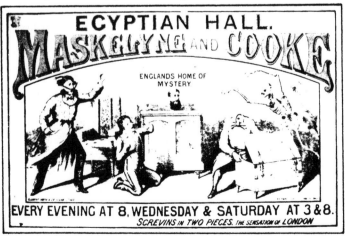

two, then passes under five cards for 't-h-r-e-e, three' and produces a three, and so on. The prearranged order of the thirteen cards for this form of trick is:

Three, eight, seven, ace, king, six, four, two, queen, knave (jack), ten, nine, five.

"To produce the card <u>with</u> the last letter of each word spelt, instead of immediately after it, the order should be:

Knave (jack), four, ace, eight, queen, two, seven, five, ten, king, three, six, nine.

"When presenting this trick, explain to your audience that it is a very old trick and so you must spell out the name <u>knave</u> instead of the name <u>jack</u> that is used today."

"TO ARRANGE TWELVE CARDS IN ROWS IN SUCH A MANNER THAT THEY WILL COUNT FOUR IN EVERY DIRECTION. This is rather a puzzle than a conjuring trick, but may sometimes serve as an interlude to occupy the minds of your audience while you are preparing for some other feat. The secret is to place nine of the twelve cards in three rows so as to form a square; then place the remaining three cards as follows: the first on the first card of the first row, the second on the second card of the second row, and the last on the third card of the last row."

"TO PLACE THE ACES AND COURT CARDS IN FOUR ROWS IN SUCH A MANNER THAT NEITHER HORIZONTALLY NOR PERPENDICULARLY SHALL THERE BE IN EITHER ROW TWO CARDS ALIKE EITHER IN SUIT OR VALUE. This also is a puzzle, and a very good one. The key to it is to begin by placing four cards of like value (say four kings) in a diagonal line from corner to corner of the intended square, then four other cards of like value (say the four aces) to form the opposite diagonal. It must be borne in mind, that of whatever suit the two center kings are, the two aces must be of the opposite suits. Thus, if the two center kings are those of diamonds and hearts, the two center aces must be those of clubs and spades; and in adding the two end aces, you must be careful not to place at either end of the line an ace of the same suit as the king at the corresponding end of the opposite diagonal. Having got so far, you will find it a very easy matter to fill in the remaining cards in accordance with the conditions of the puzzle. The sixteen cards when complete will be as I have arranged them on this table, subject, of course, to variation according to the particular cards with which you commence your task."

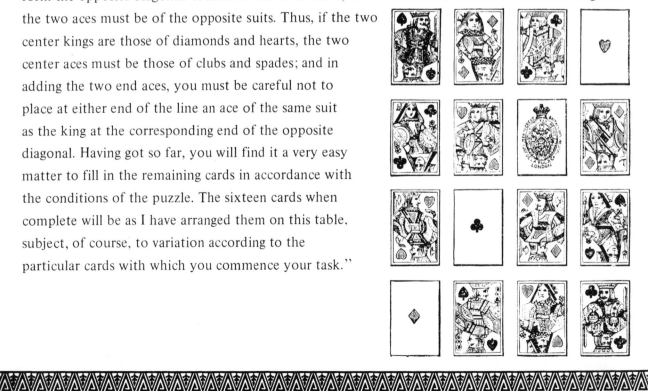

"THE CAPITAL Q TRICK. This should be classified as a numerical trick. In its simplest form it may be performed with counters, coins, or even bits of torn paper.

"The original form of the trick is as follows: The performer takes (for example) five-and-twenty counters (the precise number is immaterial) and lays them on the table in the form of a capital Q, after the manner shown in Fig. 1. He then offers to leave the room and asks some one to count, during his absence, from the tip of the tail up the <u>left</u> side of the circle, touching each counter in turn, and stopping at any one he pleases. Then to start from such last-mentioned counter and count back again <u>to the same number</u>, but this time not returning down the tail, but continuing up the right-hand side of the circle, touching each counter in succession as before. On his return to the room, the performer will indicate without fail the counter last touched, and this may be repeated as often as desired.

"The secret lies in the length of the "tail," the touching process necessarily terminating just <u>as far up the right-hand side of the circle as there are counters in the tail</u>. An example will render this clearer. Suppose that the person counting goes up to twelve, which will bring him to the counter marked <u>b</u> in the Figure. He then begins the return journey, calling that counter <u>one</u>, the next <u>two</u>, and so on till he has again counted twelve. There being in this case <u>five</u> counters in the tail, the touching process will terminate at the counter marked <u>c</u>: being the fifth from the tail up the right-hand side, and however far the counting process had been continued up the left-hand side, the return journey must still have terminated at this same counter. This arises from the fact that the counters touched on the left-hand side of the circle, are common to both the going and returning series. All that the performer therefore has to do is privately to count from <u>a</u> (exclusive) as many counters as there are in the tail, and this will bring him to the required counter. If the experiment be repeated, it is well (under the excuse of showing that the exact number of counters is immaterial), to shorten or lengthen the tail by a counter or two, or otherwise it would soon be noticed that the touching terminated at the same point, and the secret would probably be discovered."

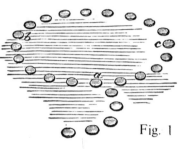

Fig. 1

"THE CARDS REVEALED BY THE LOOKING GLASS. My last item for the day is rather a joke than a feat of magic, but it will create some fun, and may often be kept up for some time without being discovered. Take up your position on one side of the room, facing a good-sized mirror or chimney glass. Make your audience stand or sit facing you, when they will, of course, have their backs to the glass. Offer the cards to be shuffled and cut. Take the top card and hold it high up, with its back to you and its face to the audience. As it will be reflected in the mirror opposite you, you will have no difficulty in naming it, or any other card in like manner, till your audience either find you out, or have had enough of the trick."

las, this, our third journey to Merlin's Isle, is over much too soon. It seems as though our ship had only landed a moment ago and that our days here, like the vacations of youth, would stretch on endlessly. Well, we had best pack our souvenirs and puzzles and magic tricks and gameboards and whatever else we have accumulated during our stay and head for the pier. This is my third trip here, and I had as much fun this time as I had during the other two trips. If you missed out on either of those excursions please turn to the last page of this book for your traveling instructions.

Last night, after our farewell dinner up at the castle, I had a chat with Merlin and he assured me that he would return again next year and that he would make sure that we would be able to attend the puzzle convention again. With that good news I take my leave until we meet again. Goodbye, and good luck.

❖❖❖❖❖❖❖❖❖❖❖❖❖❖❖❖❖❖❖❖❖❖❖❖❖❖

rofessor Hoffmann has come down to the dock to see us off, and as a going away present he has one more puzzle for us to do on our homeward journey. This is a very old puzzle, having appeared in books by Dudeny, Loyd and Hoffmann's *Puzzles Old and New*. The pieces needed to work this puzzle are depicted on pages 279, 280 and 281 for duplication.

And now, Professor, if you please!

THE CHEQUERS PUZZLE

This is a dissected puzzle of a very novel kind. It consists of a miniature chessboard, five inches square, divided into fourteen pieces, each consisting of from three to five squares, as illustrated below.

The experimenter is required, out of these fourteen segments, to construct the chessboard anew. At first sight, the task would seem to be one of the easiest possible, but any such idea very soon vanishes when the matter is put to the test. The pieces drop into position with enticing facility till the board is about three parts complete, but at that point the neophyte usually finds himself with half a dozen segments still in hand which absolutely decline to accommodate themselves to the spaces left for them.

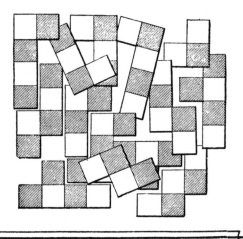

It may be mentioned, for the encouragement of the faint-hearted, that there are, according to the publishers, no less than fifty ways in which the puzzle may be solved, and it should therefore be merely a matter of time and perseverance to discover one or another of them.

While traveling through time Merlin often drops into Mr. Will Goldston's magic shop, Aladdin House. For the answers to the puzzles in this book I have decided to let the reader also journey to Aladdin House. The year is 1915. Just step up and open the door. . . . . . .

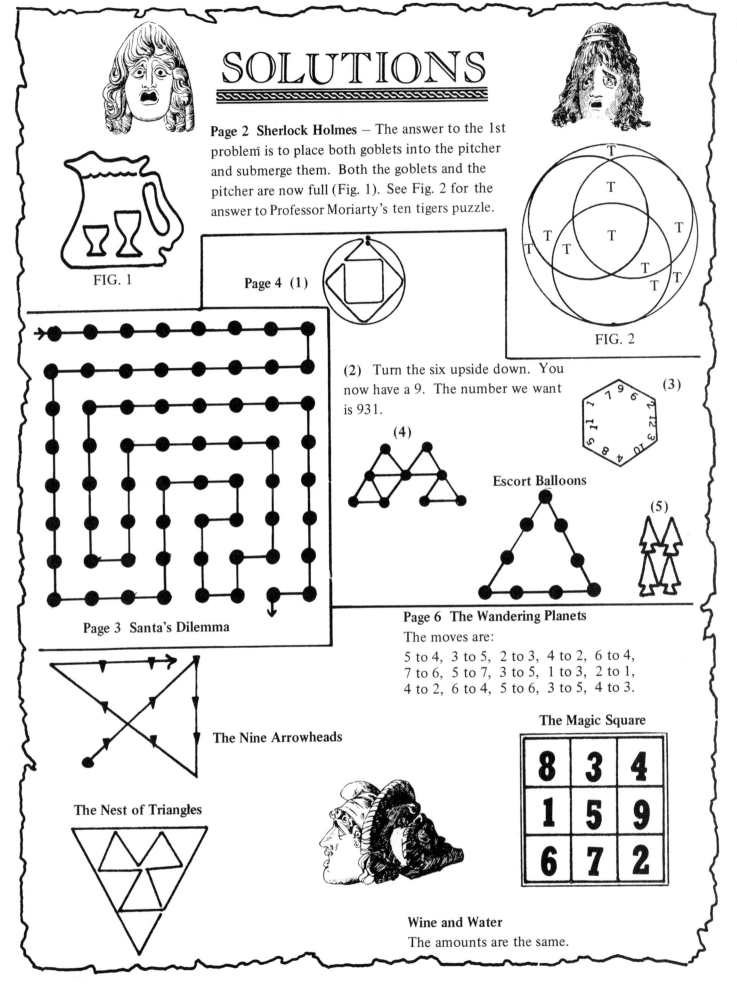

SOLUTIONS

Page 2 Sherlock Holmes — The answer to the 1st problem is to place both goblets into the pitcher and submerge them. Both the goblets and the pitcher are now full (Fig. 1). See Fig. 2 for the answer to Professor Moriarty's ten tigers puzzle.

FIG. 1

Page 4 (1)

FIG. 2

(2) Turn the six upside down. You now have a 9. The number we want is 931.

(3)

(4)

Escort Balloons

(5)

Page 3 Santa's Dilemma

Page 6 The Wandering Planets

The moves are:

5 to 4, 3 to 5, 2 to 3, 4 to 2, 6 to 4,
7 to 6, 5 to 7, 3 to 5, 1 to 3, 2 to 1,
4 to 2, 6 to 4, 5 to 6, 3 to 5, 4 to 3.

The Nine Arrowheads

The Nest of Triangles

The Magic Square

8	3	4
1	5	9
6	7	2

Wine and Water
The amounts are the same.

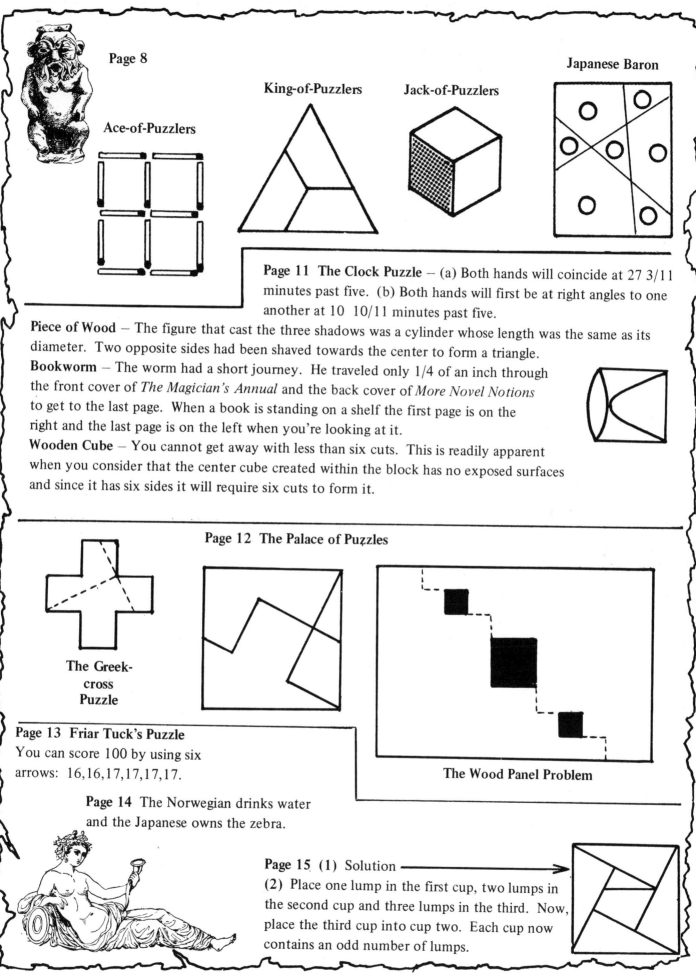

Page 8

Ace-of-Puzzlers

King-of-Puzzlers

Jack-of-Puzzlers

Japanese Baron

Page 11 The Clock Puzzle — (a) Both hands will coincide at 27 3/11 minutes past five. (b) Both hands will first be at right angles to one another at 10 10/11 minutes past five.

Piece of Wood — The figure that cast the three shadows was a cylinder whose length was the same as its diameter. Two opposite sides had been shaved towards the center to form a triangle.

Bookworm — The worm had a short journey. He traveled only 1/4 of an inch through the front cover of *The Magician's Annual* and the back cover of *More Novel Notions* to get to the last page. When a book is standing on a shelf the first page is on the right and the last page is on the left when you're looking at it.

Wooden Cube — You cannot get away with less than six cuts. This is readily apparent when you consider that the center cube created within the block has no exposed surfaces and since it has six sides it will require six cuts to form it.

Page 12 The Palace of Puzzles

The Greek-cross Puzzle

The Wood Panel Problem

Page 13 Friar Tuck's Puzzle
You can score 100 by using six arrows: 16,16,17,17,17,17.

Page 14 The Norwegian drinks water and the Japanese owns the zebra.

Page 15 (1) Solution ⟶
(2) Place one lump in the first cup, two lumps in the second cup and three lumps in the third. Now, place the third cup into cup two. Each cup now contains an odd number of lumps.

229

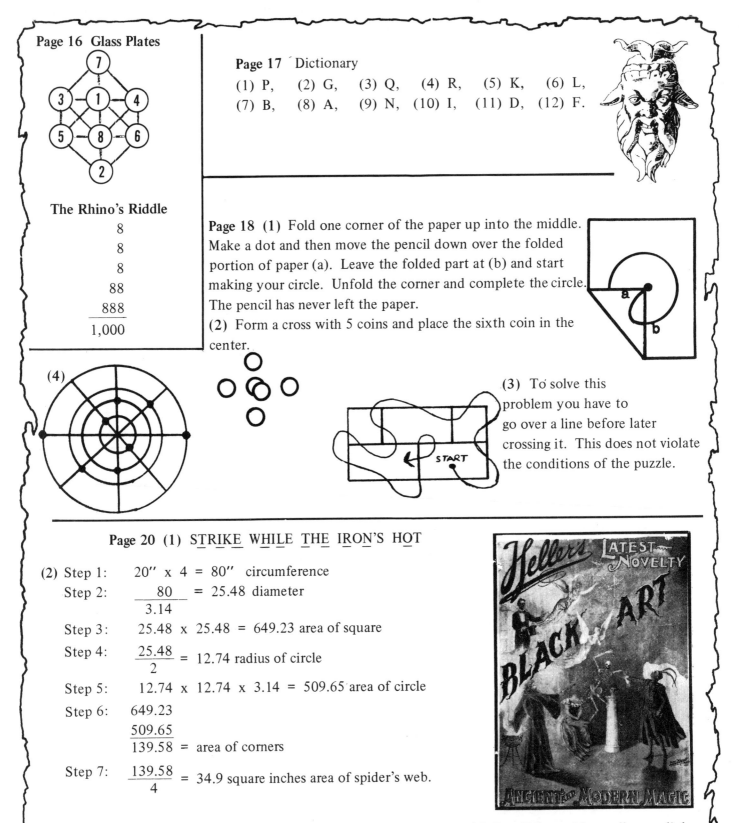

Page 16 Glass Plates

The Rhino's Riddle

$$\begin{array}{r} 8 \\ 8 \\ 8 \\ 88 \\ 888 \\ \hline 1,000 \end{array}$$

Page 17 Dictionary

(1) P, (2) G, (3) Q, (4) R, (5) K, (6) L, (7) B, (8) A, (9) N, (10) I, (11) D, (12) F.

Page 18 (1) Fold one corner of the paper up into the middle. Make a dot and then move the pencil down over the folded portion of paper (a). Leave the folded part at (b) and start making your circle. Unfold the corner and complete the circle. The pencil has never left the paper.

(2) Form a cross with 5 coins and place the sixth coin in the center.

(3) To solve this problem you have to go over a line before later crossing it. This does not violate the conditions of the puzzle.

(4)

Page 20 (1) <u>STRIKE</u> <u>WHILE</u> <u>THE</u> <u>IRON</u>'S <u>HOT</u>

(2) Step 1:   20″ x 4 = 80″ circumference

Step 2: $\dfrac{80}{3.14}$ = 25.48 diameter

Step 3:   25.48 x 25.48 = 649.23 area of square

Step 4: $\dfrac{25.48}{2}$ = 12.74 radius of circle

Step 5:   12.74 x 12.74 x 3.14 = 509.65 area of circle

Step 6: $\begin{array}{r} 649.23 \\ 509.65 \\ \hline 139.58 \end{array}$ = area of corners

Step 7: $\dfrac{139.58}{4}$ = 34.9 square inches area of spider's web.

(3) Answer: $5.25. Take the section with three links and the section with four links and have all seven links opened. These seven links can now be used to join the other seven sections together. (4) It can be done in just four moves. Jump 5 over 8, 9, 3, 1. Jump 7 over 4. Jump 6 over 2, 7. Jump 5 over 6 which leaves the last checker in the middle. (5) The answer is June 4, 1976 at 12:00 noon. For the three clocks to again show twelve o'clock at the same time it is necessary for the first clock to lose twelve hours and for the second clock to gain twelve hours. This will take exactly 720 days. Add this number of days to June 15, 1974 and we get June 4, 1976 (1976 is a leap year).

Page 22 A-10, B-9, C-27, D-24-16, E-15, F-21, G-20, H-2, I-19, J-3, K-23, L-17, M-26, N-25, O-13, P-5, Q-12, R-6, S-22, T-18, U-14, V-7, W-11, X-8, Y-4, Z-1.

Page 23 The Birdmen

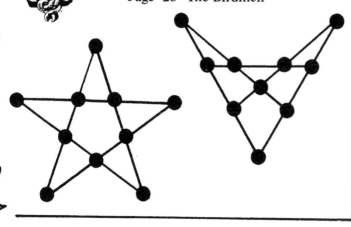

Page 24 (1) Start at any dot, count six dots and place a coin on the sixth dot. Remember which dot you *started* counting from as that's the dot you will want to place your second coin on. Start your second coin on a dot that will allow you to come to rest on the first dot. Start the third coin so that it comes to rest on the dot you started your second coin from. Continue like this for the rest of the coins. **(2)** Thirty-five triangles. **(3)** Move 2 and 3 to squares 9 and 10. Move 5 and 6 to squares 2 and 3. Move 8 and 9 to squares 5 and 6. Move 1 and 2 to squares 8 and 9.

Page 27 Cuckoo Clock — Since we do not start counting until the first strike of the clock it must take six seconds to complete the remaining five strikes. This comes to 1.2 seconds per strike. The answer to the puzzle is then 1.2 times 8 or 9.6 seconds. **Pizza Machine Box** — For solids with plane surfaces and no holes in them, the sum of the faces and the corners is two more than the number of edges. The answer to our problem is then 9 faces.

Page 29 The Farmers' Problem

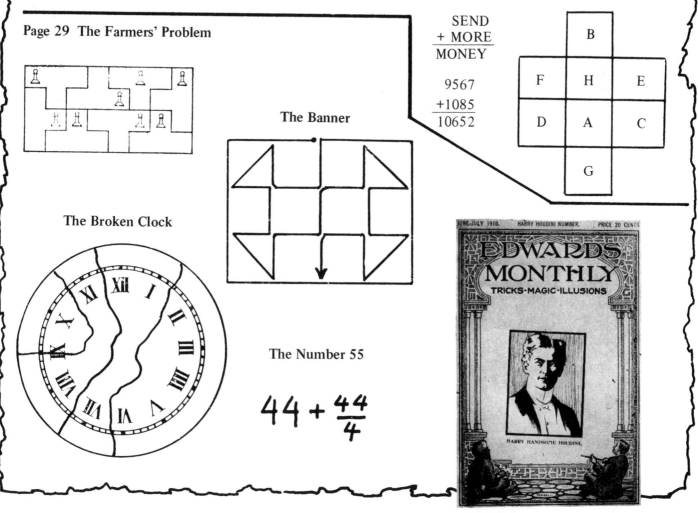

The Banner

The Broken Clock

The Number 55

$$44 + \frac{44}{4}$$

SEND
+ MORE
MONEY

9567
+1085
10652

	B	
F	H	E
D	A	C
	G	

Page 30 The "English Sixteen" Puzzle — We know of no rule for working this puzzle. There are several possible solutions. Among others, moving the men in the following order will be found to answer the conditions of the problem. The man to be moved is in each case indicated by the number of the square (page 31). It is not necessary to specify the square to which it is to be moved. As there is never more than one square vacant, the experimenter cannot go wrong in this particular. It will be observed that the number of moves is 52, which we believe to be the smallest which will suffice to transfer the whole of the men.

11, 7, 9, 8, 10, 13, 11, 14, 9, 6, 8, 5, 7, 11, 9, 10, 8, 2, 1, 6, 3, 5, 7, 4, 9, 12, 15, 17, 14, 16, 13, 15, 11, 7, 9, 14, 11, 13, 10, 8, 9, 6, 8, 2, 5, 7, 11, 9, 12, 10, 8, 9.

A Singular Subtraction — This is somewhat of a quibble. The number 45 is the sum of the digits 1, 2, 3, 4, 5, 6, 7, 8, 9. The puzzle is solved by arranging these in reverse order, and subtracting the original series from them, when the remainder will be found to consist of the same digits in a different order, and therefore making the same total — viz., 45.

$$987654321 = 45$$
$$123456789 = 45$$
$$864197532 = 45$$

A Mysterious Multiplicand — The number 37 will be found to answer the conditions of the problem. Multiplied by 3, it is 111; by 6, 222; by 9, 333; by 15, 555; by 12, 444; by 18, 666; by 21, 777; by 24, 888; and by 27, 999.

An Unmanageable Legacy — The lawyer had a horse of his own, which he drove into the stable with the rest. "Now," he said to John, "take your half." John took nine horses accordingly. James and William were then invited to take their shares, which they did, receiving six and two horses respectively. This division exactly disposed of the seventeen horses of the testator; and the lawyer, pocketing his fee, drove his own steed home again. N.B. — The above solution rests on the fact that the sum of the three fractions named, 1/2, 1/3, and 1/9, when reduced to a common denominator, will be found not to amount to unity, but only to 17/18. The addition of another horse (= 1/18) bringing the total number up to eighteen, renders it divisible by such common denominator, and enables each to get his proper share, the lawyer then resuming his own 1/18, which he had lent for the purpose of the division. In the administration of the Mohammedan Law of Inheritance, which involves numerous and complicated fractions, this expedient is frequently employed.

A Novel Century — 9 x 8 + 7 + 6 + 5 + 4 + 3 + 2 + 1 = 100.

Page 32 The Eight-Pointed Star Problem — The secret lies in working backwards throughout, each time covering the point from which you last started. Thus, placing a counter on a, draw it along the line a-d, and leave it on d. a is now the next point to be covered, and there is only one vacant line, f-a, which leads to it. Place, therefore, your second counter on f, draw it along f-a, and leave it on a. The third counter must be placed on c, drawn along c-f, and left on f. The next placed on h, and left on c. The fifth is placed on e, and left on h. The sixth is placed on b, and left on e, and the seventh placed on g, and left on b. You now have the whole seven counters duly placed, and only one point, g, left uncovered.

Can You Name It? — Answer, 20. 50 - 20 = 30. 80 - 50 = 30.

Page 32 Another Century

Answer:

$$
\begin{array}{r}
15 \\
36 \\
\underline{47} \\
98 \\
\underline{2} \\
100
\end{array}
$$

Page 33 Lucky Number – Multiply the selected number by <u>nine</u>, and use the product as the multiplier for the larger number. It will be found that the results will be respectively as under:

$$
\begin{array}{lrl}
12345679 \times & 9 = & 111\ 111\ 111 \\
'' \quad\quad\ \times & 18 = & 222\ 222\ 222 \\
'' \quad\quad\ \times & 27 = & 333\ 333\ 333 \\
'' \quad\quad\ \times & 36 = & 444\ 444\ 444 \\
'' \quad\quad\ \times & 45 = & 555\ 555\ 555 \\
'' \quad\quad\ \times & 54 = & 666\ 666\ 666 \\
'' \quad\quad\ \times & 63 = & 777\ 777\ 777 \\
'' \quad\quad\ \times & 72 = & 888\ 888\ 888 \\
'' \quad\quad\ \times & 81 = & 999\ 999\ 999
\end{array}
$$

It will be observed that the result is in each case the "lucky" number, nine times repeated.

The Hundred Bottles of Wine – He sold on the first day 2 bottles only; on the second, 5; on the third, 8; on the fourth, 11; on the fifth, 14; on the sixth, 17; on the seventh, 20; and on the eighth day, 23.

$2 + 5 + 8 + 11 + 14 + 17 + 20 + 23 = 100.$

To ascertain the first day's sale, or first term of the series, take the ordinary formula for ascertaining the sum of an arithmetical progression.

$$S = \frac{n}{2}(2a + (n-1)d)$$

Now <u>S</u> (the sum of the series), <u>n</u> (the number of terms), and <u>d</u> (the daily rate of increase), are known, being 100, 8, and 3 respectively.

Substituting these known values in the formula, that of the first term, <u>a</u>, is readily ascertained. Thus:

$$
\begin{array}{rl}
& \ \frac{8}{2} \\
100 = & \frac{8}{2}\ (2a + 21) \\
= & 4\ (2a + 21) \\
= & 8a + 84 \\
100 - 84 = & 8a \\
16 = & 8a \\
a = & 2
\end{array}
$$

Page 34 Just One Over – 61, being the least common multiple of 2, 3, 4, 5, and 6 (60) + 1.

A Weighty Matter – Seven weights are required, of 1, 2, 4, 8, 16, 32 and 64 lbs. respectively, together making 127 lbs. It will be found that, by using one, two, or more of these, any weight from 1 to 127 lbs. can be weighed.

The Expunged Numerals – The dots indicate the figures to be expunged.

$$
\begin{array}{r}
.11 \\
33. \\
\cdots \\
77. \\
\cdots \\
\hline
1111
\end{array}
$$

The Menagerie – There being 36 heads (i.e., 36 creatures in all), if all had been birds they would have had 72 feet. If all had been beasts, they would have had 144 feet. It is clear, therefore, that there were some of each. Suppose the numbers equal, the feet would then count as under:

18 birds: 36 feet
<u>18 beasts</u>: <u>72</u> feet.
36   108 feet
(being an excess of 8 over the stated number.)

Each bird added to the "bird" half (involving at the same time the deduction therefrom of one beast) produces a diminution of 2 in the number of feet. As the equal division gives an excess of 8 feet, we must therefore deduct 4 beasts and add 4 birds.

This gives us 18 + 4 = 22 birds – 44 feet
       18 – 4 = <u>14</u> beasts – <u>56</u> feet
              36   100

The Beheaded Words – The initials, as will be seen, give the word LAFAYETTE.

1. L – arch
2. A – loft
3. F – lung
4. A – bout
5. Y – ours
6. E – rase
7. T – aunt
8. T – ease
9. E – vent

Page 34 (continued) **The Two Numbers** — The required numbers are 5 and 7. For if twice the first + the second = 17, and twice the second = the first = 19, then the above added together, i.e., three times the first + three times the second must be 17 + 19 = 36, and the sum of the numbers themselves must be 36/3 = 12. And since twice the first + the second is an odd number, the second is also an odd number, and the first, being an even number (12) less an odd number, must also be an odd number. Now the only pairs of odd numbers which together make 12 are 1 and 11, 3 and 9, and 5 and 7. Of these, we find by experiment that 5 and 7 are the only two that answer the conditions; 5 x 2 + 7 = 17, and 7 x 2 + 5 = 19.

Nine Counters

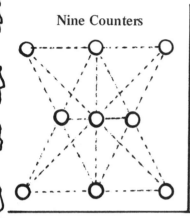

Page 36 The "Twenty-Six" Puzzle — (See Fig. 1) **Many Figures, But a Small Result** — (Reducing each fraction to its lowest denominator it

$$\frac{35}{70} + \frac{148}{296}$$ will be found to be equal to ½ and ½ + ½ = 1).

The Captives in The Tower — The boy descended first, using the cannonball as a counterpoise. The queen and her daughter then took the cannonball out of the upper basket, and the daughter descended, the boy acting as counterpoise. The cannonball was then allowed to run down alone. When it reached the ground, the daughter got into the basket along with the cannonball, and their joint weight acted as counterpoise while the queen descended. The princess got out and the cannonball was sent down alone. The boy then went down, the cannonball ascending. The daughter removed the cannonball and went down alone, her brother ascending. The latter then put the cannonball in the opposite basket, and lowered himself to the ground.

		1	4	Fig. 1
11	6	7	2	
8	10	3	5	
	9	12		

Page 35 The Chess Master — The numbers in the squares below indicate the order in which the moves are made to solve the Knight's Tour.

1	6	51	8	11	60	57	54
50	13	2	61	52	55	10	59
5	64	7	12	9	58	53	56
14	49	62	3	16	47	36	31
63	4	15	48	35	30	17	46
24	21	26	41	44	39	32	37
27	42	23	20	29	34	45	18
22	25	28	43	40	19	38	33

A Difficult Division — According to the conditions of the problem, each son's share will be seven casks (irrespective of contents), and of wine, 3½ casks. The division can be made in either of two ways; Dick and Tom each take 2 full, 2 empty, and 3 half-full casks; and Harry, 3 full, 3 empty, and 1 half-full; or Dick and Tom take 3 full, 3 empty, and 1 half-full cask; and Harry 1 full, 1 empty, and 5 half-filled casks.

Nothing Left — The required number is 118. To obtain it, work the process indicated in reverse order, as follows:

$$0 + 18 = 18$$
$$18 = 324$$
$$324 \div 3$$
$$108 + 10 = 118$$

Page 37 The Three Travellers — The plan adopted is as follows: 1. Two of the servants are sent over. 2. One of the servants brings back the boat, and takes over the third servant. 3. One of the servants brings the boat back, lands, and two of the masters go over. 4. One of the masters and one of the servants return. The servant lands, and the third master crosses with

Page 37 (continued) – the second. The position of matters is now as follows: The three masters are on the farther side with one of the servants, who is sent back with the boat, and fetches, one at a time, the other two servants.

Dropped Proverbs – 1. A stitch in time saves nine.   2. He laughs best who laughs last.   3. Children and fools speak the truth.   4. When the wine is in, the wit is out.   5. Honesty is the best policy.

A puzzle with counters

No Two In A Row

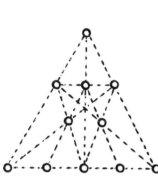

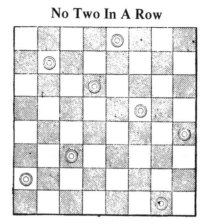

A Card Puzzle

The Four Wineglasses — Lay three of the wineglasses on the table so as to form an equilateral triangle, each side being equal to the height of a single glass. Then place the fourth glass upside down in the centre.

Page 38 The "Forty-Five" Puzzle
The first of the required numbers is 8.

$$(8 + 2 = 10)$$
The second is 12. $(12 - 2 = 10)$
The third is 5. $(5 \times 2 = 10)$
The fourth is 20. $(20 \div 2 = 10)$
$$8 + 12 + 5 + 20 = 45.$$

Squares, Product, & Difference
Answer: 11 and 15. Their product is 165, and their difference is 4. The former exceeds the latter by 161, the sum of their squares is 346, and $346 - 165 = 181$.

The Two Ages
The father was three times the age of his son 15½ years earlier, being then fifty-five and a half, while his son was eighteen and a half. The son will have reached half his father's age in three years' time, being then thirty-seven, while his father will be seventy-four.

The Shepherd and His Sheep
To ascertain the number of the flock, find in the first place the least common multiple of 2, 3, 4, 5, and 6, i.e., 60. Then take the lowest multiple of this, which, with 1 added, will be divisible by 7. This will be found to be 301, which is the required answer.

When Will They Get It?
In 420 days; 420 being the least common multiple of 1, 2, 3, 4, 5, 6 and 7.

The Two Sons
The younger son is 24½; the elder, 29¾ years old. The solution is most easily got at by means of a simple equation, thus: Let y = age of younger. Then $5\frac{1}{4}y$ = age of elder.
By the terms of the question —

$$5y + 6(y + 5\tfrac{1}{4}) = 301$$
$$5y + 6y + 31\tfrac{1}{2} = 301$$
$$11y = 301 - 31\tfrac{1}{2} = 269\tfrac{1}{2}$$
$$y = 24\tfrac{1}{2}$$

The younger son is therefore 24½ years old, and the elder $24\frac{1}{2} + 5\frac{1}{4} = 29\frac{3}{4}$.

Page 39 Crossette

It will be found that unless the experimenter proceeds, in accordance with a regular system he will fail, the count of four beginning very soon to fall upon circles already covered by coins, and so failing to meet the conditions. To solve the puzzle, after placing a coin on a given circle, *miss three before starting again.* Thus, suppose the start to be made from No. 1.

No. 4 will in such case be the first circle you will place a coin on. Miss three, and start again at 8; No. 1 will then be the one you will place a coin on. Begin again at 5 and place a coin on 8. Again at 2, and place a coin on 5. Again at 9, and place a coin on 2. Again at 6, and place a coin on 9. Again at 3, and place a coin on 6. Again at 10, and place a coin on 3. Again at 7, and place a coin on 10. You have thus placed coins on 9 out of the 10 circles. It will be observed that you place a coin at each round on the number with which you started at the previous round.

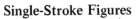

```
              1
     10           2
   9                3
   8                4
     7           5
         6
```

The Orchard Puzzle

Single-Stroke Figures

Fig. 3 may be described by tracing the lines from A to B, B to C, C to D, D to A, A to F, F to C, C to E, E to F, F to B, B to E, and E to D.

Fig. 4 may be described by starting at A, then passing along the curve AGD, from D along DEB, from B along BFC, and from C along CEA.

The Two Travellers

A, in his 2½ hours' start, has travelled 10 miles. As B gains on him at the rate of a mile an hour, it will take him ten hours to recover this distance, by which time A will have been travelling 12½ hours, and will be 50 miles from the point whence he started.

Page 40 The "Right and Left" Puzzle – You first deal with the middle row (15 to 21) after the manner described in The Wandering Planets Puzzle (see page 6). You then move the white counter now occupying space 25 into the central space (18), and deal in like manner with the fourth row (22 to 28), leaving space 25 vacant. Pass the counter occupying 11 into this space, and you are then in a position to deal with the second row (8 to 14). When space 11 is again vacant, move the counter occupying space 4 into it, and you are then enabled to deal with the uppermost line (1 to 7). Pass the counter occupying space 18 into space 4, and that occupying space 32 into space 18. You are now in a position to rearrange the last row (29 to 35). You have then a vacant space (32) in the centre of the bottom row. Move the counter occupying space 25 into this space, then pass that occupying 11 into 25, and finally move the counter now in 18 to 11.

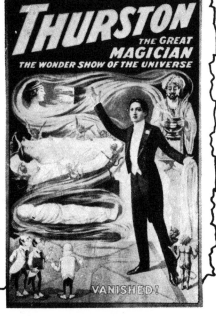

236

Page 42 The Treasure at Medinet

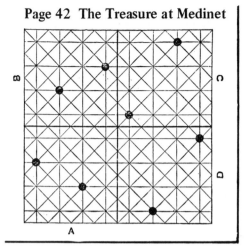

The Market Woman and her Stock

Her original stock was 40 apples. Her first customer, buying half her stock, and giving back 10, left her with 30; the second, buying one-third of 30, and giving her back 2, left her with 22; and the third, buying half of these, and giving her back 1, left her with 12. To solve the problem, however, it is necessary (unless algebra be used) to work the process backwards. Take away 1 (given back by the last boy) from her ultimate remainder, 12, thus leaving 11. It is clear that as he purchased half her stock, she must before he did so have had 22 apples. Of these, 2 had been given back to her by the second boy, so that prior to his so doing she must have had 20. As he bought one-third of her stock, the number previous to his purchase must have been 30. Of these 30, 10 were given back to her by the first boy, prior to which she must have had 20; and as this 20 represents half her original stock (for the first boy bought the other half), she must at the outset have had 40.

Page 43 The Three Arabs

The first Arab was entitled to seven, and the second to one only of the eight coins. For, the consumption being equal, each person ate 8/3 (2 2/3) loaves. Of the portion eaten by the stranger the first Arab contributed 2 1/3 loaves, while the second contributed 1/3 loaf. The former therefore contributed seven parts, while the second contributed one only, and the proper division of the money was seven coins to the first, and one to the second.

The Three Market Women

They began by selling at the rate of three apples for a penny. The first sold ten pennyworth, the second eight pennyworth, and the third seven pennyworth. The first had then left three apples, the second five, and the third six. These they sold at one penny each, receiving, therefore, in the whole —

The first,   10¢. + 3¢. = 13¢.
The second,   8¢. + 5¢. = 13¢.
The third,   7¢. + 6¢. = 13¢.

An Aggravating Uncle

The number of soldiers was 58.

On examination of the conditions of the puzzle, it will be found that in each case, whether divided by 3, 4, 5, or 6, there are always two short of an even division. All that is needed, therefore, is to find the least common multiple of 3, 4, 5, and 6, and deduct 2 from it. The l.c.m. of 3, 4, 5, and 6 is 60, and 60 – 2 = 58, the required number.

The False Scales

Answer: 12 lbs. Problems of this class are solved by ascertaining the square root of the product of the two weights. In this case 9 x 16 = 144, and the square root of 144 is 12, the required answer.

The Divided Square

Suppose A B C D (Fig. 1) represents the square to be divided. Find the centre of each side, represented by the letter E F G H. Draw straight lines from H to D, D to F, A to G, and E to C. Cut the cardboard through the lines thus marked. This will give us nine segments, which we will distinguish accordingly by the numbers 1 to 9 inclusive. Rearrange the various segments as shown in Fig. 2.

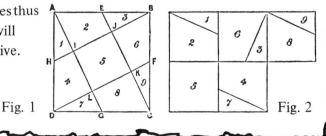

Fig. 1   Fig. 2

Page 44 The Triangle — Push the point of the long loop through the ring <u>a</u> (see Fig. 1), then pass it over the angles <u>b</u>, <u>c</u>, and <u>d</u>, in succession; this done, it may be drawn out clear through <u>a</u>. To reengage it, reverse the process.

The Interlaced Triangles — Hold the puzzle by the corner <u>a</u>, and fold back the upper part behind the lower. Push the movable triangle (with the ring upon it) to the top of the upright from which it hangs, and then pass the ring along down the two uprights now folded together, and up the two slanting portions to <u>a</u>. Again open the puzzle, and push the ring along the two horizontal wires to <u>b</u>. Fold the puzzle again, and slide the ring down along the double wires to <u>c</u>, then upwards in a perpendicular direction, and it will be free.

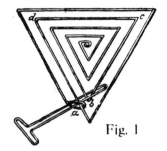

Fig. 1

To put it on again, repeat the process in the opposite direction.

The United Hearts — Pass the loop <u>a</u> of the left-hand heart through the ring <u>b</u> of the right-hand heart, and over the ring <u>c</u>, in the direction shown by the arrow, when the two will come apart. They may be joined again by reversing the process.

Page 45 The Heart — On closely examining this puzzle it will be seen that in the centre the cord forms a loop, which passes round the opposite portion. Draw the ball close up to the heart; then by means of the "slack" thus gained draw out the loop as far as possible. Pass it down through the centre hole, then through the next two holes, and back again to the front through the bottom hole. Finally slip the loop over the ball. Draw back the loop, which is now disengaged from the rest of the cord, and all will come off together.

To replace the cord, pass the loop first from the front through the bottom hole, up through one of the adjoining pair of holes, and back again through the other, then through the next pair in like manner. You now have the loop brought to the front. Pass it down through the centre hole and up through the bottom hole, then over the ball, and draw it back again. Pull down the ball as far as the cord permits, and all will be as at first.

The Chinese Ladder — This, though at first sight it appears somewhat formidable, is in reality a very simple puzzle. Take the ladder in the left hand, with the small bead and knot undermost at the same side. Drawing the cord moderately taut, twist it twice round the lower right-hand end of the ladder. Then pass the needle up through the lower hole on the same side, through the first counter, and so on till you reach the top; then, in the same way, down the holes and through the counters on the opposite side. You have now exactly reversed the process by which the counters were threaded into position, and if you were to release the hitch you made round the lower end of the ladder and pull on the cord in its now doubled condition, it would be drawn clean out, and the counters would fall from it. You are, however, required to keep the counters still on the cord. To effect this, you must hitch the end, still drawn tightly, round the other foot of the ladder, and then thread the remaining portion, with the aid of the needle, through each counter in succession (this time not passing through the holes in the ladder). This done, unfasten your two hitches, and draw away the doubled cord. It will now come clear away from the ladder, but the counters will be left upon it, according to the conditions of the puzzle.

The Imperial Scale — To get the ring off, draw up the central loop a couple of inches; pass it through the hole <u>a</u>; pass it under the bead at that corner, and draw it back again *outside* the cord. Repeat the same process at the b corner, and the loop will be outside both cords. Draw it up a little further, and pass it over the *central knot,* then down through the holes c and d in succession *(over the bead, and draw back under).* The loop will now no longer embrace the standing part of the central cord, but will lie loose on the scale, and the ring will be free. Care must be taken not to twist the loop during the foregoing operations.

To work the ring on again, draw the loop through the hole a, under the bead, and up again outside the cord. Repeat at the corner b. You will now have the loop outside two of the cords. Pass it over the general knot at top, down through c, outside the cord, over the bead, and up again inside. Repeat at d, and the ring will be secure.

If the puzzle be homemade (and it is a very easy matter to make it) it will be found an improvement to have the centre cord of a different colour from the four others. By adopting this plan there is much less risk of getting the cords "mixed" in passing the loop through the corner holes.

The Cross-Keys or Three-Piece Puzzle — The three pieces of which the puzzle is composed are shaped as a, b, and c (Fig. 1) respectively. To put them together, take a upright between the forefinger and thumb of the left hand. Through the slot push b, with the crosscut uppermost, till the farther edge of the central slot comes all but flush with the outer face of a. Then take c, with the short arm of the cross towards you, and lower it gently down over the top of a, the uncut centre portion (next the short arm of the cross) passing through the crosscut in b. You have now only to push b onward through a till the transverse cut is hidden, and the cross is complete.

To separate the parts, reverse the process.

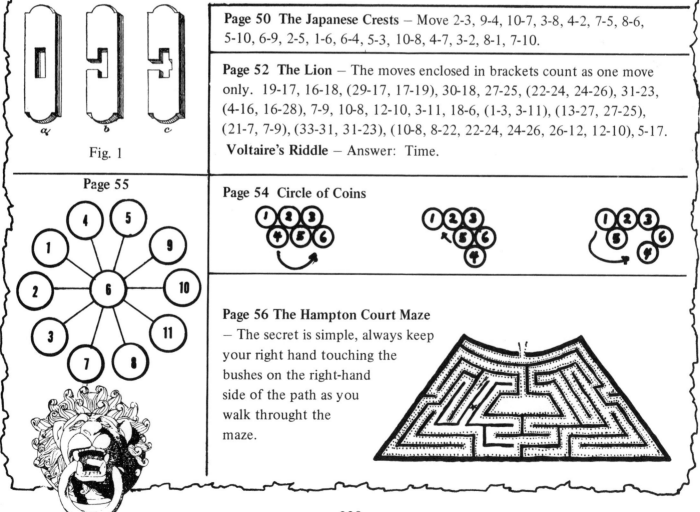

Fig. 1

Page 50 The Japanese Crests — Move 2-3, 9-4, 10-7, 3-8, 4-2, 7-5, 8-6, 5-10, 6-9, 2-5, 1-6, 6-4, 5-3, 10-8, 4-7, 3-2, 8-1, 7-10.

Page 52 The Lion — The moves enclosed in brackets count as one move only. 19-17, 16-18, (29-17, 17-19), 30-18, 27-25, (22-24, 24-26), 31-23, (4-16, 16-28), 7-9, 10-8, 12-10, 3-11, 18-6, (1-3, 3-11), (13-27, 27-25), (21-7, 7-9), (33-31, 31-23), (10-8, 8-22, 22-24, 24-26, 26-12, 12-10), 5-17.

Voltaire's Riddle — Answer: Time.

Page 55

Page 54 Circle of Coins

Page 56 The Hampton Court Maze — The secret is simple, always keep your right hand touching the bushes on the right-hand side of the path as you walk throught the maze.

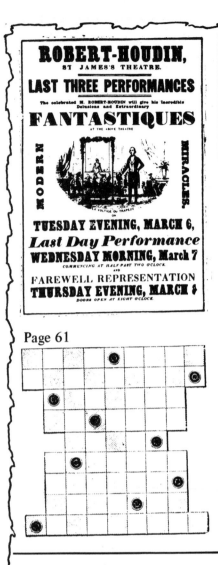

Page 61

Page 59 The Earl's Puzzle — Answer: Move 12-15, 10-12, 15-10, 9-14, 6-13, 3-12, 12-15, 15-10, 1-3, 4-2, 10-3, 2-4, 5-3.

Alice's Alphabet Puzzle —

$$\frac{A \quad EF \quad HI \quad KLMN \qquad T \quad VWXYZ}{BCD \quad G \quad J \qquad OPQRS \quad U}$$

Answer: All the letters made with straight lines are above the line while the letters made with curved lines are below the line.

Page 63 — The secret move that the red forces must make before they can capture the monster is to ignore the black piece and move out directly towards position 1. Entering position 1 by way of position 3 and leaving by 2 or entering by 2 and leaving by 3 bestows upon the red side the power to defeat the powers of darkness. Your opening moves, disregarding what moves black may make, should be; 26-24, 24-20, 20-19, 19-15, 15-11, 11-7, 7-3, 3-1, 1-2. After making the last move, 1-2, it is time for the red forces to go on the attack. Pursue the black piece, pushing him always away from position 1 in the northwest corner. From this point on it will only be a matter of time before you capture the enemy. If he gets around you and manages to pass through position 1 you will have to return and go through position 1 to regain your advantage. One last puzzle: see if you can analyze this game and come up with the reason that makes position 1 so important in delivering certain victory to the red side.

Page 64 The Sphinx —

1. Write twelve in Roman numerals — XII. Halve the number by drawing a line horizontally across its center. The upper half is VII.

2. $6\frac{6}{6}$ 3. An icicle.   4. $99\frac{99}{99}$ (=100)   5. Don't pay your water bill.

6. The last of the five received his herring in the dish.

7. Debt.   8. This is another of the "catches" dependent upon the use of Roman numerals. One six (VI) is placed above another six, but the latter in an inverted position (ΛI), the combination making XI.

9. An echo.   10. The puzzle is solved by cracking a nut, showing your interlocutor the kernel, and then eating it.

11. You place in the person's left hand his own right elbow, which, obviously, he cannot take in his right hand.

12. Write nineteen in Roman numerals — XIX. Remove the I and you have XX.

Page 65 — Pick up glass number 4 and pour the contents of the glass into glass 1 and replace glass number 4 back in position 4.

Page 66 Alice in Puzzleland — (1) a. Weigh 2 eggs against one another and mark one H (heavier) and mark one L (lighter). b. Next weigh 2 more eggs in the same way marking them h and l. c. Weigh H against h. (Let's say H is heavier). The order of weight so far is H, h, l. We will come back to L later. d. In no more than two weighings you can determine the placement of the 5th egg. e. Getting back to L, it is now possible to find its position in no more than two weighings using the knowledge that L is lighter than H.

Page 66 (continued)

(2)

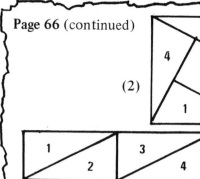

(3) Alice asked, "If I had asked you yesterday, 'Which is the path that will lead me to the house of the Mad Hatter?' what would your answer have been?"

(4)

8	9	1
3		4
5		7
2	10	6

(5)

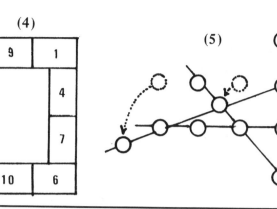

Page 68 — The moves are: 10-5, 1-8, 11-6, 2-9, 12-7, 3-4, 5-12, 8-3, 6-1, 9-10, 7-6, 4-9, 12-7, 3-4, 1-8, 10-5, 6-1, 9-10, 7-2, 4-11, 8-3, 5-12.

Page 70 Rupert's Riddle — I, do, met, shot, timed, desist, methods, moistest, Methodist, Methodists.

Whaler's Cove

	8 gal.	5 gal.	3 gal.
Start —	8	0	0
1 —	3	5	0
2 —	3	2	3
3 —	6	2	0
4 —	6	0	2
5 —	1	5	2
6 —	1	4	3
7 —	4	4	0

The Golfing Problem

The solution depends on the source of the river beginning on the golf course itself.

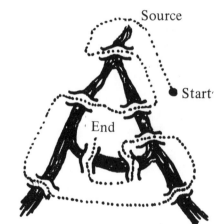

Page 72 Tom Thumb's Travels — Engine T pushes car B up into C. T then goes around and pushes car A up and couples it on to B. T then pulls B and A down into right siding. T goes around up into C and pushes A on to main track. T leaves B on right siding, goes and gets A and pushes it up into left siding.

The answer to the second problem is: T pushes A up into C. T goes around and pushes B against A. T pulls B and A down to main track and pushes both cars up past right siding. T leaves A there, brings B back to left siding and pushes B up to C. T goes around to right siding and pulls B down into right siding. T leaves B there, goes and couples up to A and pulls, then pushes A into left siding. T goes back to main track.

Page 74 The Coins of Odin

The Impossible Coin Puzzle

Place the four coins as shown. Stand the 5th coin upright.

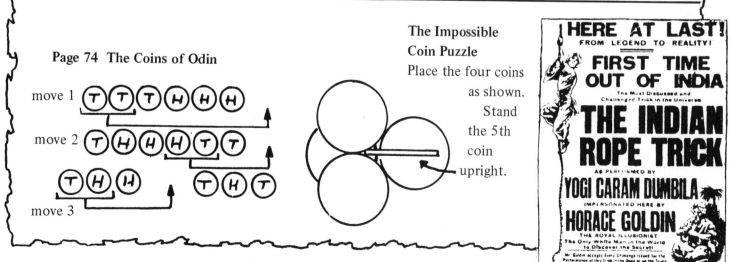

241

Page 75 Nine Coins – Place three coins on each side of the balance scale, holding the remaining three in your hand. If the scale does not balance, you have located the group of three which contains the heavier coin. If the scale balances, the group of three in your hand contains the heavier coin. Now, from the group of three containing the heavier coin, select two and place one on each side of the scale. If they do not balance, you have located the heavier coin. If they balance, the heavier coin is the one remaining in your hand.

Twelve Coins – The counterfeit coin could be either heavier or lighter than the other coins. You must find the answer in only 3 weighings. The schematic diagram gives you the answer. The result of all comparisons (in boxes) is based on comparing the top figure(s) to the bottom figure(s). L stands for *light*.

H stands for *heavy*.

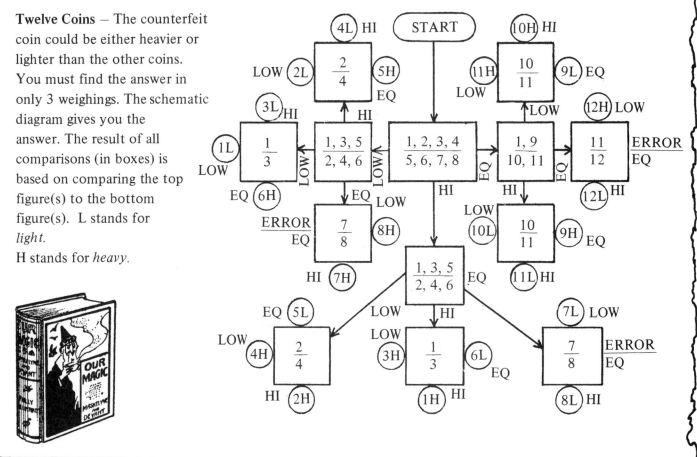

Page 77 (1) Let a few drops of water fall on the broken part of the match. In a few minutes the wood will swell causing the ends to move apart. When they have moved far enough the coin will fall into the bottle.

(2)

(3) Put your finger on the center coin of the vertical column at the far left. Move the coin around the coins to the other side and place it against the center coin of the vertical column at the far right. Push the coin to the left moving the whole center row of coins to the left until all the red and black checkers line up under one another.

(4) 27 lbs.

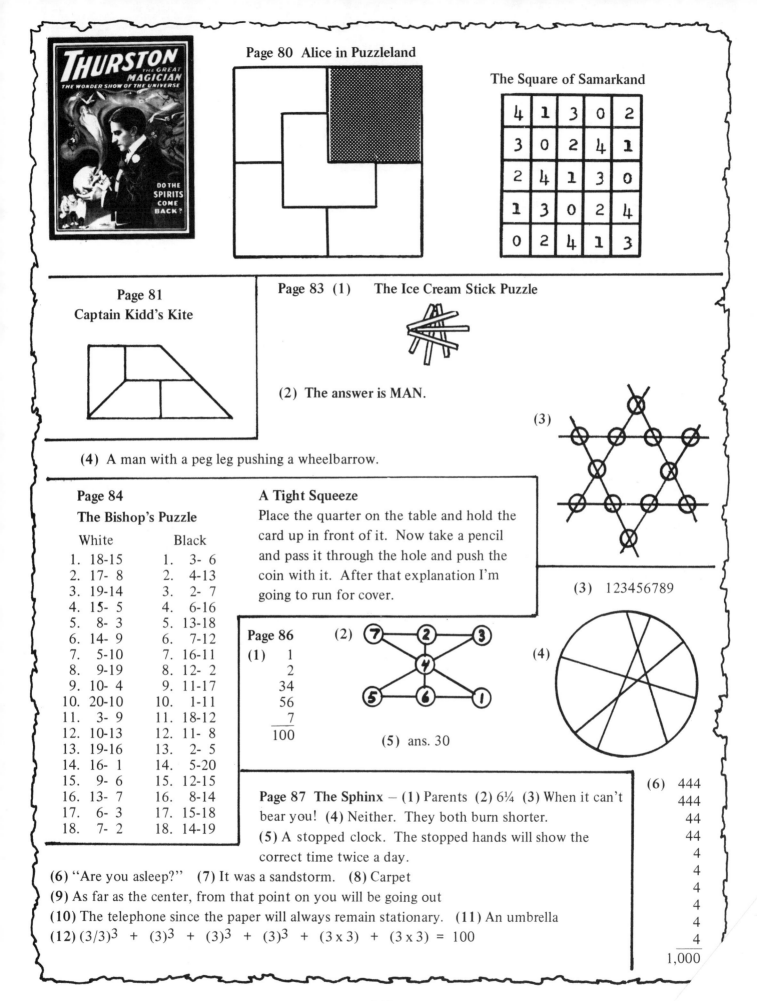

Page 80 Alice in Puzzleland

The Square of Samarkand

4	1	3	0	2
3	0	2	4	1
2	4	1	3	0
1	3	0	2	4
0	2	4	1	3

Page 81
Captain Kidd's Kite

Page 83 (1)   The Ice Cream Stick Puzzle

(2) The answer is MAN.

(3)

(4) A man with a peg leg pushing a wheelbarrow.

Page 84

The Bishop's Puzzle

White	Black
1. 18-15	1. 3- 6
2. 17- 8	2. 4-13
3. 19-14	3. 2- 7
4. 15- 5	4. 6-16
5. 8- 3	5. 13-18
6. 14- 9	6. 7-12
7. 5-10	7. 16-11
8. 9-19	8. 12- 2
9. 10- 4	9. 11-17
10. 20-10	10. 1-11
11. 3- 9	11. 18-12
12. 10-13	12. 11- 8
13. 19-16	13. 2- 5
14. 16- 1	14. 5-20
15. 9- 6	15. 12-15
16. 13- 7	16. 8-14
17. 6- 3	17. 15-18
18. 7- 2	18. 14-19

A Tight Squeeze
Place the quarter on the table and hold the card up in front of it. Now take a pencil and pass it through the hole and push the coin with it. After that explanation I'm going to run for cover.

Page 86
(1)   1
        2
       34
       56
        7
      ─────
      100

(2)

(5) ans. 30

(3)   123456789

(4)

(6)   444
      444
       44
       44
        4
        4
        4
        4
        4
     ─────
     1,000

Page 87 The Sphinx — (1) Parents (2) 6¼ (3) When it can't bear you! (4) Neither. They both burn shorter.
(5) A stopped clock. The stopped hands will show the correct time twice a day.
(6) "Are you asleep?"   (7) It was a sandstorm.   (8) Carpet
(9) As far as the center, from that point on you will be going out
(10) The telephone since the paper will always remain stationary.   (11) An umbrella
(12) $(3/3)^3 + (3)^3 + (3)^3 + (3)^3 + (3 \times 3) + (3 \times 3) = 100$

Page 87 (continued) **(13)**

45 pennies	=	45¢
1 quarter	=	25¢
2 dimes	=	20¢
2 nickels	=	10¢
		$1.00

(14) The trip starts and ends at the South Pole.

(15) Because its capital is always Dublin.

(16) Because he is no better.

Page 88 – The knights' moves enclosed in brackets count as one move only.
(1-6), (3-8-1), (9-4-3-8), (7-2-9-4-3), (6-7-2-9), (1-6-7), (8-1).

Page 89

(1) White to move and win – 15-10, 24-6, 7-2, 12-19, 2-27.

(2) White to move and win – 22-17, 21-25, 17-21, 10-14, 18-9, 25-30, 21-25, 30-21, 9-6, 21-17, 6-2, 17-14, 2-7.

(3) Black to move and win – 22-26, 30-14, 17-10.

(4) Black to move and win – 27-24, 28-19, 26-23, 19-26, 30-16.

Page 91

(2) $2 + \dfrac{22}{22} - \dfrac{2}{2}$

(3) There are 1,296 different rectangles. Of these 204 are squares. The general formula is that a board of squares contains $\dfrac{(n^2 + n)^2}{4}$ rectangles, of which $\dfrac{2n^3 + 3n^2 + n}{6}$ are squares and $\dfrac{3n^4 + 2n^3 - 3n^2 - 2n}{12}$ are rectangles that are not squares.

(1)

(4)

Page 92 Doodle-Words –
(1) Thin Ice. (2) Bottom (or half) Dollar.
(3) Sitting Bull. (4) Dance Step.
(5) Closed Circuit. (6) Fat Chance.
(7) Open End. (8) Upper Crust.
(9) Hang-up. (10) Double-bed.
(11) Waterfall.

Page 93 The Rhino's Riddle – Rupert tipped the barrel towards himself until the water inside was about to pour out. (line A-A) Rupert then looked inside. If he could see any part of the bottom of the barrel then he knew that it was less than half-full (Fig. B). If he could just see the far corner at the bottom (Fig. A) then he knew it was exactly half-full. If it was more than half-full (Fig. C) then all he would see was the side of the barrel.

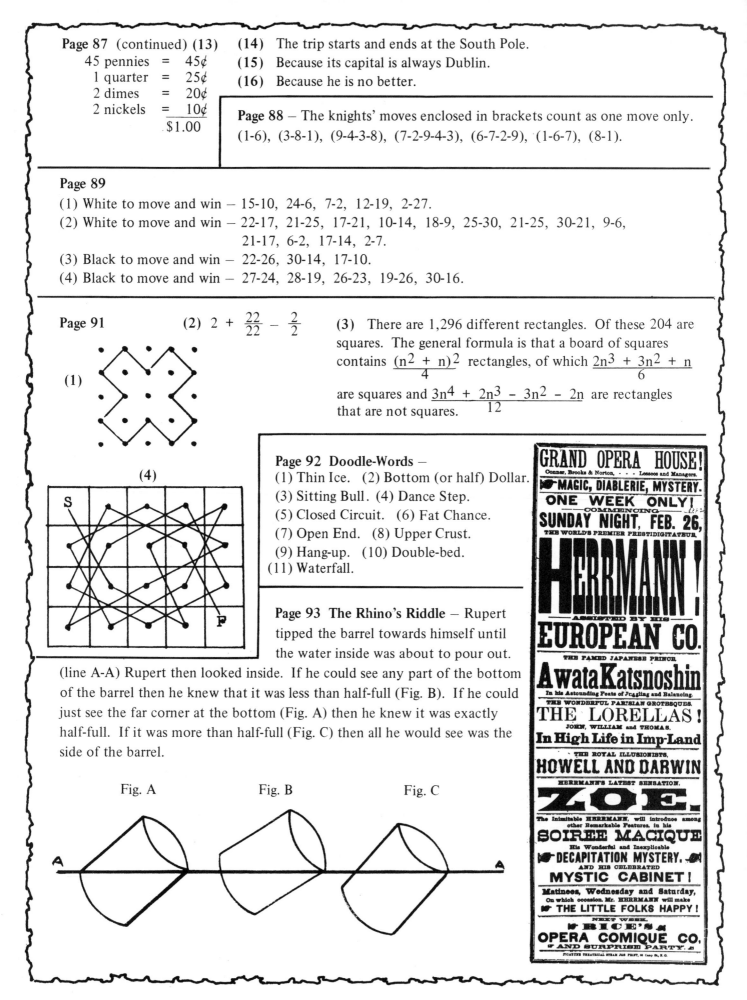

Fig. A   Fig. B   Fig. C

(3) Where Did The Square Go?

(4) The Artist's Dilemma

Page 96

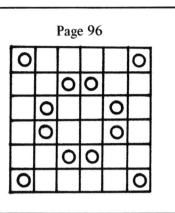

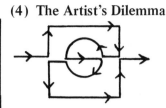

Page 97 Single-Stroke Figure — Figure 1 may be described, according to the conditions of the puzzle, by starting at the point E, thence carrying the pencil from E to A, from A to B, from B to C, from C to D, and from D to E; then from E to B, B to D, D to A, and A to C.

Page 98 The Magic Cards — The seven cards are drawn up on a mathematical principle,

The Entangled Scissors — Pass the loop through the opposite bow, and over the ends of the scissors, when they will be free.

in such manner that the *first numbers of those in which a given number appears,* when added together, indicate that number.

Suppose, for instance, that the chosen number is 63. This appears in cards I, II, III, IV, V and VI. The key numbers of these are 1, 2, 4, 8, 16 and 32; and $1 + 2 + 4 + 8 + 16 + 32 = 63$.

If the number 7 is selected, this appears only in cards I, II and III, whose key numbers are 1, 2 and 4 = 7.

The principle of construction seems at first sight rather mysterious, but it is simple enough when explained. The reader will note, in the first place, that the first or "key" numbers of each card form a geometrical progression, being 1, 2, 4, 8, 16, 32, 64. The total of these is 127, which is accordingly the highest number included.

It is further to be noted that by appropriate combinations of the above figures *any* total, from 1 to 127, can be produced.

The first card consists of the alternate numbers from 1 to 127 inclusive. The second, commencing with 2 (the second term of the geometrical series), consists of alternate groups of *two* consecutive figures — 2, 3; 6, 7; 10, 11, and so on. The third, beginning with 4, the third term of the series, consists of alternate groups of *four* figures — 4, 5, 6, 7; 12, 13, 14, 15; 20, 21, 22, 23; and so on. The fourth, commencing with 8, consists in like manner of alternate groups of *eight* figures. The fifth, commencing with 16, of alternate groups of *sixteen* figures. The sixth, commencing with 32, of alternate groups of *thirty-two* figures; and the last, commencing with 64, of a single group, being those from 64 to 127 inclusive.

It will be found that any given number of cards arranged on this principle will produce the desired result, limited by the extent of the geometrical series constituting the first numbers.

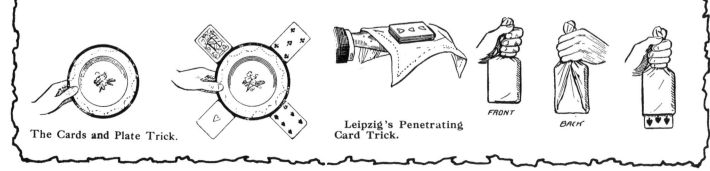

The Cards and Plate Trick.

Leipzig's Penetrating Card Trick.

FRONT

BACK

In Volume 1 of *Merlin's Puzzler,* when it came time to supply the reader with the answers to the puzzles, we journeyed across time and space to the magic shop of Mr. Will Goldston. Once again we will make that journey, but this time we will visit the magic department that Mr. Goldston managed for the A.W. Gamage department store in Holborn, London, England.

The time is 1911. It is just down this aisle and to the right.

MANAGER & BUYER WILL GOLDSTON.

SOLUTIONS

Page 101 The Coin Under The Glass – Lightly scratch with your index finger the table cloth in front of the glass. This will cause the coin to slide across the table in the opposite direction. Keep this up until the coin moves out from under the glass.

Page 103 – (1) Bend the Straw near the bottom and push it into the bottle. You can then wedge the straw in the bottle and lift it up.

(2) The Flatland Puzzle

(3) The Team Buttons Puzzle

(4) The Drummer – 51 rectangles.

Page 104 Captain Kidd's Kite – 11 squares

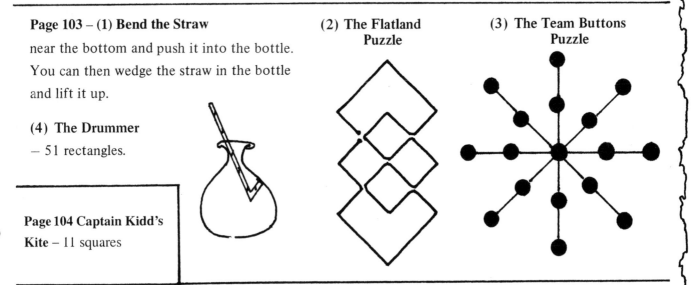

Page 106 (1) Making Things Even – Johnny had seven pennies and Tommy had five pennies. **(2) A Rejected Proposal** – Johnny had eight pennies and Tommy had four pennies. **(3) Father and Son** – In four years and a half, when the son will be sixteen and a half, the father forty-nine and a half. When the son reaches 16, the father will be 49 – i.e., still a little more than three times the son's age. But when the son reaches 17, his father will be 50, which is not quite three times 17. It is, therefore, clear that the required age is between those two points, and a little reflection will show that only the ages stated exactly answer the conditions of the problem. **(4) The Walking Match** – They will meet in an hour, by which time <u>A</u> will have gone round the circle exactly five times, <u>B</u> four times, <u>C</u> three times, and <u>D</u> twice. **(5) The Three Legacies** – As the amount of each share is to correspond with length of service, it is plain that the housemaid will receive one share, the parlourmaid three, and the cook six – in all, ten shares. The value of a single share is therefore one-tenth of $700, or $70, which is the portion of the housemaid, the parlourmaid receiving $210, and the cook $420.

Page 107 – See page 104.

Page 109 (1) An Easy Creditor – The amount of the first payment was $20. To ascertain such amount, let x = the first payment. Then according to the conditions of the puzzle –

$$x + \frac{x}{2} + \frac{3x}{4} + \frac{x}{4} + \frac{2x}{5} + 2 = 60$$

Page 109 con't – Multiplying by 20, the least common multiple of the various denominators,

$$20x + 10x + 15x + 5x + 8x + 40 = 1200$$
$$58x = 1200 - 40 = 1160$$
$$x = 20$$

(2) The Over-Polite Guests – To obtain the answer, all that is needed is to find the number of permutations of seven objects (7 x 6 x 5 x 4 x 3 x 2 x 1 = 5040). It would take, therefore, 5040 days, or nearly fourteen years, to exhaust the possible positions.

Page 110 The Double Bow and Ring – Bend the two bows together, so that the one shall partially cross the other. Get the ring between the two joints, pull it downwards over the two inner wires, and the trick is done.

Page 107– The Royal Aquarium Thirteen Puzzle

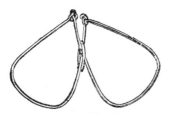

(2) The Egyptian Mystery – The secret here lies in the proper manipulation of the moveable loop a. Get this into the position shown to the right. Then fold the puzzle in half; lift the ring so as to bring it over the two curved ends on the opposite side; work it up to the centre, down the opposite curve and up again to the top, a in its present position offering no obstacle to you doing so. When the ring reaches the top at the left-hand side, it is free.

Page 111 The Stanley Puzzle – To get the ring off, fold the loop backwards against the Stanley medallion, as shown in the figure. Then push the ring upward into the horseshoe-shaped space, and then work the outer portion of its circumference round the medallion from left to right, till it reaches the position shown in the diagram. When it reaches this point, it is free. The solution seems almost childishly simple when known, but the puzzle will, notwithstanding, give a good deal of trouble to any one trying it for the first time.

(2) The Ashantee Horseshoe – Take the second piece of wire in your hand, and with its point gently raise the horseshoe to a slightly more vertical position, so that the upper end of the first piece of wire, that which is holding the horseshoe propped up, shall fall forward onto the second piece of wire. By slightly raising the second piece of wire you shall lock all three items together, and they may be lifted without difficulty.

(3) The Latin Cross Puzzle – The segments are arranged as shown in the figure on the right.

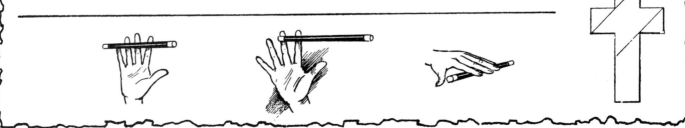

Page 111 con't. The Diabolical Cube — Stand the piece _c_ (the one which looks like a flight of steps) up on end, and beside it the piece _a_, with its projecting portion uppermost, but farthest away from the highest step of _c_. Against the nearer side of _c_ place the square block _e_, and stand the small block _f_ on end beside it. The state of things will now be as shown in the figure. Fix _d_ in beside _a_, with one of its projections pointing downward and the other resting on _f_. You will find that you have now only room left for the remaining piece, _b_, whose cut-out central space just fits the projecting top of _c_. Place this in position, and the cube is complete.

Page 112 (1) A Puzzling Inscription — The letter E, which, inserted at the proper intervals, makes the inscription read as under:

PERSEVERE YE PERFECT MEN,
EVER KEEP THESE PRECEPTS TEN.

(3) A Puzzle With Coins — Lay out nine counters in three rows of three each, so as to form a square. This done, distribute the remaining three as follows: place one counter on the first of the first row, another on the second of the second row, and the third on the last of the third row.

(2) Dropped-Letter Proverbs

    (a) Faint heart never won fair lady.
    (b) Birds of a feather flock together.
    (c) He who goes a borrowing goes a sorrowing.
    (d) Take care of the pence, and the pounds will take care of themselves.

(4) A Bridge Problem — The three matches are interlaced as shown in the illustration on the right, one resting on the brim of each wineglass. The superincumbent weight binds them together, so that they will sustain a fourth wineglass without difficulty.

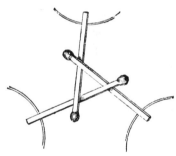

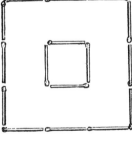

(5) A Square Puzzle — Take away the matches forming the inner sides of the four corner squares, when you will have left two squares only, the one in the center of the other.

Page 113 (1) Six Into Three — Take away two matches forming each of the lower corners, and the center match from the top row. This will leave three squares.

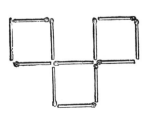

Page 113 con't (2) Six into Two — Take away the four matches forming the inner sides of the four squares to the left, and the two matches forming the outer sides of the lower square to the right. You will then have only two squares left, a larger and a smaller, as

(3) Five Into Three — First take away the three matches which form the outer sides of the upper left-hand square. Next, remove the two matches forming the outer sides of the upper right-hand square, and the two matches forming the outer sides of the lower left-hand square. You have then left two squares, lying diagonally. With four of the matches you removed, form a third square in continuation of the diagonal line (see illustration to the left).

(4) The Balanced Pencil — You have merely to dig the blade of a half-open penknife in the pencil, a little above the point, and to open or close the blade, little by little, till you find that the balan e is obtained. The precise angle must be ascertained by experiment, as it will vary with the length and weight of the two articles. When you have discovered it, the pencil may be balanced, as shown in the figure.

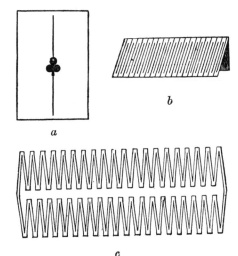

a

b

c

(5) The Cut Playing Card — Fold the card down the centre, and cut through the line thus made to within a quarter of an inch of each end. The card will then be as Fig. a. Next, with a sharp penknife, or scissors, cut through both thicknesses, alternately to right and left, but each time stopping within a quarter of an inch of the edge, as in Fig. b. The cuts should be about an eighth of an inch apart. The card when opened will be as Fig. c. Open it out still further, when it will form an endless strip, of such a size as to pass easily over a person's body.

(6) The Balanced Quarter — The first step is to bend the paper clip into the form shown in Fig. a. Use the narrow loop of this as a clip to hold the quarter, bending the wire closer and closer till you have the coin secure. Hang the ring on the hook at the opposite end of the wire, and then proceed to balance it as shown in our illustration. A good many trials will probably be necessary before you are able to ascertain the precise point to which to apply the pin; but, this once found, you may even set the coin spinning (by gently blowing upon the ring) without destroying its equilibrium.

a

Page 113 con't (7) **Water Bewitched** — Fill a wineglass with water to the brim. Lay a piece of card flat upon it, and turn it over, keeping the card meanwhile in place with the hand. When the glass is inverted the card will not fall, though the hand be removed, neither will the water run out, being kept in position by atmospheric pressure. Place the glass thus inverted on a smooth wooden table, near the edge, and cautiously draw away the card. The water will still not run out so long as the glass is not moved, but the moment any one lifts it the whole will be spilt.

Page 114 The John Bull Political Puzzle — No absolute rule can be given for the solution of this puzzle, as the number and direction of the moves will necessarily vary according to the position in which the nine counters happen to be placed at the outset. We propose to take a couple of specimen positions, and if the reader duly studies the modus operandi in these two cases, he should have little difficulty in finding appropriate solutions for other positions. Distinguishing the counters for facility of reference as follows:

Red Conservative as R.C.
White　　　" 　as W.C.
Blue　　　" 　as B.C.
Red Liberal　　as R.L.
White　" 　　as W.L.
Blue　" 　　as B.L.
Red Unionist　as R.U.
White　" 　　as W.U.
Blue　" 　　as B.U.

we will suppose that the original (haphazard) position is as follows:

On spot 1 (see Fig. Page 16) B.C.
" 　" 　2　　　　　　　B.U.
" 　" 　3　　　　　　　W.C.
" 　" 　4　　　　　　　R.L.
" 　" 　5　　　　　　　W.L.
" 　" 　6　　　　　　　W.U.
" 　" 　7　　　　　　　B.L.
" 　" 　8　　　　　　　R.U.
" 　" 　9　　　　　　　R.C.

The puzzle may then be solved as follows:

Move R.C. from 9 to 10
" 　R.U. 　" 　8 to　9
" 　W.U. 　" 　6 to　8
" 　B.C. 　" 　1 to　6
" 　W.C. 　" 　3 to　1
" 　B.U. 　" 　2 to　3
" 　R.L. 　" 　4 to　2
" 　B.C. 　" 　6 to　4
" 　W.L. 　" 　5 to　6
" 　B.C. 　" 　4 to　5
" 　R.U. 　" 　9 to　4
" 　R.C. 　" 　10 to　9.

Page 116 To Balance an Egg — Have the egg boiled hard. Thrust the two forks into the cork, one on each side, so that they shall form an angle of about 60 degrees to each other. Hollow slightly the lower end of the cork, so that it may adapt itself with tolerable exactness to the larger end of the egg. Hold the stick, ferule upwards, firmly between the knees. Place the egg on end upon the ferule and then the cork upon the egg. After one or two attempts, you will find that the combination rest in equilibrium. (2) **Silken Fetters** — This is a very simple matter, though, like a good many of the puzzles it is perplexing enough till you know "how it's done." Let the gentleman pass the loop of his own ribbon through the loop which encircles one of the lady's wrists, over the hand, and back again, when it will be found that they are freed from the link which united them. Their individual bonds must, of course, be removed by untying in the ordinary way.

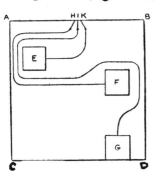

Page 117 (1) The Three Fountains — This, though at first sight perplexing, is really a very simple problem. The illustration at the left represents one method out of two or three for the solution of the problem.

(2) The Penetrative Quarter — Fold the paper exactly across the center of the hole; then take it in both hands, and ask some one to drop the quarter into the fold. Let it rest just over the hole, its lower edge projecting below.

Bend the corners of the paper slightly upwards, as indicated by the drawing. This elongates the opening, and, if the movement be continued, the quarter will, after a second or two, fall through by force of its own weight. The paper remains uninjured.

(3) The Singular Quarter — Take hold of two diagonally opposite corners of the handkerchief, with the thumb on the upper surface of each, and stretch vigorously. The handkerchief will be found to form a tense fold, or "overlap," on either side of the coin; and if the handkerchief, still in this condition, be lifted into a perpendicular position, the quarter will remain gripped in the fold, and will not fall.

(4) The Balanced Quarter — The first step is to fix the needle, point upwards, in the cork of the wine bottle. The next, to cut a slit, a quarter of an inch deep, across the top of the smaller cork, and to press the quarter as far as it will go into the cut so made. (The diagram is hardly accurate in this particular. The slit in the cork should be deep enough to admit about one half the diameter of the quarter.) Holding the cork with the coin downwards, thrust the two forks into it (one on either side) in an upward direction, at an angle of about 30 degrees to the center of the cork. Now bring the edge of the coin carefully down upon the point of the needle, and, if the forks are properly adjusted, it will remain balanced, and the cork may even be spun round at considerable speed with little fear of displacing it.

(5) The Three Peanuts — This is a very ancient "sell," but it still finds victims. The performer's undertaking is performed by simply putting on the hat selected. No one can deny that the three peanuts are thereby brought under the hat.

Page 118 (1) The Mysterious Obstacle — You perform your undertaking by clasping the person's hands round the leg of a low piano, or other object too bulky to be dragged through the doorway.

(2) The Portrait — The portrait represented the speaker's son, as will be seen after a moment's consideration. The speaker says in effect, "The father of that man is my father's son"; in which case the father of the subject must be either a brother of the speaker, or himself. He has already told us that he has no brother. He himself must therefore be the father, and the portrait represents his son.

(3) The Egg and The Cannonball — You place the egg on the floor, in one corner of the room, in which position the walls on either side make it impossible to touch it with the cannonball.

(4) A Curious Window — The window was diamond-shaped. By enlarging it to a square, its area is

Page 118 con't – exactly doubled, without increasing either its height or width. A window shaped as an isosceles or right-angled triangle will equally answer the conditions of the puzzle.

(5) **Arithmetical Enigma** – Seven – Even – Eve.

(6) **Necessity the Mother of Invention** – Push the cork in.

(7) **Easy, When You Know It** – Seven and one.

Page 119 (1) A Singular Subtraction

SIX	IX	XL
IX	X	L
S	I	X

(2) **The Vanishing Number** – The number is 888. When halved it becomes $\dfrac{000}{000} = 0$

(3) **An Interesting Question** – This is a mere "sell." The answer is "Letters." In the word "twenty" there are six letters, in the word "six" three, and so on. (4) **The Mouse** – There were nine ears of corn in the box. The mouse brought out three ears at each journey, but two of them were his own.

(5) **A Reversible Fraction** – $\dfrac{6}{9}$. Turn the paper upside down, so as to bring the denominator into the place of the numerator, and vice versa. The fraction will still be $\dfrac{6}{9}$.

(6) **The Three Counters** – Remove one of the end counters and transfer it to the opposite end. You have not touched the middle counter, but it is no longer in the middle. (7) **Magic Made Easy** – The spectators naturally prepare themselves for some more or less adroit feat of jugglery, but you perform your undertaking by simply crossing the closed hands. The right hand (and the coin in it) is now where the left was previously, and vice versa.

Page 120 (1) The Endless Chain Puzzle – The figure at the right shows the proper arrangement of the various segments.

(2) **The "Spots" Puzzle** – We will assume that the finished assembly will be as shown here, the six being to the front, and, consequently, the one to the rear; the two at top, consequently the five at bottom; and the four to the left, consequently the three to the right, on the side concealed from view. The lower stratum will consist of three bars as follows.

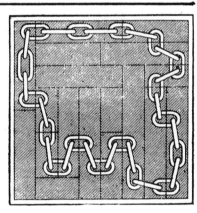

The Hinder bar: Two spots on under side, and one on the end to the left.

Middle: One spot in center of under side. Otherwise blank.

Front: Two spots on under side, two in front, and one on each end.

We next come to the middle layer; and here most people give themselves a good deal of unnecessary trouble by taking it for granted that all the nine bars must lie in the same direction. As a matter of fact, the three at top and three at bottom should lie parallel, but the three in the middle at right angles to them. This middle layer is formed as follows –

Left-hand: Bar with one spot on end towards front.

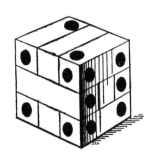

Page 120 con't. – Otherwise blank.

Middle: Bar with spot on hinder end. Otherwise blank.

Right-hand: Bar with spot on forward end, and one in center of right-hand side.

(These, as we have said, are to be laid across the three bars already placed.)

Upper layer: Back. Spot on each end, and one on upper side to the right. Further side blank.

Middle: Blank throughout.

Front: Two spots on front, one on the end to the left, and one on the top, at the same end.

These last three bars being laid on the top, parallel to the bottom section, the die will be complete, having the appearance shown in the figure.

(3) Fixing The Ring – Let the lady hold the cord at about three inches from the upper end. The gentleman passes the ring over it, then takes hold of the upper end of the cord and draws it through the lady's fingers to within an inch or two of the opposite end. The cord is held slack, the ring hanging in the center. The gentleman then passes the end he holds round the opposite portion of cord, draws it through the loop thus formed, and the trick is done.

Page 121 (1) The Thirty-Six Puzzle – The six counters are so removed as to leave the remainder shown here.

Page 122 (1) Riddle – "Campbell's Elephant Soup."

(2) Mr. Puff's Puzzle –

(3) The Rhino's Riddle – $3^2 = 4 + 5$.

Page 123 (1) 10-7, 1-17, 29-25, 3-10, 25-22. White wins.

(2) 9-14, 17-10, 2-7, 10-3, 16-12. Black wins.

(3) 19-16, 11-27, 18-15, 10-26, 32-5. White wins.

(4) 11-16, 19-15, 22-18, 14-23, 16-19, 23-16, 12-10. Black wins.

Page 124 (1) Outside.

(2) A dead one. **(3)** A bald head. **(4)** Silence. **(5)** Noah. He made the Ark Light on Mount Ararat.

(6) When they make 22. **(7)** A leek. **(8)** Hailing taxis. **(9)** Samson. He brought down the house.

(10) Unquestionably. **(11)** A man on horseback. **(12)** When it is going down. **(13)** The pavement.

(14) A lyre. **(15)** May. It only has 3 letters. **(16)** Finding half a worm. **(17)** Madam, I'm Adam.

(18) In the river basin.

Page 125 (1) (D), **(2)** (R), **(3)** (L), **(4)** (Q), **(5)** (I), **(6)** (O), **(7)** (N), **(8)** (F), **(9)** (J), **(10)** (C), **(11)** (A), **(12)** (G).

Page 127 (1) No Two In The Same Row

JS	JH	JD	JC
QS	QH	QD	QC
KS	KH	KD	KC
AS	AH	AD	AC

(2) Things are looking up! – Consider the cards as being numbered 1, 2, and 3. On the first move turn over cards 2 and 3. On the second move turn over cards 1 and 3, and on the third move turn over cards 2 and 3.

(3) The Five Pairs Puzzle – Consider the cards as being numbered from left to right, 1 through 10. The moves would then be: Card 4 on card 1; card 6 on 9; card 8 on 3; card 2 on 7; and card 5 on 10.

Page 129 (1) 75 Triangles.

(2)

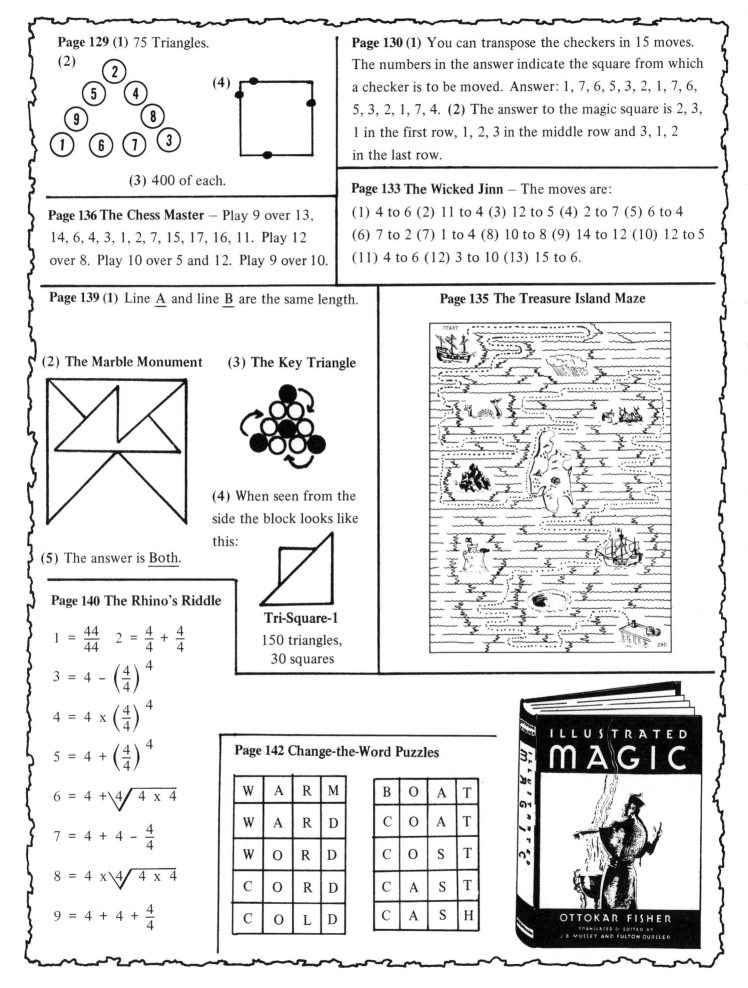

(4)

(3) 400 of each.

Page 136 The Chess Master – Play 9 over 13, 14, 6, 4, 3, 1, 2, 7, 15, 17, 16, 11. Play 12 over 8. Play 10 over 5 and 12. Play 9 over 10.

Page 130 (1) You can transpose the checkers in 15 moves. The numbers in the answer indicate the square from which a checker is to be moved. Answer: 1, 7, 6, 5, 3, 2, 1, 7, 6, 5, 3, 2, 1, 7, 4. **(2)** The answer to the magic square is 2, 3, 1 in the first row, 1, 2, 3 in the middle row and 3, 1, 2 in the last row.

Page 133 The Wicked Jinn – The moves are:

(1) 4 to 6 (2) 11 to 4 (3) 12 to 5 (4) 2 to 7 (5) 6 to 4 (6) 7 to 2 (7) 1 to 4 (8) 10 to 8 (9) 14 to 12 (10) 12 to 5 (11) 4 to 6 (12) 3 to 10 (13) 15 to 6.

Page 139 (1) Line **A** and line **B** are the same length.

(2) The Marble Monument

(3) The Key Triangle

(4) When seen from the side the block looks like this:

Tri-Square-1
150 triangles,
30 squares

(5) The answer is **Both**.

Page 140 The Rhino's Riddle

$1 = \dfrac{44}{44}$ $2 = \dfrac{4}{4} + \dfrac{4}{4}$

$3 = 4 - \left(\dfrac{4}{4}\right)^{4}$

$4 = 4 \times \left(\dfrac{4}{4}\right)^{4}$

$5 = 4 + \left(\dfrac{4}{4}\right)^{4}$

$6 = 4 + \sqrt{4 \times 4}$

$7 = 4 + 4 - \dfrac{4}{4}$

$8 = 4 \times \sqrt{4 \times 4}$

$9 = 4 + 4 + \dfrac{4}{4}$

Page 135 The Treasure Island Maze

Page 142 Change-the-Word Puzzles

W	A	R	M
W	A	R	D
W	O	R	D
C	O	R	D
C	O	L	D

B	O	A	T
C	O	A	T
C	O	S	T
C	A	S	T
C	A	S	H

ILLUSTRATED
MAGIC

OTTOKAR FISHER
TRANSLATED & EDITED BY
J B MUSSEY AND FULTON OURSLER

Page 142 con't

S	T	A	R
S	E	A	R
F	E	A	R
F	E	A	T
F	E	E	T

M	O	R	E
L	O	R	E
L	O	S	E
L	O	S	S
L	E	S	S

F	I	S	H
F	I	S	T
F	I	A	T
F	E	A	T
M	E	A	T

Page 143 (1) The Rearranging Bee — (A) Denmark (B) Bulgaria
(C) Ethiopia (D) Honduras (E) Rumania (F) England (G) Liechtenstein
(H) Afghanistan (I) West Germany (J) Pakistan
(2) Ant, Moth, Gnat, Mite, Fly, Flea, Lice, Wing, Pest, Wasp
(3) Soup to Fish
(4) Surf into Turf.

S	O	U	P
S	O	U	R
P	O	U	R
P	O	U	T
P	O	S	T
P	A	S	T
F	A	S	T
F	I	S	T
F	I	S	H

Page 151

② ③ ①

④

If <u>B</u> had seen two black helmets he would have known that he was wearing a white helmet, and have said so. Since <u>B</u> had said nothing <u>C</u> knew that he couldn't have a black helmet on, so <u>C</u> declared first, giving Merlin the reason why he could not be wearing a white helmet.

Page 156 (1) see below. **(2)** The 50 coins trick — 45 pennies, 1 quarter, 2 dimes, and 2 nickels. **(3)** Put your face down close to the dime and blow on it. A good hefty gust of wind should get it off the plate. Pick a plate with a small sloping rim. **(4)** 22 + 2 = 24. **(5)** Live.

Page 158 The Black Widow (1) As long as he was Abel. **(2)** A joke. **(3)** They don't go without winding. **(4)** Scrap iron. **(5)** A donkey. **(6)** $6 \times 6 + \frac{66}{66} = 37$
(7) One time. After the first time the number is not 135 anymore. **(8)** None, the hole is empty. **(9)** $9 + \frac{99}{9} = 20$. **(10)** When it is 8 o'clock and you add 6 hours to it, the answer is 2 o'clock. **(11)** Because it makes Ma Mad. **(12)** To keep his wig warm.
(13) Because it makes the butterfly. **(14)** A timetable. **(15)** In the dictionary.
(16) None. You have to pour them into the pot.

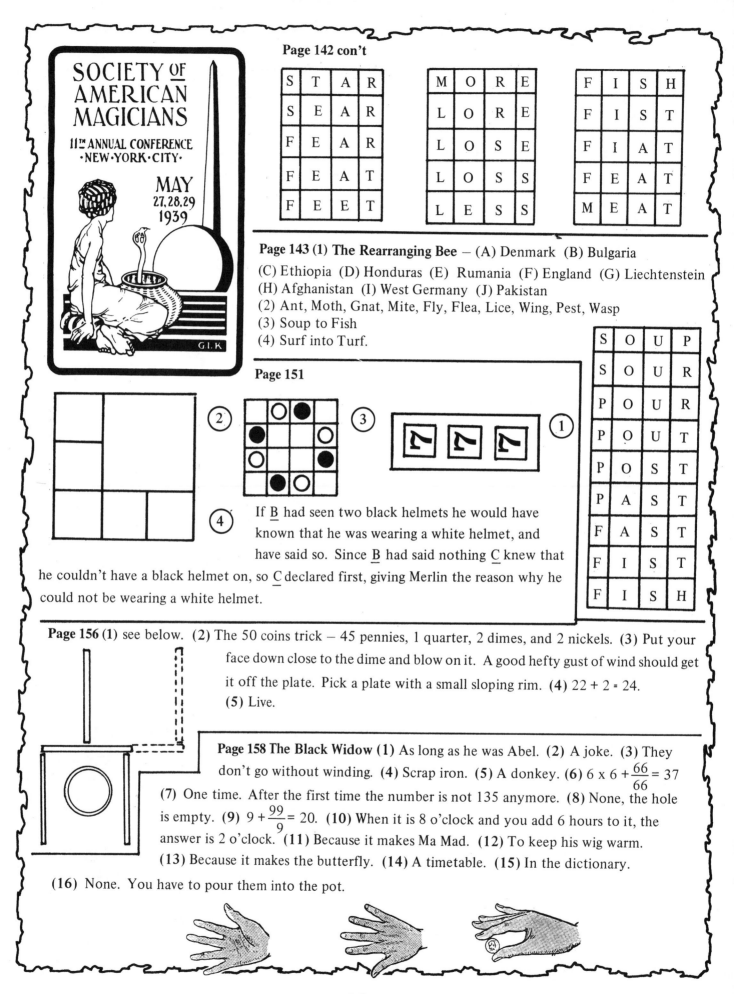

Page 159 The Man In The Iron Mask — The man with the Black mask.

Page 161 (1) The Space Ship — Starting at command center 2 go by way of the following route: 2, E, N, H, 3, J, N, M, 4, L, 3, G, 2, C, 1, B, N, K, 3, I, N, F, 2, D, N, A, 1. **(2)** $\frac{77}{.77} = 100$.

(3) The Three Squares   **(4)** First move reverse the 2nd and 3rd coins; Second move reverse the 3rd and 4th coins; Third move reverse the 4th and 5th coins.

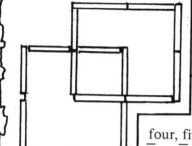

Page 163 (1) Road, Goad, Goal, Coal, Coil. **(2)** Bell, Sell, Sill, Silt, Sift.
(3) Call, Mall, Male, Mate, Mute. **(4)** Fire, Fore, Ford, Cord, Cold.
(5) Raft, Rant, Rang, Ring, Wing.

Page 167 (1) 25, 6, 19. **(2) The Rhino's Riddle** — The next letter in line is <u>N</u>. Each letter is the first letter of a number. The numbers are <u>one</u>, <u>two</u>, <u>three</u>, <u>four</u>, <u>five</u>, <u>six</u>, <u>seven</u>, <u>eight</u>, <u>nine</u>. It was a simple progression.

Page 164 The Rhino's Riddle

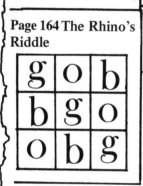

Page 169 (1) The secret to this puzzle/game is to be the player that goes first. You place your first card on the exact center of the table. Now, wherever your opponent places a card on the table you place your next card in exactly the same place on the opposite side of the table. In this way if he can find a place to put down a card, then there must be a spot vacant on the other side of the table for you to place a card. If he cannot find an open spot then you are the winner. **(2)** Turn the nine card upside-down making it into a six. Now arrange the cards as follows:

(3) You will find 19 different squares indicated in the drawing below. There are 9 squares of the four <u>A</u>'s type, four squares of the <u>B</u>'s type, four squares of the <u>C</u>'s type and two squares of the <u>D</u>'s type.

To render the cross "squareless," remove the circles marked "E." It will then be impossible to form any of the above squares.

1	3
8	6
2	4
7	5
18	18

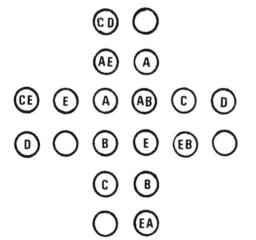

Page 170 – A-7, B-19, C-8, D-13, E-20, F-1, G-26, H-21, I-2, J-17, K-25, L-5, M-9, N-23, O-4, P-24, Q-10, R-3, S-22, T-11, U-6, V-15, W-18, X-16, Y-14, Z-12.

Page 171 The Royal Feast — There being 180 heads (i.e., 180 creatures in all), if all had been birds they would have had 360 feet. If all had been beasts, they would have had 720 feet. It is clear, therefore, that there were some of each. Suppose the numbers equal, the feet would then count as under:

90 birds:	180 feet	
90 beasts:	360 feet	
180	540 feet	

(being an excess of 40 over the stated number.)

Each bird added to the "bird" half (involving at the same time the deduction there of one beast) produces a diminution of 2 in the number of feet. As the equal division gives an excess of 40 feet, we must therefore deduct 20 beasts and add 20 birds.

This gives us 90 + 20 = 110 birds − 220 feet

90 − 20 = 70 beasts − 280 feet

180   500

The Rhino's Riddle

$$\frac{8888}{8.888} \text{ and } \frac{8888-888}{8}$$

Page 174

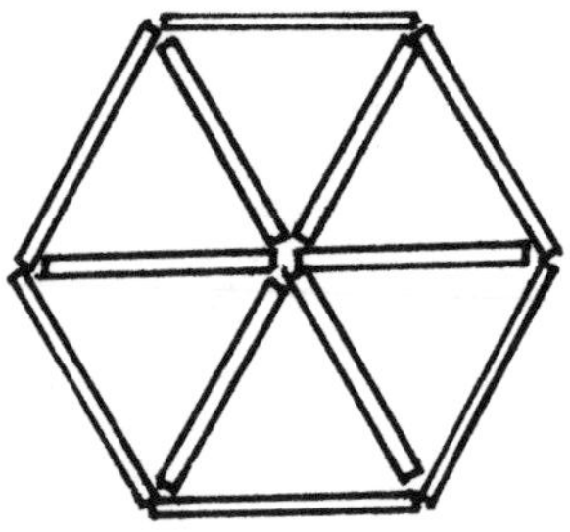

Page 173 (1) Loosen the central loop and pass the key through it. Next, pull the two hanging strands downwards until the loops at the back of the cardboard come through the hole to the front of the puzzle. These loops can then be put through the key. After doing that you can slide the key over so that it hangs on the right loop. Pull the loops back through the hole and the puzzle is solved.

(2) The Division Puzzle

```
      971
53 ) 51463
     477
     376
     371
      53
      53
```

(3) The New Houses Puzzle — The electric pipe for house 2 was run under house 3.

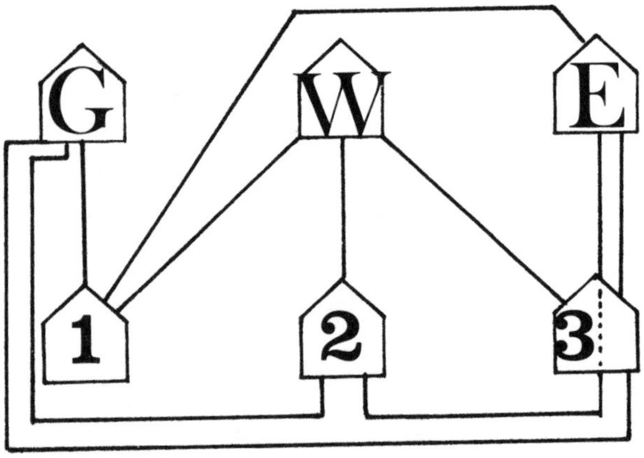

Page 176 — The path taken by Holmes and Watson is shown in the diagram below. When he got to the room marked b Holmes put one foot onto the spot marked with a star, thus entering it but at the same time he kept his other foot in room b so that technically he did not leave it. He snapped on the switch in the room with the star and the door swung open and out tottered inspector Lestrade. Good old Holmes, he had saved the day again.

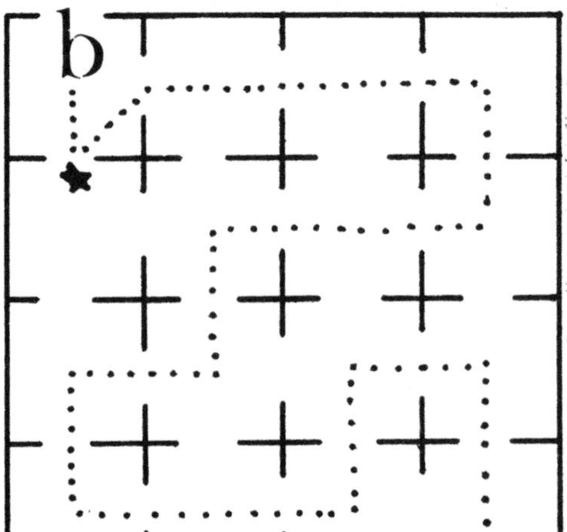

Page 177 (1) The ten moves are: Black 1 to 3; Black 6 to 8; Red 4 to 1; Red 9 to 6; Black 2 to 4; Black 7 to 9; Red 5 to 2; Red 10 to 7; Black 3 to 5; Black 8 to 10.

(2) The Greek Cross Puzzle – Draw four lines from the corners of the square to the centers of the opposite sides. Cut out the pieces marked <u>a</u> and position them in the areas marked <u>b</u>.

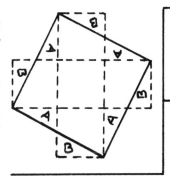

Page 178 – Start by moving 8 to 10 and play as follows, always remove the checker you jumped over: 9 to 11, 1 to 9, 13 to 5, 16 to 8, 4 to 12, 12 to 10, 3 to 1, 1 to 9 9 to 11.

Page 181 (1) Place three of the coins in a triangle so that each coin is touching the other two coins. Now, place the fourth coin in the center, on top of the other three coins. Since every coin is now touching every other coin, the coins are all equidistant from each other. **(2)** You change DEAL to SHOT in the following manner: DEAL, MEAL, MEAT, MOAT, BOAT, BOOT, BOON, SOON, SOOT, SHOT. **(3) The Babylonian Arithmetic** puzzle – 1 2 3 – 4 5 – 6 7 + 8 9 = 100. **(4) The Sign of Sid**

Page 184 – (1-L), (2-D), (3-O), (4-P), (5-B), (6-Q), (7-J), (8-G), (9-E), (10-M), (11-I), (12-R).

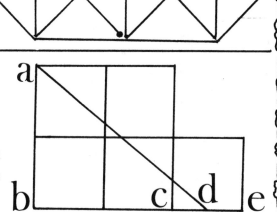

Page 185 The Chicken-man

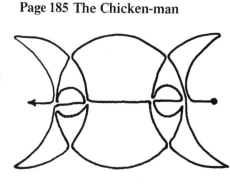

The Surveyors Puzzle – Draw a straight line from point <u>A</u> to point <u>D</u>. Point <u>D</u> is the mid point of line <u>C – E</u>. This gives us the triangle <u>A – B – D</u> which is half of the rectangle made up of side <u>AB</u> and side <u>BD</u>.

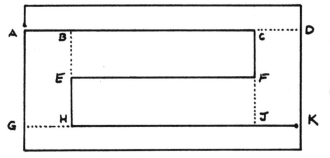

Page 186 (1) The four "dotted" lines in the diagram on the right are the lines that the "Steam Man" had to go over twice. His route was: <u>A</u> to <u>D</u>, <u>D</u> to <u>C</u> and back to <u>D</u>, <u>D</u> to <u>G</u>, <u>G</u> to <u>H</u> and back, <u>G</u> to <u>B</u>, <u>B</u> to <u>E</u> and back, <u>B</u> to <u>F</u>, <u>F</u> to <u>J</u> and back, and <u>F</u> to <u>K</u>.

Page 187 The Golf Puzzle – The two shots that Dashing Dan plays are 150 yard drive and a 125 yard approach shot. The holes are made in the following manner: 150 yards: 1 drive, 300 yards: 2 drives, 250 yards: 2 approach, 325 yards: 3 drives, 1 approach back, 275 yards: 1 drive, 1 approach, 350 yards: 4 approaches, 1 drive back, 225 yards: 3 approaches, 1 drive back, 400 yards: 1 drive, 2 approaches, 425 yards:

Page 187 con't – 2 drives, 1 approach. **The Archery Range** – The Hood sisters put 2 arrows in the 25 circle, 2 arrows in the 20 circle, and 2 arrows in the 3 circle.

Page 188 (1) The Square Board – The least number of pieces the puzzle can be done in is two. Cut out the piece outlined by the dotted line, turn it end for end and replace it in the board. The hole will now be in the center of the board. **(2) The Perplexing Pyramid Puzzle** – You will find 31 different equilateral triangles in Ector Pendragon's painting. **(3) The Jumbo Puzzle**

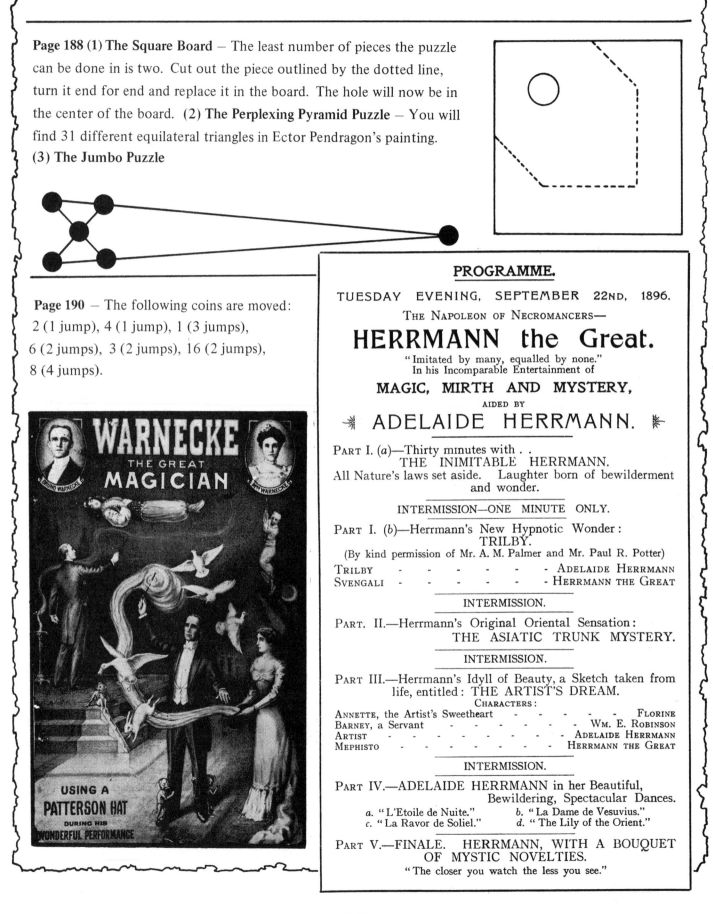

Page 190 – The following coins are moved:
2 (1 jump), 4 (1 jump), 1 (3 jumps),
6 (2 jumps), 3 (2 jumps), 16 (2 jumps),
8 (4 jumps).

Page 191 – (1) (F), (2) (N), (3) (C), (4) (R), (5) (P), (6) (I), (7) (D), (8) (J), (9) (M), (10) (B), (11) (Q), (12) (G).

Page 192 – (1) Solitaire Problems

No. 1. From 3 to 1
   2.   ''   12 to 2
   3.   ''   13 to 3
   4.   ''   15 to 13
   5.   ''   4 to 6
   6.   ''   18 to 5
   7.   ''   1 to 11
   8.   ''   31 to 18
   9.   ''   18 to 5
 10.   ''   20 to 7
 11.   ''   3 to 13
 12.   ''   33 to 20
 13.   ''   20 to 7
 14.   ''   9 to 11
 15.   ''   16 to 18
 16.   ''   23 to 25
 17.   ''   22 to 20
 18.   ''   29 to 27
 19.   ''   18 to 31
 20.   ''   31 to 33
 21.   ''   34 to 32
 22.   ''   20 to 33
 23.   ''   37 to 27
 24.   ''   5 to 18
 25.   ''   18 to 20
 26.   ''   20 to 33
 27.   ''   33 to 31
 28.   ''   2 to 12
 29.   ''   8 to 6
 30.   ''   6 to 19
 31.   ''   19 to 32
 32.   ''   36 to 26
 33.   ''   30 to 32
 34.   ''   26 to 36
 35.   ''   35 to 37

(3) The Triplets

No. 1. From 17 to 19
   2.   ''   31 to 18
   3.   ''   19 to 17
   4.   ''   16 to 18
   5.   ''   30 to 17
   6.   ''   6 to 19
   7.   ''   10 to 12
   8.   ''   19 to 6
   9.   ''   2 to 12
 10.   ''   4 to 6
 11.   ''   21 to 19
 12.   ''   7 to 20
 13.   ''   19 to 21
 14.   ''   22 to 20
 15.   ''   8 to 21
 16.   ''   32 to 19
 17.   ''   28 to 26
 18.   ''   19 to 32
 19.   ''   36 to 26
 20.   ''   34 to 32

(2) The Curate and His Flock.

No. 1. From 6 to 19
   2.   ''   4 to 6
   3.   ''   18 to 5
   4.   ''   6 to 4
   5.   ''   9 to 11
   6.   ''   24 to 10
   7.   ''   11 to 9
   8.   ''   26 to 24
   9.   ''   35 to 25
 10.   ''   24 to 26
 11.   ''   27 to 25
 12.   ''   33 to 31
 13.   ''   25 to 35
 14.   ''   29 to 27
 15.   ''   14 to 28
 16.   ''   27 to 29
 17.   ''   19 to 21
 18.   ''   7 to 20
 19.   ''   21 to 19

Page 195 The Wolf, The Goat, and The Cabbages

This is a very simple problem.

It is solved as under:
1. He first takes across the goat and leaves him on the opposite side.
2. He returns and fetches the wolf, leaves him on the opposite side, and takes back the goat with him.
3. He leaves the goat at the starting point and takes over the basket of cabbages.
4. He leaves the cabbages with the wolf and, returning, fetches the goat. <u>Or,</u>
1. He takes over the goat.
2. He returns and fetches the cabbages.
3. He takes back the goat, leaves him at the starting point, and fetches the wolf.
4. He leaves the wolf on the opposite side with the basket of cabbages and goes back to fetch the goat.

Page 196 Passing The Gate – He had at the outset 61 cents. On the first day he pays a penny at the gate, spends 30 cents, and pays a penny on going out, leaving him with 29 cents.

The second day he pays a penny on entering, spends fourteen cents, and after paying a penny on going out is left with thirteen cents.

The third day he brings in 12 cents, spends six cents, and is left, on going out, with five cents.

The fourth day he brings in four cents, spends two cents, and after paying the toll to go out, is left with one penny only.

Page 196 con't – To solve the problem, the calculation must be worked backwards. Thus, on the fourth day he pays a penny on coming out and has still one left, together making two cents. He had spent *half* his available money in the town. The total must therefore on that day have been four cents, exclusive of the penny he paid to come in. This gives us five cents as the amount with which he came out the previous evening. The penny he paid to get out brings this amount to six cents, and as he had first spent a like amount, he must previously have had twelve cents, exclusive of the penny to come in.

By continuing the same process, it is easy to arrive at his original capital.

---

(2) A Feat Of Divination – All that is necessary is to deduct 25 from the final sum named. This will give a remainder of two figures, representing the points of the two dice.

Thus, suppose that the points thrown are 6 and 1, and that the thrower selects the former to be multiplied. The figures will then be as follows:

$$(6 \times 2 + 5) \times 5 + 1 = 86$$
$$86 - 25 = 61$$

which, as will be seen, corresponds with the points of the two dice.

If the thrower had selected the 1 as the starting point of the process, the only difference in the result would be that the two digits would come out in reverse order. Thus:

$$(1 \times 2 + 5) \times 5 + 6 = 41$$
$$41 - 25 = 16$$

The same process, in a slightly modified form, is equally applicable to three dice. In this case the steps are as under:

Multiply the points of the first die by 2;
Add 5;
Multiply the result by 5;
Add the points of the second die;
Multiply the total by 10;
Add the points of the third die;

On the final result being announced, the operator subtracts from it 250, when the remainder will give the points of the three dice.

Thus, suppose the points of the three dice to be 5, 4, and 2. Then –
$5 \times 2 + 5 = 15$; $15 \times 5 = 75$; $75 + 4 = 79$; $79 \times 10 = 790$; $790 + 2 = 792$.
And $792 - 250 = 542$, giving the three numbers required.

(3) Hidden Proverbs – The five proverbs are as follows:

A rolling stone gathers no moss.
Too many cooks spoil the broth.
A live dog is more to be feared than a dead lion.
You cannot eat your cake and have it.
Peace hath her victories, no less renowed than war.

To read them, first find the central letter, which is <u>A</u>. This begins the first proverb. Immediately below this will be found <u>R</u>, to the left of this <u>O</u>, and above the <u>O</u> two <u>L</u>'s. To the right of the last <u>L</u> are the letters <u>I</u> <u>N</u>. The <u>G</u>, completing the word "rolling," comes next below the <u>N</u>, and below this, <u>S</u>, the initial of the next word, "stone." From the <u>S</u>,

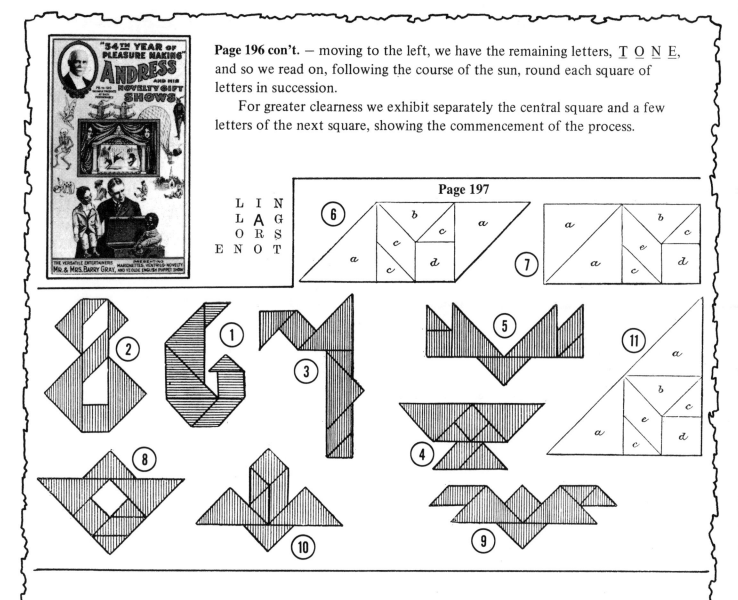

Page 196 con't. — moving to the left, we have the remaining letters, <u>T</u> <u>O</u> <u>N</u> <u>E</u>, and so we read on, following the course of the sun, round each square of letters in succession.

For greater clearness we exhibit separately the central square and a few letters of the next square, showing the commencement of the process.

```
L I N
L   G
O   S
R
E N O T
     A
     R
     S
```

Page 197

Page 198 (1) **The "Five and Five" Puzzle** — For the sake of brevity, we will distinguish the red and black counters by the letters <u>r</u> and <u>b</u> respectively. They will then stand at the outset as under:

```
                b r b r b r b r b r . .
Position after 1st move;  b       r b r b r b r r b
     "      "  2nd  "     b b r r b r       b r r b
     "      "  3rd  "     b b r       r r b b r r b
     "      "  4th  "     b b r r r r r b b       b
     "      "  5th  "     . . r r r r r b b b b b
```

(2) **The "Six and Six" Puzzle** — They will stand at the outset as under:

```
                b r b r b r b r b r b r . .
Position after 1st move;  b       r b r b r b r b r r b
     "      "  2nd  "     b b r r       b r b r b r r b
     "      "  3rd  "     b b r r r b b r b       r r b
     "      "  4th  "     b b r r r       r b b b r r b
     "      "  5th  "     b b r r r r r r b b b       b
     "      "  6th  "     . . r r r r r r b b b b b b
```

(3) **A Long Family** — Their respective ages are as follows: the youngest 3, and the eldest 24. Here again the assistance of algebra is needed for a ready solution. Let x = the age of the youngest (15th).

263

Page 198 con't. — Then 8x = the age of the eldest. And by the terms of the question —

8x = (x + 1½ + 1½ + 1½ + 1½ + 1½ + 1½ + 1½ + 1½ + 1½ + 1½ + 1½ + 1½ + 1½ + 1½)

    = x + 21

7x = 21

 x = 3: the age of the youngest,

and 8x = 24: the age of the eldest.

(4) How to Divide Twelve among Thirteen — It will be found that, counting as described in the problem, the person standing <u>eleventh</u> from the point at which you begin will be excluded. The distributor will therefore begin ten places farther back, or (which is the same thing) three places farther forward, in the circle. Thus, if <u>x</u> (see Fig. 1) be the person to be excluded, the distributor will begin to count at the point <u>a</u>. The numbers placed against the various places show the order in which the gifts will be distributed and the men drop out of the circle.

Fig. 1

Page 199 (1) The Three Jealous Husbands — For the sake of clearness, we will designate the three husbands <u>A</u>, <u>B</u>, and <u>C</u>, and their wives <u>a</u>, <u>b</u>, and <u>c</u>, respectively. The passage may then be made to the satisfaction of the husbands in the following order:

   1. <u>a</u> and <u>b</u> cross over, and <u>b</u> brings back the boat.

   2. <u>b</u> and <u>c</u> cross over, <u>c</u> returning alone.

   3. <u>c</u> lands and remains with her husband, while <u>A</u> and <u>B</u> cross over. <u>A</u> lands, <u>B</u> and <u>b</u> return to the starting point.

   4. <u>B</u> and <u>C</u> cross over, leaving <u>b</u> and <u>c</u> at the starting point.

   5. <u>a</u> takes back the boat and <u>b</u> crosses with her.

   6. <u>a</u> lands and <u>b</u> goes back for <u>c</u>.

(2) The Four Jealous Husbands — The answer to this version is: (Distinguishing the four husbands as <u>A</u>, <u>B</u>, <u>C</u>, and <u>D</u>, and the four wives as <u>a</u>, <u>b</u>, <u>c</u>, and <u>d</u>, respectively.)

   1. <u>a</u>, <u>b</u>, and <u>c</u>, cross over; <u>c</u> brings back the boat.

   2. <u>c</u> and <u>d</u> cross over and <u>d</u> brings back the boat.

   3. <u>A</u>, <u>B</u>, and <u>C</u> cross over; <u>C</u> and <u>c</u> bring back the boat.

   4. <u>C</u>, <u>D</u>, and <u>c</u> cross over.

   5. <u>c</u> takes back the boat and fetches <u>d</u>.

(3) A Loan and a Present — The remainder in this case will be one-half of the amount added by way of "present." This is very easily demonstrated.

   Let <u>x</u> equal the number thought of; then 2x + 14 will equal that number <u>plus</u> the imaginary loan and present. Half that amount being professedly given to the poor, will leave a remainder of <u>x</u> + 7, and on the repayment of the imaginary loan the figures will stand as <u>x</u> + 7 – x (= 7), the value of <u>x</u> having no bearing whatever on the result.

(4) The Shepherdess and her Sheep — The numbers are 7, 14, 28, and 56 respectively. By the terms of the question, it appears that the numbers in the four folds are in geometrical progression, with a common ratio of 2. Taking experimentally the smallest possible such progression, we find it to be

Page 199

(4) con't — 1 + 2 + 4 + 8 = 15. But the total of the actual progression is stated to be 105. Dividing this by 15, we have as quotient 7, which we use as a common multiplier to bring the series up to the required total. Thus:

$$7 \times 1 = 7$$
$$7 \times 2 = 14$$
$$7 \times 4 = 28$$
$$7 \times 8 = \underline{56}$$

Total 105

Page 200 (1) Locked Out — The Count took up one of the boards and placed it across one corner of the moat. He then took up the other board and walked out to the middle of the first board, from which point he was able to place the second board on the corner of the island, forming a safe passage to his villa.

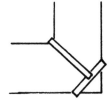

(2) Apples and Oranges — As each child had 3 more oranges than apples, and this caused a difference of 33 (48 – 15) in the number left over, it follows that the number of children must have been 11. As each child received 12 apples, and there were 48 over, the total number of apples must have been (11 x 12) + 48 = 132 + 48 = 180. As each child received 15 oranges, and there were 15 over, the total number of oranges must have been (11 x 15) + 15 = 165 + 15 = 180. **(3) The Devil's Bridge:** Figure 1 shows how the four knives are interlocked to support the fifth glass.

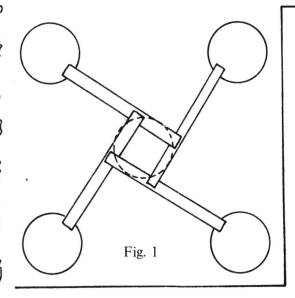

Fig. 1

Page 201 (1) The Carpenter's Puzzle — He cuts the board as shown in Fig. 2-viz: — from a to b (halfway across); from c to d, and then along the middle from b to d. He then reunites the two pieces as shown in Fig. 3.

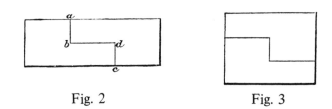

Fig. 2   Fig. 3

(2) The Extended Square — The card is cut as indicated in a. The upper part is then shifted backward one step to form the shape b, or two steps to form c.

Fig. 4

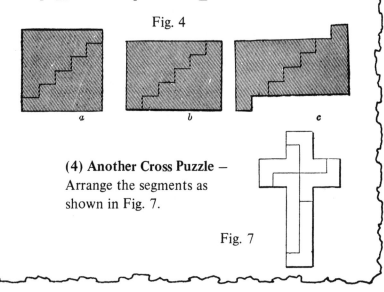

a   b   c

(4) Another Cross Puzzle — Arrange the segments as shown in Fig. 7.

Fig. 7

(3) The Two Squares — First divide the larger square by pencil lines from a to b and c to d, then cut from e to c and from c to f (Fig. 5). The card will now be in three pieces which, duly rearranged, will form a square, as shown in Fig. 6.

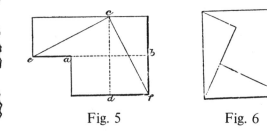

Fig. 5   Fig. 6

265

Page 202 (1) **A Remarkable Division** — The only three persons who shared in the gift were related to each other as son, father, and grandfather. Each is necessarily a son (of somebody), while the two elder are fathers also. (2) **A Distinction and a Difference** — There is a difference of twenty; twice twenty-five being fifty, while twice five, and twenty, make thirty only.

(3) **A Sum in Subtraction** — The answer is 56 quarts; twenty four-quart bottles holding 80 quarts, while four-and-twenty quart bottles hold 24 quarts only.

(4) **Multiplication Extraordinary** — Answer: 1 1/5. 1 1/5 x 5 = 6.

(5) **A Question in Notation** — Answer: 13212.

(6) **A Singular Subtraction** — The propounder of this puzzle should be wearing gloves, and the problem is solved by taking them off. The ten fingers of the gloves are taken from the ten fingers of the hand, and the latter still remain.

(7) **The Flying Half-Dollar** — Place yourself so as to bring one hand just over the mantlepiece and drop the coin contained in such hand upon the latter. Then, keeping the arms still extended, turn the body round till the other hand comes over the coin. Pick it up, and you have solved the puzzle, both coins being now in one hand.

(8) **The Draper's Puzzle** — It took him 59 seconds. Most people are apt to say 60, forgetting that the 59th cut separates the last two lengths and that, therefore, a 60th cut is unnecessary.

(9) **The Charmed Circle** — The circle is drawn on the clothes of the victim, round the waist.

(10) **Arithmetical Enigma** — L stands for 50 (Roman numerals), the zero for the letter O, and V for 5, while E is one-fifth of eight (e i g h t), the whole forming the word LOVE.

Page 203 (1) **The Abbot's Puzzle** — The secret lies in increasing or diminishing, as the case may require, the number of persons in the corner cells, each of which counts twice over, and so, to a person as doddering as the abbot must be assumed to have been, seems at first sight to increase the general total. Thus when the four monks absented themselves, the remaining twenty were rearranged as in Fig. 1; and when they returned with four other persons, the twenty-eight were disposed as in Fig. 2. When four more visitors arrived, the thirty-two were distributed as in Fig. 3; and when the final four arrived, the party, now numbering thirty-six, were arranged as in Fig. 4.

Fig. 1

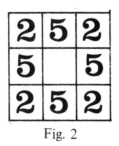
Fig. 2

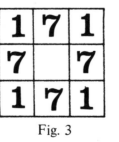
Fig. 3

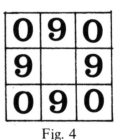
Fig. 4

(2) **A Complicated Transaction** — William had 48 quarters, and Thomas 30. The arithmetical solution of this question is somewhat intricate, but by the algebraic method it is simple enough.

Thus: Let w = William's number,

and t = Thomas' number.

Page 203 con't – Then the state of William's finances at the close of the transaction will be represented by $\underline{w} - \underline{t} + (\underline{w} - \underline{t})$, and by the terms of the question this = 36. We also have it stated in the question that the joint finances $\underline{w} + \underline{t} = 36 + 42 = 78$, so that $\underline{w} = 78 - \underline{t}$.

Reducing the first equation to simpler form, we have:

$$2\underline{w} - 2\underline{t} = 36$$
$$\text{or } \underline{w} - \underline{t} = 18$$
$$\text{and } \underline{w} = 18 + \underline{t}$$

Comparing the values of $\underline{w}$ thus ascertained, we have:

$$18 + \underline{t} = 78 - \underline{t}$$
$$2\underline{t} = 78 - 18 = 60$$
$$\underline{t} = 30$$

and $\underline{w}$ being $= 18 + \underline{t} = 18 + 30 = 48$.

Page 204 (1) A Geometric Problem – The counters must be placed as shown in Fig. 1.

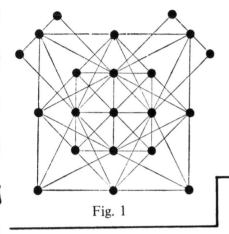

Fig. 1

(2) The Captain and His Company – The captain orders the two children to pass to the farther side. One of them then brings back the boat, lands, and a soldier crosses alone to the farther side. The second child then brings back the boat.

The state of things (save that one man has crossed) is now just as at first, the boat and the two children being on the hither side of the stream. The process is repeated until the whole of the company have passed over.

Page 205 (1) The Pen and Wheel – To detach the pen, draw the pen close up, or nearly, to the wheel, so as to make the "loop" as long as possible. Pass this under and over the spokes, side by side with the protion already wound, finally passing it through the hole in the center and over the pen, then draw it back again in the same direction and the cord will be free from the wheel. In all puzzles of this class, wherever a loop has to be passed over a knot, ball, or other obstacle, special care must be taken that the loop is clear, i.e., that the two cords constituting it are not twisted. If the loop be passed in a twisted condition over the ball, the result is "confusion worse confounded," and the difficulty of the puzzle proportionately increased. This caution is especially necessary in the case of this puzzle, the successive passages under and over the spokes rendering such twisting a very likely occurrence. In such case the cord, when drawn back again, will be found rather more entangled than it was in the first instance. To reinstate the cord and pen, reverse the process.

(2) The Chinese Zigzag – To reconstruct the block, you must follow as closely as possible, but in reverse order, the process by which it was taken to pieces. First put together one of the external layers, and, having completed this, lay it, with the flat side undermost, to form the bottom of the block. Then put together the layer next in order, and slide it into position, and in like manner with the two remaining layers.

Fig. 2

Page 205 con't — A novice usually endeavors to reconstruct the block haphazardly, so to speak, instead of layer by layer, under which conditions success is impossible.

Fig. 2 shows the four layers in readiness for the final reconstruction, b sliding (from left to right, or vice versa) over a, and d c over b in like manner.

Page 206 (1) Transformations — (A) Hand; hard; lard; *lord; ford; fort; Foot. (B) Sin; son; won; Woe. (C) Hate; have; lave; Love. (D) Black; slack; stack; stalk; *stale; shale; whale; while; White. (E) Wood; wool; cool; Coal. (F) Blue; bile; pile; pine; Pink. (G) Cat; cot; cog; Dog. (H) More; lore; lose; loss; Less. (I) Rose; lose; lost; list; lilt; Lily. (J) Shoe; shot; soot; Boot. *These are examples of a necessity, which frequently arises, of interposing a move which does not directly aid the transformation, but indirectly as a link with some more desirable word. In the first example, the word "food" might (in place of "fort") form the intermediate step between "ford" and "foot."

(1) A Difficult Placement — This is a quibble dependent on the special wording of the problem. You begin by distributing the counters in three rows of three each, forming a square, and then place the remaining counter on the center one. You have now four rows of four each; but as each row can be counted in two different directions, i.e., from right to left or left to right, and vertical rows upwards or downwards — you are enabled to count four in eight different directions, as required by the problem.

Page 207 The Two Corks — The secret lies in the position of the hands as they are brought together. The uninitiated brings them together with the palms of both turned towards the body, with the consequence we have described. To solve the puzzle, turn the palm of the *right hand inward,* and that of the *left hand outward,* in the act of seizing the corks. They will then not get in each other's way, but may be separated without the least difficulty.

Page 212 (1) The Rum Riddle — Any four-legged table or chair. You cannot raise just one leg off the floor without raising at least one other leg. **(2) A Square Deal For Mr. Bang** — See Fig. 2.

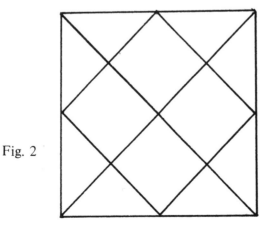

Fig. 2

Page 215 Puzzle Rock

(1)   8384
      803
      626
       50
        8
   9871

(2) 98765
     1234
  99,999

(3)

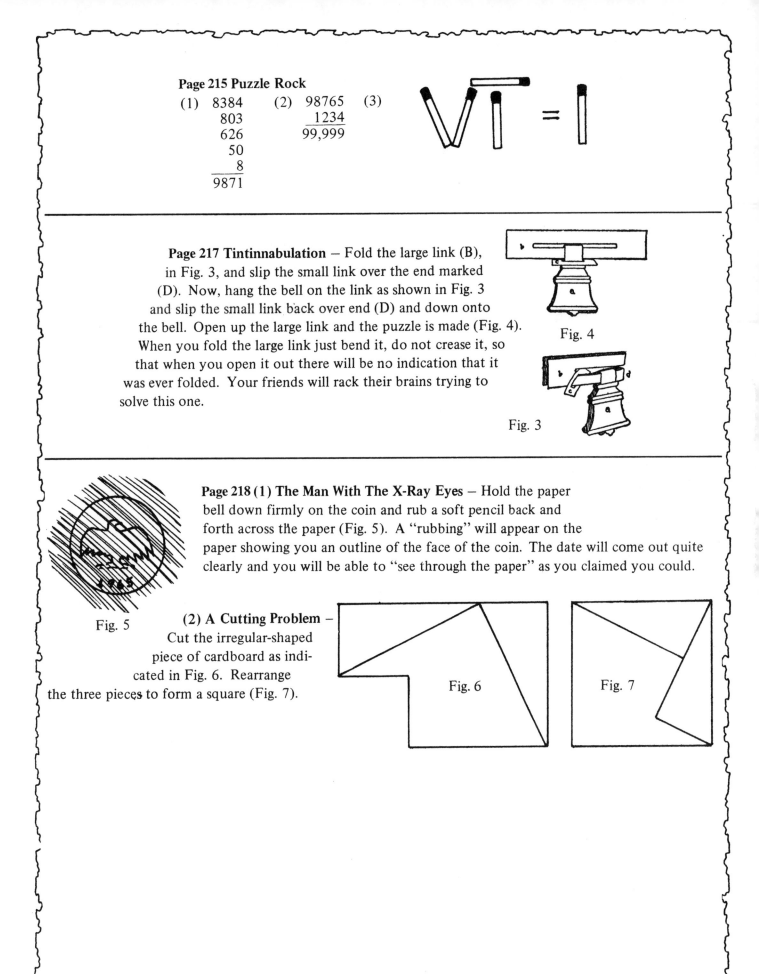

Page 217 Tintinnabulation — Fold the large link (B), in Fig. 3, and slip the small link over the end marked (D). Now, hang the bell on the link as shown in Fig. 3 and slip the small link back over end (D) and down onto the bell. Open up the large link and the puzzle is made (Fig. 4). When you fold the large link just bend it, do not crease it, so that when you open it out there will be no indication that it was ever folded. Your friends will rack their brains trying to solve this one.

Fig. 4

Fig. 3

Page 218 (1) The Man With The X-Ray Eyes — Hold the paper bell down firmly on the coin and rub a soft pencil back and forth across the paper (Fig. 5). A "rubbing" will appear on the paper showing you an outline of the face of the coin. The date will come out quite clearly and you will be able to "see through the paper" as you claimed you could.

Fig. 5

(2) A Cutting Problem — Cut the irregular-shaped piece of cardboard as indicated in Fig. 6. Rearrange the three pieces to form a square (Fig. 7).

Fig. 6

Fig. 7

Page 220 (1) Get Off the Earth — Sam Loyd never really explained how this puzzle worked. The best explanation that has been given to date is that the 13 Chinamen merge into 12 Chinamen and that in the process each Chinaman becomes slightly larger than he was before. When I asked Merlin if he had a better solution to the problem he just shrugged his shoulders and went on reading, so for the time being I am going to stand by the above answer. **(2) The Fore And Aft Puzzle** — The winning moves are:

(1)	11-9	(9)	12-9	(17)	8-10	(25)	17-14	(33)	9-4	(41) 8-10
(2)	7-11	(10)	15-12	(18)	5-8	(26)	15-17	(34)	11-9	(42) 9-8
(3)	4-7	(11)	11-15	(19)	7-5	(27)	11-15	(35)	7-11	(43) 14-19
(4)	9-4	(12)	7-11	(20)	3-7	(28)	13-11	(36)	3-7	(44) 11-14
(5)	10-9	(13)	9-7	(21)	1-3	(29)	10-13	(37)	6-3	(45) 7-11
(6)	8-10	(14)	14-9	(22)	4-1	(30)	8-10	(38)	9-6	(46) 9-1
(7)	6-8	(15)	16-14	(23)	9-4	(31)	2-8	(39)	12-9	
(8)	9-6	(16)	10-16	(24)	14-9	(32)	4-2	(40)	10-12	

(3) The Bell And The Durango Kid — When the Durango Kid started hauling on the rope he found himself going up in the air the same distance as the bell was going up. When the bell was four feet off of the ground so was Durango. No matter how fast or how slow he hauled on the rope, he went up the same distance above the ground as the bell did on its side. They both arrived at the tower together, which after all is what the Reverend wanted.

Page 226 The Chequers Puzzle — We have not undertaken to verify the fifty ways in which it is said that this puzzle may be solved, but we append two, leaving the remaining 48 to the ingenuity of our readers. It will be seen that the two solutions given are radically different.

270

The following pages contain full-size drawings of many of the outstanding puzzles found in this book. To fully enjoy these problems I suggest that you take these pages down to your local copy store and reproduce them on standard 64-pound "business card" stock. With these sturdier props you can try your skills at solving these classic problems from the past. You'll also have hours of fun using them to challenge and stump your friends with.

for duplication

from page 98

I.

1	33	65	97
3	35	67	99
5	37	69	101
7	39	71	103
9	41	73	105
11	43	75	107
13	45	77	109
15	47	79	111
17	49	81	113
19	51	83	115
21	53	85	117
23	55	87	119
25	57	89	121
27	59	91	123
29	61	93	125
31	63	95	127

II.

2	34	66	98
3	35	67	99
6	38	70	102
7	39	71	103
10	42	74	106
11	43	75	107
14	46	78	110
15	47	79	111
18	50	82	114
19	51	83	115
22	54	86	118
23	55	87	119
26	58	90	122
27	59	91	123
30	62	94	126
31	63	95	127

III.

4	36	68	100
5	37	69	101
6	38	70	102
7	39	71	103
12	44	76	108
13	45	77	109
14	46	78	110
15	47	79	111
20	52	84	116
21	53	85	117
22	54	86	118
23	55	87	119
28	60	92	124
29	61	93	125
30	62	94	126
31	63	95	127

IV.

8	40	72	104
9	41	73	105
10	42	74	106
11	43	75	107
12	44	76	108
13	45	77	109
14	46	78	110
15	47	79	111
24	56	88	120
25	57	89	121
26	58	90	122
27	59	91	123
28	60	92	124
29	61	93	125
30	62	94	126
31	63	95	127

V.

16	48	80	112
17	49	81	113
18	50	82	114
19	51	83	115
20	52	84	116
21	53	85	117
22	54	86	118
23	55	87	119
24	56	88	120
25	57	89	121
26	58	90	122
27	59	91	123
28	60	92	124
29	61	93	125
30	62	94	126
31	63	95	127

VI.

32	48	96	112
33	49	97	113
34	50	98	114
35	51	99	115
36	52	100	116
37	53	101	117
38	54	102	118
39	55	103	119
40	56	104	120
41	57	105	121
42	58	106	122
43	59	107	123
44	60	108	124
45	61	109	125
46	62	110	126
47	63	111	127

VII.

64	80	96	112
65	81	97	113
66	82	98	114
67	83	99	115
68	84	100	116
69	85	101	117
70	86	102	118
71	87	103	119
72	88	104	120
73	89	105	121
74	90	106	122
75	91	107	123
76	92	108	124
77	93	109	125
78	94	110	126
79	95	111	127

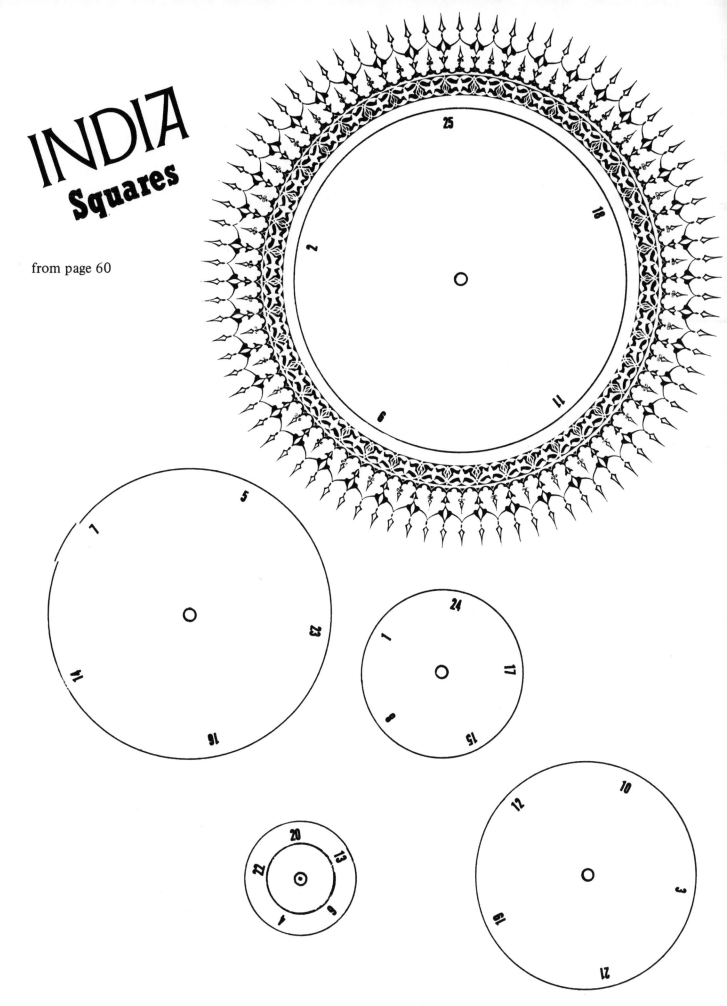

INDIA
Squares

from page 60

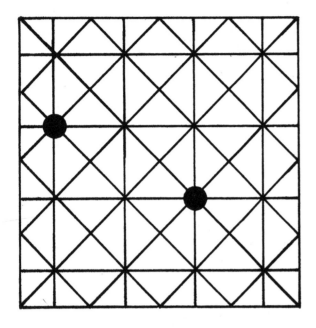

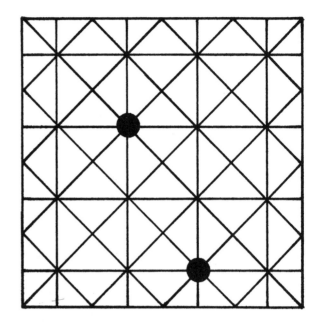

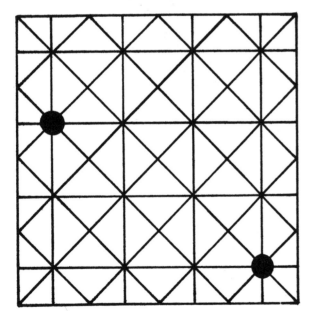

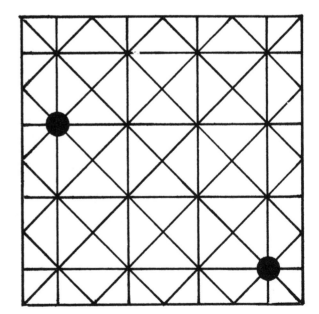

The Latin Cross Puzzle From page 111

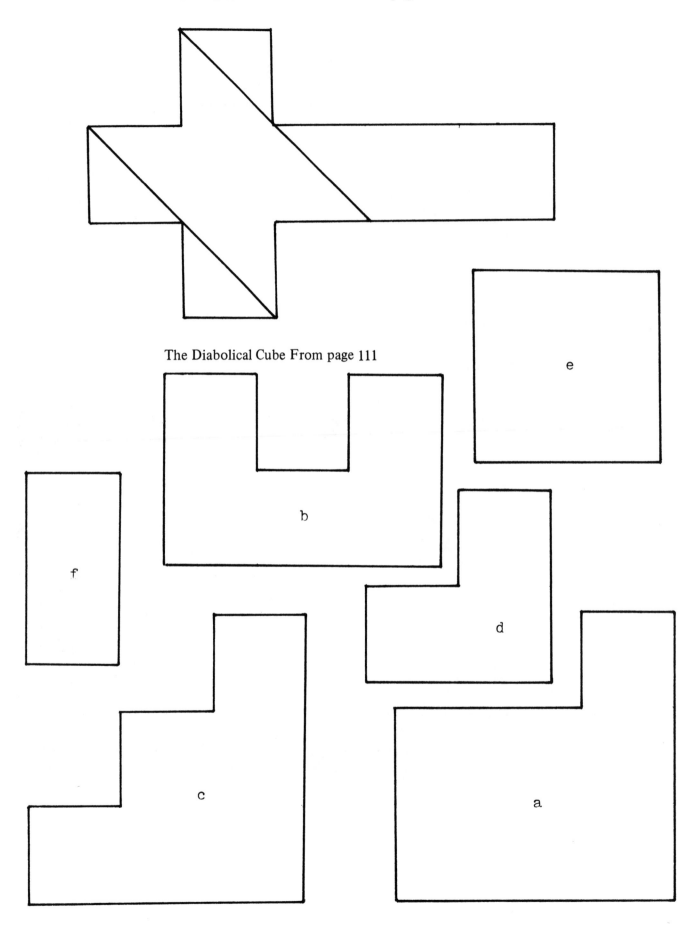

The Diabolical Cube From page 111

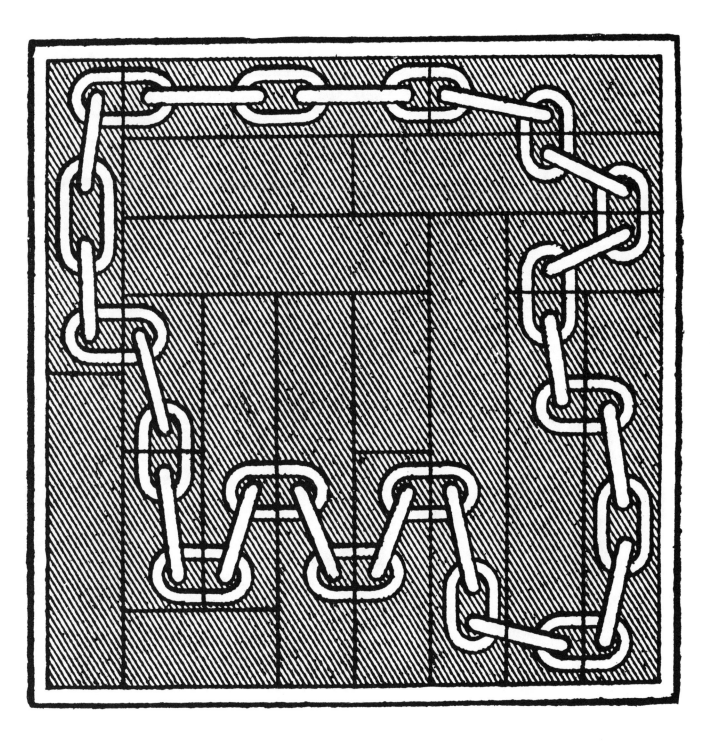

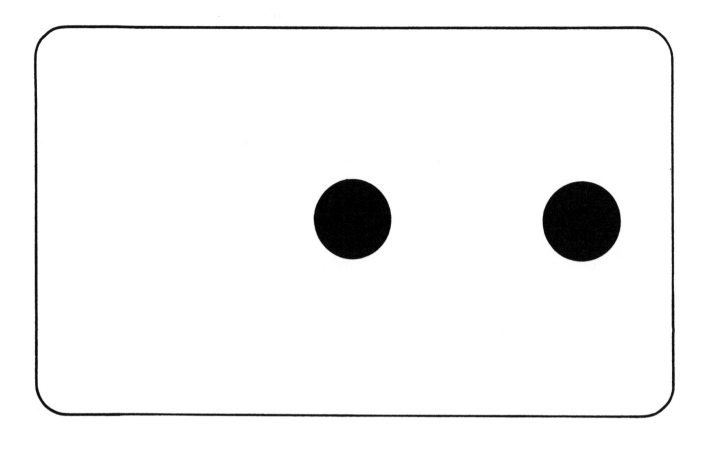

The Card With Many Sides From page 146

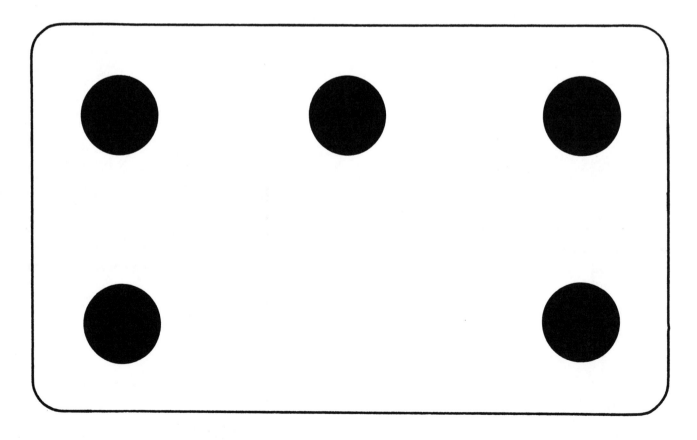

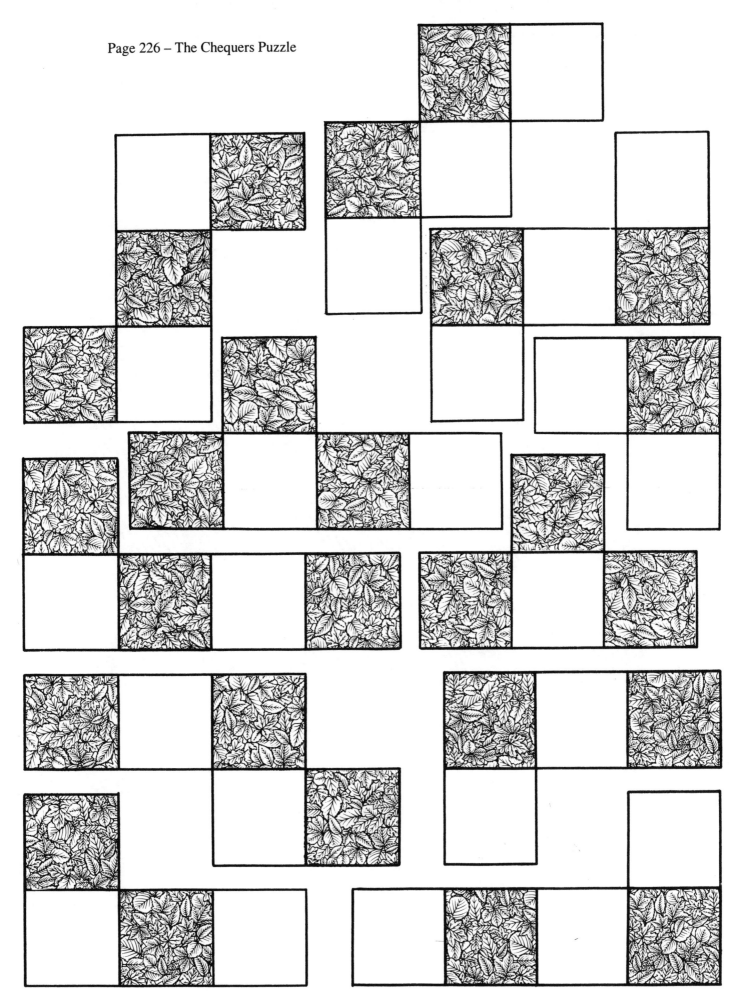

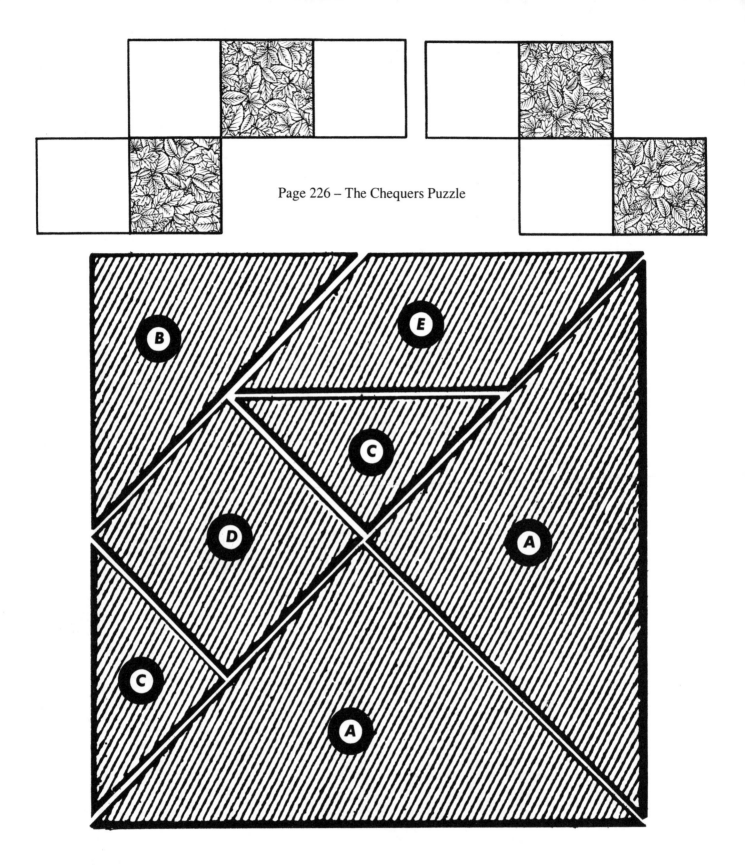

Page 226 – The Chequers Puzzle

THE ANCHOR PUZZLE

Duplicate this page and glue it onto a piece of cardboard. Cut the
pieces out and try to do the puzzles on Page 197.

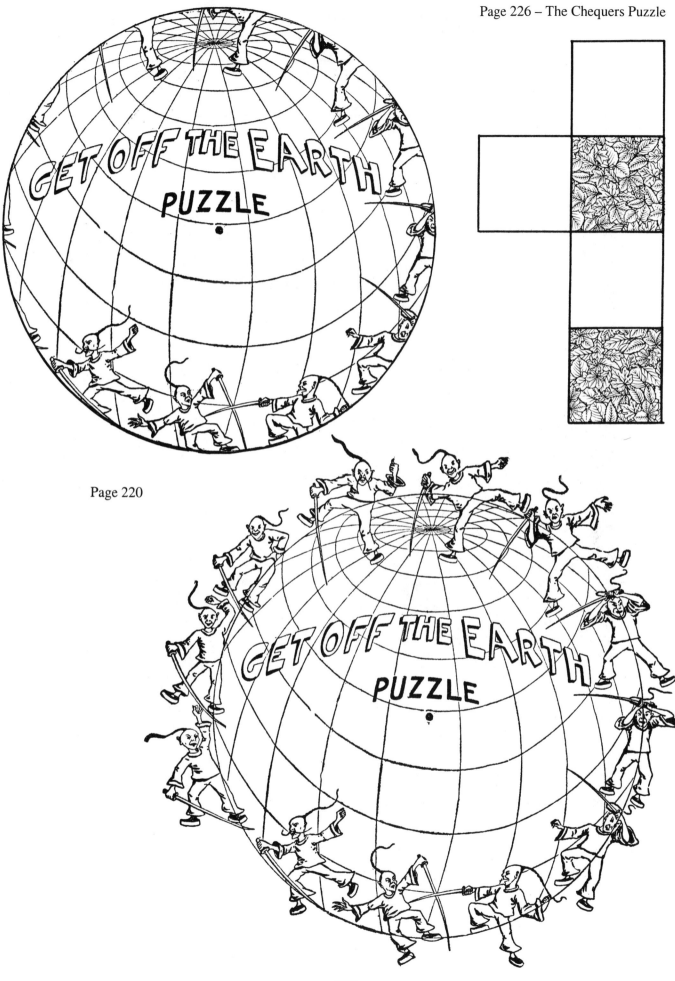

Page 220

AN A "MAZING PUZZLE"

See Page 195 for instructions on how to use this puzzle. To construct it, first duplicate this page, then cut out the puzzleboard. Cut along the outside border line. Next, cut out a piece of cardboard 5 inches by 4¾ inches. Finally, fold the puzzleboard along line x———x and glue both sides to the cardboard (see figure at right).

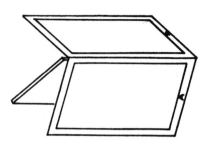

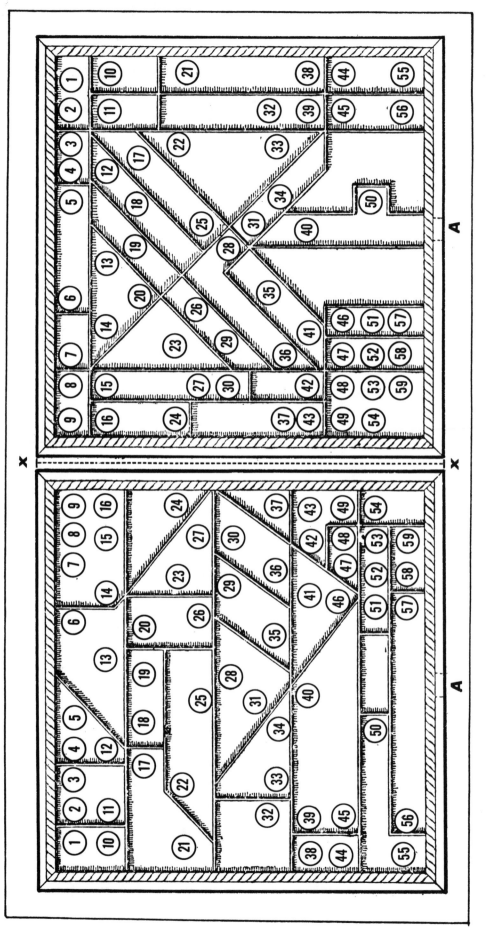

INDEX